THE GENERATION OF 1898 IN SPAIN

THE GENERATION OF 1898 IN SPAIN

~~DONALD~~ Bobby LeeSHAW

Reader in Hispanic Studies, University of Edinburgh

LONDON & TONBRIDGE
ERNEST BENN LIMITED

BARNES & NOBLE BOOKS
NEW YORK

First published 1975 by Ernest Benn Limited
25 New Street Square, Fleet Street, London, EC4A 3JA
and Sovereign Way, Tonbridge, Kent, TN9 1RW
and Harper & Row Publishers Inc.
Barnes & Noble Import Division
10 East 53rd Street, New York 10022

Distributed in Canada by
The General Publishing Company Limited, Toronto

© Donald L. Shaw 1975

Printed in Great Britain

ISBN 0 510–32290–5

ISBN 06–496208–3 (U.S.A.)

To Andrew and Silvia

CONTENTS

CONTENTS

LIST OF ABBREVIATIONS

AG   Anales Galdosianos
BH   Bulletin Hispanique
BHS   Bulletin of Hispanic Studies
BSS   Bulletin of Spanish Studies
CA   Cuadernos Americanos
CCMU   Cuadernos de la Catedra de Miguel de Unamuno
CHA   Cuadernos Hispanoamericanos
FMLS   Forum for Modern Language Studies
Hisp   Hispania
HR   Hispanic Review
In   Ínsula
KFLQ   Kentucky Foreign Language Quarterly
MLJ   Modern Language Journal
MLN   Modern Language Notes
MLQ   Modern Language Quarterly
MLR   Modern Language Review
NRFH   Nueva Revista de Filología Hispánica
OC   Obras completas
PMLA   Publications of the Modern Language Association of
America
PhQ   Philosophical Quarterly
PQ   Philological Quarterly
PSA   Papeles de San Armadans
REH   Revista de Estudios Hispánicos
RHi   Revue Hispanique
RHM   Revista Hispánica Moderna
RL   Revista de Literatura
RLC   Revue de Littérature Comparée
RO   Revista de Occidente
RoN   Romance Notes
RR   Romanic Review
RyF   Razón y Fe
SGOP   Machado: Soledades, Galerías y otros poemas

Chapter 1

ORIGINS AND DEFINITIONS

I. THE CUBAN QUESTION

The loss of Spain's colonial possessions in continental Latin America in the early nineteenth century was greeted in the mother country with comparative indifference; but the emergence of a liberation movement in Cuba aroused intransigent opposition. Cuba had come to be seen as virtually part of Spain. Its economic importance, especially for Catalonia, was considerable. Spain also realized that to lose Cuba would inevitably mean the loss of Puerto Rico and the Philippines, and with them the last shreds of her international prestige. Finally, since it was clear that the United States was actively supporting the Cuban rebels, and as early as 1848 had offered to buy Cuba for 15 million pesetas, any retreat on the part of Spain was regarded as a sell-out to North America.

War broke out between the separatists and Spain in Cuba in 1868 and dragged on until peace was patched up a decade later. A number of concessions were then made to Cuban autonomy. In 1893 a far-reaching bill of reforms aimed at solving the Cuban problem was presented to the Madrid parliament by the leading Conservative Antonio Maura, but it was rejected. War broke out afresh in 1895 and was bitterly maintained until in January 1898 Spain began to apply a fresh series of measures which had gone through parliament in late 1897 granting a large degree of autonomy to the island. On 19 April 1898 the United States, alleging *inter alia* danger to her citizens and Spanish responsibility for the sinking of the battleship *Maine* on the 15th in the harbour at Santiago, presented a formal ultimatum and a few days later opened hostilities. Her navy, equipped with modern ships and cannons, blew the antiquated Spanish ships out of the water at Cavite in the Philippines on 1 May and at Santiago de Cuba on 3 July. Spain, whose war party had assured the nation of an easy victory, was humiliatingly defeated. She was forced by the Treaty of Paris on 10 December 1898 to agree to Cuban independence and to sign over Puerto Rico and the Philippines to the United States.

The defeat came as a paralysing shock to a country which, since the restoration of the monarchy after the Republic of 1873, had tended to cultivate delusions of national grandeur. There was no violent public reaction; Spain appeared benumbed. To some Spaniards she seemed apathetic. The lack of positive national response to the disaster seemed worse than the disaster itself. Francisco Silvela, the future Conservative Prime Minister, published his famous article 'Sin pulso' in the Madrid newspaper *El Tiempo* (16 August 1898) accusing the country of culpable passivity. Some younger writers and intellectuals, however, felt a pressing need to mount an all-out attack on the old governing establishment and all that it stood for, including responsibility for the defeat. Foremost were the members of the Generation of 1898. It is perhaps relevant to notice that none of them had taken any part in the fighting. With the exception of Ramiro de Maeztu, all had in fact avoided military service.

II. ORIGINS OF THE NAME; EARLY INTERPRETATIONS

The earliest significant reference to a new generation arising in Spain after 1898 seems to have been made by the historian and politician Gabriel Maura during a polemic with the young writer and philosopher Ortega y Gasset.[1] In an article in the newspaper *Faro* on 23 February 1908 Maura referred to 'la generación que ahora llega; generación nacida intelectualmente a raíz del desastre'. Four years later Andrés González Blanco in his *Historia de la novela en España* suggested the name 'la Generación del Desastre'! However, the real credit for the popularization of the name 'The Generation of 1898' must be given to one of its members, José Martínez Ruiz, *Azorín*. In 1910 he wrote a brief note 'Dos generaciones' (*Obras completas*, Madrid, 1954, IX, 1136–40) contrasting his own generation with a still younger one of unspecified membership which he accused of commercialism and pornographic writing. At this stage he regarded the critical year as 1896 and included in his own generation, besides himself: Valle-Inclán, Baroja, Unamuno, Maeztu, Benavente, and Darío. It was not until 1913 in a series of articles headed 'La Generación de 1898' that he accepted this name for the group and proceeded to develop his earlier remarks. Later these articles formed part of *Clásicos y modernos* (*Obras completas*, II, 896–914). Despite assertions to the contrary, Azorín does not appear to have invented the name 'Generation of 1898', but merely took over a term already in use. He now repeated his earlier list of members, but added a further name, that of the essayist and playwright Manuel Bueno (1873–1936). A year later, in 'Aquella generación' (*La Esfera*, 25 April 1914, uncollected) he included more details and extended the membership to include the novelist and critic Silverio Lanza (Juan Bautista Amorós, 1856–1921).

Though Azorín's articles are of basic historical importance in establishing the Generation as a recognizable entity, from the standpoint of today they present serious deficiencies. In regard to membership they overlook Ganivet and Antonio Machado, while objections may be raised against the inclusion of Benavente, Valle-Inclán, and most of all Darío, who was the leader in his own right of a quite different movement, *modernismo*, which had grown up in his native Latin America and spread to Spain. Manuel Bueno and Silverio Lanza, like José M. Salaverría, who had just as much right as they to figure in the list,[2] have since fallen into obscurity and must now be regarded as dead stars in this literary constellation.

Azorín's attempt to describe the main preoccupations of his Generation opens a much wider field of discussion. What struck him most about his companions was their disinterested, semi-Romantic idealism and their rebellious spirit of protest. Their outlook, he suggested, found expression in two important directions. The first was purely literary and derived from 'un profundo amor al arte y un hondo prurito de protesta contra las "formulas" anteriores'. The young writers of the Generation possessed a new, more 'objective', vision of reality; a new interpretation of Spain's artistic tradition; a new interest in the Spanish landscape; and a new literary style. Much of the literary renovation which these novelties represented was due in Azorín's opinion to the fertilizing effect of an entirely new set of foreign influences. The second direction in which he saw the Generation's spirit manifesting itself was towards social and political criticism. Since the seventeenth century a long succession of Spanish writers had denounced the decadence of their country. The disaster of 1898 produced a fresh upsurge of criticism from this group of young intellectuals.

Ever since their formulation in 1913 these two approaches to the Generation of 1898, in terms of 'renovación estética' and 'la regeneración de España', have, separately or together, dominated critical response to the Generation's work. But it must be categorically stated that they do not add up to an understanding of the Generation, still less of its importance in European literature as a whole. No approach based on them affords even an adequate point of departure for defining membership of the group. If the desire to regenerate Spanish literature is to be the criterion, we are forced into the position adopted by some critics, notably Ricardo Gullón,[3] of rejecting any distinction between *modernistas* and *noventayochistas* and lumping all the *fin de siglo* writers in Spain into one (extremely heterogeneous) body. To take up such a position is to overlook or minimize differences which elsewhere in literary criticism would be regarded as fundamentally important. Understandably it is a position which has not been widely accepted. If the desire to regenerate Spain is to be regarded as basic, we have some difficulty in differentiating the Generation from a slightly earlier group of men like Joaquín Costa, Macías Picavea, Francisco Silvela, Lucas Mallada, and Damián Isern, who were the main contributors to what Azorín called 'toda esa bibliografía regeneradora'. Once more the criterion is not selective enough. It also leaves open the question why, outside the essay and a few poems, the bulk of the Generation's writings were not directly concerned with social or political questions.

We remain with the final possibility of combining the two interpretations and defining the Generation as a group of innovatory young creative writers who at one time or another took an interest in the regeneration of their country. Though rarely stated so baldly, this is, to judge by the main body of critical opinion, still widely accepted as a working description of the Generation of 1898. It is flexible enough to allow the inclusion of everyone whom Azorín originally mentioned except Darío, but narrow enough to exclude such obvious non-members as Juan Ramón Jiménez, Manuel Machado, Blasco Ibañez, Villaespesa, or Marquina. It is unquestionably Azorín's principal legacy to later critics of the Generation. Other members of the Generation also added their comments. The first to do so was Ramiro de Maeztu in the magazine *Nuevo Mundo* in March 1913. His two brief articles, 'El alma de 1898' and 'La obra de 1898' (reproduced like most of the others referred to here in L. Granjel's valuable *Panorama de la Generación del 98*, Madrid, 1959), add little to Azorín's beyond mentioning Ganivet. But Maeztu asked two very pertinent questions which criticism was very slow to follow up. The first was: if the Generation of 1898 was as aggressively critical of society as Azorín declared, why was it not actively revolutionary? The second was: why was there no agreement about which of the national problems was the most serious? We shall return to both of these questions in what follows. In the Madrid newspaper *El Imparcial* (31 January 1916) Miguel de Unamuno published 'Nuestra egolatría de los del '98', later included in his volume of essays, *Libros y autores españoles contemporáneos* (*Obras completas*, Madrid, 1958, V, 418–25). Though avoiding the issue of membership, he too mentioned Ganivet, but seemed dubious about Valle-Inclán. Likewise he saw political protest as the basic characteristic of the Generation, but insisted that the main positive feature of the group was the discovery by each individual member, after the shake-up of 1898, of his own unique personality. In two lectures: 'Divagaciones de autocrítica', later included in *Divagaciones apasionadas* (1924), and 'Tres generaciones', given in 1926 (*Obras completas*, Madrid, 1948, V, 568–84), Pío Baroja for his part gruffly denied the existence of a Generation of 1898 as a unified and identifiable group. But he went on to postulate instead a 'Generation of 1870' of unspecified membership, though it included historians and scientists as well as literary writers. Baroja's lectures, like the articles of Maeztu and Unamuno, are patently derivative from Azorín's 1913 pronouncements. They underline afresh the Generation's idealism, its preoccupation with social justice, and its aggressive hostility to the old directing class. They add references to its bohemian ways, pessimism, lack of common purpose, and eventual collapse. Surprisingly Baroja all but ignores the question of literary innovation. But he reintroduces the question of *modernismo* which Azorín had mentioned in passing. Azorín had simply taken the name over from the novelist Pereda's entry-speech to the Spanish Academy of Letters in 1897 where it was employed as a carpet-bag term of abuse applying indiscriminately to young anti-conformist writers of all types.

III. *Modernismo* AND *Noventayochismo*

Between 1897 and 1924, however, the word *modernismo* as the name of a literary movement had assumed an importance comparable with the phrase 'The Generation of 1898' and had begun to acquire a relatively well-defined meaning. It referred to the movement which had grown up in Latin America beginning in the 1880s first in prose and then more importantly in poetry, under the leadership of the Cuban writer and patriot José Martí (1853–95) and the great Nicaraguan poet Rubén Darío (1867–1916). In contrast to the writers of the '98 group in Spain, who were basically preoccupied with the national problem, the *modernistas* were self-consciously cosmopolitan in outlook. Like Pater and Wilde in Britain and the Parnassians in France, the *modernistas* were aggressively devoted to conscious aestheticism, to Art as the supreme absolute, to Beauty as the overriding ideal, and to radical formal innovation in prose-writing and poetry as the means of its achievement. They exalted creative imagination and fantasy as opposed to realist observation and to the accepted canons of high nineteenth-century bourgeois literature. Signs of a similar orientation had been visible in Spanish poetry since the *Rimas* (1868) of Bécquer, and later poets including Manuel Reina (1856–1905), Ricardo Gil (1855–1908), and Salvador Rueda (1857–1933) evolved strikingly in the *modernista* direction before its full impact from abroad had been felt. *Modernismo* exerted a marked influence on the earliest work of Antonio Machado, Juan Ramón Jiménez, and Valle-Inclán, but all of them sooner or later shifted away from it, leaving it to lesser writers like Manuel Machado, Villaespesa, and Marquina, in whose work it persisted longer. Long before Baroja's reference to it in 1924 it had already run its course as a movement of poetry in Spanish and had been replaced everywhere except in provincial Latin America by the cluster of newer, even more radically innovatory groupings of poets which are collectively known as *la vanguardia*.[4]

The time was therefore ripe for a new approach to the definition of the Generation of 1898 based on an attempt to differentiate it from *modernismo* in Spain. In 1925 Aubrey Bell in *Contemporary Spanish Literature* and Rafael Cansinos Assens in *La nueva literatura* began timidly to distinguish the two movements. Ángel Valbuena Prat in 1930 took the plunge as far as poetry was concerned. His *La poesía española contemporánea* established Antonio Machado and Unamuno as poets of the Generation and demonstrated the greater proximity to *modernismo* of Valle-Inclán and certain others. But it fell to Pedro Salinas in 'El concepto de generación literaria aplicada a la del 98' (1935) and his companion essay on *modernismo* (1940), both collected in his *Literatura española siglo XX* (Mexico, 1949), to make the first major advance from Azorín's original position. The *modernistas*, Salinas argued, limited their aims chiefly to 'la renovación del concepto de lo poético y de su arsenal expresivo'. The Generation of 1898, on the other hand, 'no se limita al propósito de reformar el modo de escribir poesía o el modo de escribir en general, sino que aspira a conmover hasta sus cimientos la conciencia nacional, llegando a las mismas raíces de la vida espiritual'. 'Verdades, no bellezas, es lo que van buscando', he concluded.

This distinction, though fiercely attacked by Federico de Onís, Juan Ramón Jiménez, and others, is now generally accepted and was explored in greater detail by Guillermo Díaz-Plaja in a book of major importance: *Modernismo frente a '98* (1951). He advanced two conclusions. The first stressed the separation of the two movements: 'Se trata de que as posible establecer dos grupos', Díaz-Plaja wrote,

en las que para lo político, lo social, lo estético y lo ético se propugnan soluciones radicalmente distintas. Es algo mas que una disensión estilística, que una diversa forma literaria; es una radicalmente opuesta actitud ante la vida y ante el arte. (p. 108)

The second established the membership of the Generation, divided into two *promociones*: one, slightly older, consists of Unamuno (b. 1864) and Ganivet (b. 1865); to the other, slightly younger, belong Baroja (b. 1872), Azorín (b. 1873), Maeztu (b. 1874), and Antonio Machado (b. 1876). Benavente, Valle-Inclán, Juan Ramón Jiménez, Manuel Machado, and others are similarly divided into two age-groups of *modernistas*. In my view, neither of these conclusions can be seriously disputed. What still remained to be done was to examine comparatively the work of the members of the Generation of 1898 with a view to investigating the most basic question of all: the group's *Weltanschauung*, its underlying 'actitud ante la vida', which is the clue to its unity. Here, notwithstanding the importance of Pedro Laín Entralgo's *La Generación del 98* (1945), the most perceptive work was Hans Jeschke's *La Generación del 98*, originally in German (Halle, 1934) and not translated until 1954. Since then several books on the Generation have appeared, notably by Luis Granjel in 1959 and by Ramón Sender in 1961,[5] but the work begun by Jeschke has not been systematically continued. Many aspects of the religious and philosophic position of individual writers have, however, in the meantime received careful study, especially in the cases of Ganivet, Machado, and Unamuno.

IV. ORIGINS OF THE IDEOLOGY

Salinas's references to 'la conciencia nacional' and to 'la vida espiritual' not only take us back to Maeztu's so far unanswered questions about the Generation of 1898 but also provide the key to the present phase of criticism of the group. To understand why this is so involves an attempt to clarify the relationship between the Generation and Romanticism. Azorín from the first emphasized the closeness of this relationship. Maeztu, in 'Romanticismo' (*El Sol*, 5 March 1921), fully agreed. Unamuno, in the prologue to his novel *Niebla* (1914), confessed to 'el más desenfrenado romanticismo'. Baroja, in *El tablado de Arlequín* (1904), declared, 'Soy por mis aficiones literarias y artísticas ... un romántico'. Romanticism, as no one has explained better than Camus,[6] represents the great watershed of modern sensibility. The world view of many Romantic writers recognized the collapse of previously accepted absolute values and traditional modes of thought on which the stability of individual and social life had been supposed to depend. With the emergence of this world view a new age of doubt, anxiety, and even anguish, in which we still live, came into being. In Spain Larra, the most intellectually alert of the country's Romantic writers, was well aware of what was happening. A 'spirit of analysis', he wrote, had destroyed old-established beliefs and produced a state of profound unrest. 'Mucho me temo', he announced prophetically, 'que nos hallamos en una de aquellas transiciones en que suele mudar un gran pueblo de ideas'.[7]

The traditionalist Catholic reaction which followed the brief triumph of the movement failed to prevent the Spanish intellectual minority from receiving the heritage of Romantic insight. The philosophy of K. C. F. Krause imported from Germany by Julián Sanz del Río undoubtedly owed much of its popularity in the 1860s and 1870s to its promise of a positive answer to a spreading intellectual and spiritual malaise. But with the advent of Positivism and the systematic pessimism of Schopenhauer, Krausism collapsed. In the 1880s Spain seemed to be in a state of complete ideological disarray which stood in marked contrast to her overwhelming national tradition of collectively accepted religio-political beliefs and absence of dissenting minorities. It was against this background that the intellectual formation of the men of the Generation of 1898 took place.

The first to analyse and protest against it was Ángel Ganivet, whose work will be examined in the next chapter. In 1889 while at Madrid University he wrote a short thesis, *España filosófica contemporánea*, which is the first important document produced by a member of the Generation to deal with the problem of Spain. Six years before Unamuno's *En torno al casticismo*, eight years before Ganivet's own *Idearium español*, and ten years before Maeztu's *Hacia otra España*, it already formulated the interpretation of the national situation which was to dominate the thinking of the entire group. Instead of seeing it as an economic, social, or political problem, Ganivet saw it as an essentially *spiritual* one. For this reason he deliberately ignored measures such as agrarian reform, industrialization, or the redistribution of political power, designed to deal with Spain's difficulties in a concrete, practical way. Instead he located the root of the problem in the national mentality: 'el modo de ser interno del sujeto colectivo' (*Obras completas*, Madrid, 1943, II, 594) and specifically in the absence within that mentality of an 'idea directiva', a positive ideological or spiritual consensus. Hence he had no difficulty in concluding that Spain had fallen prey to 'un estado patológico intelectual', was spiritually prostrate, and desperately needed fresh affirmative beliefs, or what he called 'ideas madres'. Unfortunately Ganivet had no clear idea of what the required ideas might be. Though the need is asserted to 'grabar en todas las inteligencias unas mismas ideas acerca de las cuestiones más transcendentales para la vida' (665), the nature of these ideas is never stated.

Despite the fact that Ganivet's thesis remained unknown and unpublished until 1930, its approach to the problem of Spain was uniformly followed by the other members of the Generation of 1898, every one of whom accepted that what the country was facing was above all a 'crisis of conscience'. When in 1895, three years before the disaster, Unamuno published *En torno al casticismo*, he already asserted that Spain was undergoing a deep crisis. Once more what is interesting is his interpretation of the crisis, which is identical with Ganivet's: a lack of 'corrientes vivas internas en nuestra vida intelectual' (*Obras completas*, Madrid, 1958, III, 288), so that Spain presented a picture of 'páramo espiritual'. Subordinating material progress and *europeización*, he advocated the rediscovery of 'las verdades eternas de la eterna esencia' (*OC* III, 184), which he too elsewhere called *ideas madres* (*OC* I, 325). When in December 1901 Azorín, Baroja, and Maeztu brought out their own manifesto on national regeneration,[8] Unamuno refused to join them on the grounds that they were calling for practical reforms instead of trying to 'modificar la mentalidad de nuestro pueblo'. Yet once more the striking thing is the emphasis the three laid on Spain's spiritual bankruptcy and the consequent lack of an 'ideal común'. Years later Pérez de Ayala was still interpreting the problem as a 'crisis de conciencia hispánica' and seeking a solution in terms of 'normas eternas' (i.e., *ideas madres*) valid alike for the individual and the collectivity.

Other people saw things quite differently. In 1898 General Polavieja issued a famous manifesto calling for modern agrarian, industrial, and mercantile policies. In 1899 the *Liga Nacional de Productores* called for vastly increased spending on the economic substructure of roads, railways, and canals, reforms in taxation, education, and land-holding, and the establishment of some form of social security. In 1903 the Conservative Prime Minister Francisco Silvela resigned office because public demands for internal economic reconstruction prevented him from strengthening the armed forces. Plainly the problems of Spain after her defeat in 1898 were those of poverty, underdevelopment, social injustice, regional separatism, lack of investment, inadequate education, and a crying need for changes in the political power-structure. Yet in the face of these problems the Generation of 1898 called for spiritual reconstruction as the first priority!

With the highly debatable exception of Baroja's first trilogy, *La lucha por la vida*, not a single prominent work of the Generation deals with urban poverty. With the exception of Azorín's 'La Andalucía trágica' not a single work deals with peasant life. Apart from a few speeches and articles by Unamuno and Maeztu the problem of regional separatism is ignored. There is no memorable attempt, unless we count Baroja's *César o nada* as one, to explore critically or satirically the corridors of political power; Azorín's political commentaries, though critical, are now forgotten. And where is the Generation's protest against flagrant social injustice? To be sure, we find it sporadically in the earliest 'committed' journalistic writings of Unamuno, Azorín, and Maeztu; but, as we shall see, they very rapidly grew disillusioned with the class struggle. The question remains: what is the relevance to all these problems of the *ideas madres* which the Generation devoted its energies to seeking?

In brief, the Generation of 1898 made the mistake of seeking an abstract and philosophical answer to the pressing practical and concrete problems posed by the state of Spain. To consider briefly why its members did so is the best way to clarify the perspective in which their work must be viewed. The most important reason is that they thought of the problem instinctively in terms of their own individual spiritual preoccupation. As individuals they were deeply aware of the collapse of absolute values which the Romantics had been among the first to perceive. Jeschke, in the first book on the Generation by a non-Spanish critic, saw at once that 'la falta de fe a causa del escepticismo radical es el rasgo fundamental de los noventayochistas'.[9] They saw the national problem as the collective form of their own private dilemma and hence projected on to it their own hoped-for solution. Historically this had always been the Spanish approach. Carlos Blanco Aguinaga in his brilliant but partisan book *Juventud del 98* (Madrid, 1970) rightly emphasizes that 'el conflicto España-Europa, en el que se confunden ambiciones (o necesidades) económico-políticas (la "materia") y valores espirituales, suele presentarse como si fuese exclusivamente un conflicto de valores' (p. 12) with decisive advantage to the anti-progressive side of the argument. Like the rest of Europe at a much earlier stage of the history of ideas, Spain still tended to translate the issues raised by progress in any major field into issues of ultimate values, using mental categories derived in the end from distinctions between orthodoxy and heterodoxy. The men of the Generation of 1898 continued to think in terms of spiritual salvation instead of temporal reorganization.

Reinforcing this instinctive tendency were the examples of the most influential movements and figures of the time. If by the end of the century Krausism was already a thing of the past, an influence emerging directly from it, that of Francisco Giner and the *Institución Libre de Enseñanza*, was very much a thing of the present. Sanz del Río in 1844 had explained his determination to introduce Krausism into Spain precisely on the grounds that it would revitalize the nation's spiritual life. In 1880 his greatest disciple, Giner, inaugurated the *Institución* with a speech insisting on 'la necesidad de redimir nuestro espíritu'. Subsequently he saw in the disaster of 1898 a 'señal, y no más, de una disolución espiritual y material que viene de muy lejos'.[10] The order of the adjectives is noteworthy. The case of Joaquín Costa (1844–1911), acknowledged, especially by Maeztu, as an outstanding influence on the Generation of 1898, is even more indicative. His famous slogan 'escuela y despensa' and his call for a tough-minded dictatorship to carry out his reform programme seem eminently practical and concrete. Yet he too at bottom agreed with Giner. In his farewell political speech on 22 February 1906, he declared that the first priority must be given, not to social measures, but to regenerating individuals: 'renovar interiormente todo el hombre... crear hombres, hacer hombres'.[11] Another major influence, at one time thought of as a possible leader of the '98 group, the great novelist Benito Pérez Galdós, is no less a case in point. 'Like some of the more advanced [!] thinkers of his time', writes Berkowitz, his principal biographer, 'he came to believe that social reforms cannot be brought about by revolutionary changes in institutions, but only by a spiritual and intellectual reorientation of human beings'.[12] Galdós's reference in his essay 'Soñemos, alma, soñemos' (1903) to a 'sueño constitutivo' in every nation reveals a patent concern for that vague collective consensus which Ganivet had already called 'una idea directiva' and which was to survive as Ortega's concept of 'un mañana colectivo'.

We must also take into account the intractable problem of Spain's poverty of material resources and the Generation of 1898's lack of specialist knowledge in this field. The factors which have since assisted Spain to achieve some of the goals they dreamed of: massive foreign investment, a hugely profitable tourist industry, large remittances of foreign currency by emigrant workers in Europe, were beyond the imagination of the men of 1898. Trapped inside Costa's narrow formula of educational and agrarian reform, for which the capital did not exist, the *noventayochistas* became discouraged and turned their thoughts another way. One by one, Ganivet, Unamuno, Azorín, and Maeztu either renounced the Europeanizing ideal and practical reforms in favour of a *Volksgeist*-mystique in which regeneration was to come from within, from the 'alma española' operating at the spiritual level, or else subordinated the former to the latter. Machado, whose views on practical *regeneracionismo* are conjectural, also accepted the racial mystique. Baroja, after 1901, simply gave up hope of any social amelioration.

V. THE SOCIOLOGICAL FACTOR

Finally we must glance briefly at the social position of the Generation of 1898. The middle class in Spain to which its members belonged was small, closed, and self-perpetuating. It stood in a client-relationship with the ruling oligarchy, and though privileged, had little power for political decision-making. Situated near the lower end of this class, as an economically depressed intelligentsia outside traditional allegiances, the Generation was strategically positioned to re-examine accepted political ideas and to formulate new social goals. Sociologically speaking the role of its members as *regeneradores* should have been that of detaching the public from belief in the nationalistic, traditional myth in the name of which both governing parties at the time ruled, and replacing it with a new one based on the idea of *europeización*. But there were enormous obstacles in the way. Possessing no inherited wealth, the men of the Generation were financially vulnerable. Publishing books was not a major source of income. All Unamuno's early books were brought out at his own expense. In 1907 Baroja was offered only 500 pesetas for the serial rights of *César o nada*, one of his longest novels. The Generation's main instrument for propagating its ideas, the press, was for the most part in conservative hands. Azorín was dismissed three times from journalistic posts because of the radical tone of his articles. Political backing could have helped, but here there were fresh difficulties. If there was one idea on which the Generation was completely united, it was that nothing could be expected of the old political power-groups. But no acceptable alternative emerged. Costa's Agrarian League, the movement for 'Revolution from above' led by Maura, the Republican-Socialist alliance of 1907, and Ortega's *Liga de Educación Política Española* (1914) all failed successively to gather political momentum and the country gradually slid towards military dictatorship under Primo de Rivera.

The only really viable alternative was straight socialism. But the Spanish Socialists were Marxist in inspiration, doctrinaire in outlook, and maximalist in intention. Various members of the Generation found sentimental anarchism, with its vague humanitarian idealism, more congenial, but it led them nowhere. We cannot overlook the view expressed by Tierno Galván and Pérez de la Dehesa that the real reason behind the Generation of 1898's reluctance to accept its role as the intellectual spearhead of a left-wing movement was its fear of becoming involved with a genuinely revolutionary force. The *noventayochistas'* allegiance was to the middle class; their work principally reflects the world of the middle class; their target audience was middle class. The conclusion suggests itself that by eventually postulating the primacy of ideals, beliefs, and spiritual forces over concrete social ones, they found a stance which had no threatening social implications. The first major critic to perceive how this played into the hands of those who maintained the *status quo* was Pérez de Ayala in his essay 'El 98' in *Política y toros* (*Obras completas*, Madrid, 1969, III, 1016–19). Politically isolated as the Generation of 1898 was, its phase of direct social commitment remained brief and ineffectual. It produced chiefly propaganda in the extreme left-wing press on behalf of political and economic objectives, combined with destructively critical attacks on the incapacity of the old governing class, the frivolity of the younger generation, the cult of the past, and the apathy of the present. Maeztu acknowledged in 1910: 'Cuando cesamos de dar gritos para volver las miradas a nuestro alrededor, nos encontramos dolorosamente con que las cosas seguían como antes'.[13]

VI. THE PHILOSOPHIC PROBLEM

Meanwhile the assumption, already visible, that the real problem lay in the rediscovery of life-directing ideals and beliefs, led the Generation of 1898 directly to philosophy. Its members read, not in a spirit of intellectual curiosity, but in the hope that somewhere, like Sanz del Río with Krause, they might stumble across a thinker who could set them on the road towards fresh certainties. Ganivet began the search, with the characteristic demand that a philosophy must be evolved which would have 'tendencias prácticas' contributing directly to 'la obra común de reconstrucción (*Obras completas*, II, 657). Unamuno, in the opening of *El sentimiento trágico de la vida*, made an identical demand for a philosophy with an immediate practical application to life. Baroja fell into line with his statement in his essay 'Palabras nuevas' (*OC* V, 1117–21): 'La filosofía como cuestión de escuela no me interesa nada . . . lo que me importa son las direcciones que puede dar a la vida'. All were scrutinizing philosophy in search of the same thing: the *ideas madres* on which to rebuild at one and the same time their own confidence in existence and their country's confidence in its future.

From this point of view, what the Generation of 1898 found going on in philosophy was disastrously negative. Orthodox Catholic thought, even if the *noventayochistas* had been prepared to examine it seriously, was at a low ebb. On the other side the collapse of Krausism had opened the way to a split between followers of the German tradition and Positivists. The former found themselves confronted with the systematic pessimism of Schopenhauer, who was to become indisputably the major philosophical influence on the Generation of 1898; the latter were now heavily influenced by post-Darwinian thought, especially that of Herbert Spencer, which had brought into vogue the biological model of society, and the 'struggle for life'. The prestige of experimental scientific method, divorced alike from revealed beliefs and philosophic speculation, had been enormously enhanced by the work of men like Pasteur, Claude Bernard, and Haeckel. In the 1890s to the welter of influences were added those of William James, Marx, and Anarchist theorists, particularly Kropotkin. Nietzsche, whose influence, especially on Baroja, Azorín, and Maeztu, was for a time second only to that of Schopenhauer, remained unknown in Spain before the end of the century, as did Bergson.

What the rest of the Generation, like Ganivet in 1889, soon discovered was that, just as the philosophical writers of the Enlightenment had eroded the basis of religious confidence in the eighteenth century, so Kant and later critical philosophy had shattered the foundations of comfortable rational absolutes. The achievements of science and the idea of evolutionary progress in man and society seemed to offer some hope, but it was heavily offset by the realization that neither scientists nor prophets of social betterment had convincing answers to ultimate why-questions. For the men of the Generation of 1898 the unavoidable issues were those of truth, duty, and finality. Their aim, as we have seen, was practical: to find a basis for action. They sought reassurance that an unchanging, universal criterion of judgement existed, that there was some kind of ethical absolute to safeguard the direction which action might take, and that action itself could be ultimately purposive. To this end they adopted an attitude to literature very different from that of the *modernistas*. Writing was seen, not as primarily concerned with the creation or expression of beauty, but rather as a method of investigating man's existential situation, a means of access to truth, with potentially valid results. The *noventayochistas* aimed not so much at reflecting or refining reality as at exploring it purposively, with the hope, that is, of illuminating some corner of it which concealed an answer to their problems.

VII. MEMBERSHIP

The test of membership of the Generation is therefore, in my view, bound up with three considerations: participation in a personal quest for renewed ideals and beliefs; interpretation of the problem of Spain in related terms, i.e., as a problem of mentality, rather than as political or economic and social; and acceptance of the role of creative writing primarily as an instrument for the examination of these problems. On this basis neither Benavente nor Valle-Inclán fits in. Benavente, though originally a left-wing sympathizer like the others and a fellow-contributor to Anarchist and Socialist newspapers, shows little sign in his work of accepting either the Generation's interpretation of the Spanish problem or its broader spiritual preoccupations. Valle-Inclán's case is more complex; but Sumner Greenfield and Anthony Zahareas's acceptance of his 'apparent lack of interest in Spanish problems during 1895–1908', and their agreement that 'he was also very sceptical about such '98 ideological attitudes as *agonía, intrahistoria, abulia* and *españolismo* . . . he never participated in the obsessive process of soul-searching which, with Unamuno and others, tended towards introversion',[14] seem to me to be both factually correct and to point towards Valle-Inclán's exclusion from the group. Ganivet's initial formulation of the position hitherto outlined makes him in spite of his premature death a full member of the Generation of 1898. The fact that he died a month before Cuba achieved independence from Spain, which is probably why Azorín failed to mention him in 1913, supports the view that there would have been a Generation of 1898 even if the 'disaster' had never happened. The membership of Unamuno, Baroja, and Antonio Machado requires no qualification. That of Azorín and Maeztu is equally acceptable, though perhaps subject to limits of time in the case of the former, and to the narrower range of his interests and creative talent in the case of the latter. Pérez de Ayala's early novels and his later explanation of the intention behind them form a near-perfect illustration of our general argument, but the second phase of his work marks a transition. Ortega y Gasset's intellectual pre-occupations were, as we shall see, in essence identical with those of the Generation of 1898, but the tone of his response to them is radically different. It initiated a brief revival of confidence among a certain section of his country's intellectual minority. By basing the present study on these authors, it is hoped to present a coherent picture of Spain's first fully modern generation of writers.

NOTES

1. See Rafael Marquina, 'El bautista de la 98', *La Gaceta Literaria*, 15 November 1931.
2. See Francisco Caudet Roca, *Vida y obra de J. M. Salaverría* (Madrid, 1972).
3. See especially, *La invención del 98 y otros ensayos* (Madrid, 1969).
4. For a broader discussion of the issues raised here see Max Henríquez Ureña, *Breve historia del modernismo* (2nd ed., Mexico, 1962); Guillermo Díaz-Plaja, *Modernismo frente a 98* (Madrid, 1951); Gustav Seibenmann, 'Reinterpretación del modernismo', in *Spanish Thought and Letters in the Twentieth Century*, ed. G. Bleiberg and E. Inman Fox (Nashville, 1966), 497–511; D. L. Shaw, '*Modernismo*, A Contribution to the Debate', *BHS*, XLIV (1967), 195–202; and Richard Cardwell's useful introduction to his edition of Gil's *La caja de música* (Exeter, 1973).
5. Luis Granjel, *Panorama de la Generación del 98* (Madrid, 1959); Ramón Sender, *Los noventayochos* (New York, 1961).
6. Albert Camus, *L'homme révolté* (Paris, 1951), esp. 38–75: 'La révolte métaphysique'. For the connection with Spanish Romanticism and links with the '98 see E. A. Peers, *A History of the Romantic Movement in Spain* (Cambridge, 1940), II, ch. 8; A. del Río, 'Present Trends in the Conception and Criticism of Spanish Romanticism', *RR*, XXXIX (1948), 220–48; and my own article: 'Towards the Understanding of Spanish Romanticism', *MLR*, XLVIII (1963), 190–5.
7. José María de Larra, *Artículos completos* (Madrid, 1943), 425.
8. Reproduced by Granjel, op. cit., 220–3.
9. Hans Jeschke, *La Generación del 98 en España* (Madrid, 1954), 87.
10. María Dolores Gómez Molleda, *Los reformadores de la España contemporánea* (Madrid, 1966), 372.
11. ibid. For more on Costa and the '98 see Ramiro de Maeztu, 'Debemos a Costa' in *Los intelectuales y un epílogo para estudiantes* (Madrid, 1966); Enrique Tierno Galván, *Costa y el regeneracionismo* (Barcelona, 1961); and Rafael Pérez de la Dehesa, *El pensamiento de Costa y su influencia en el 98* (Madrid, 1966).
12. H. C. Berkowitz, *Pérez Galdós: Spanish Liberal Crusader* (Madison,

1948), 92. For more on Galdós and the '98 see Berkowitz, 'Galdós and the Generation of 1898', *PQ*, XXI (1942), 107–20; Ricardo Gullón, *Galdós, novelista moderno* (Madrid, 1960), esp. 141–5; Gustavo Correa, 'El sentido de lo hispánico en *El caballero encantado* de Pérez Galdós y la Generación del '98', *Boletín del Instituto Caro y Cuervo* (Bogota), XVIII (1963), 14–28; and Richard Cardwell, 'Galdós' Early Novels and the *Segunda Manera*', *Renaissance and Modern Studies* (Nottingham), XV (1971), 44–62.

13. Ramiro de Maeztu, *La revolución y los intelectuales* (Madrid, 1911), 24. For a more detailed discussion of the sociological interpretation of the Generation of 1898 see my chapter on the movement in *Literature and Western Civilization*, ed. Anthony Thorlby, VI (London, 1975).

14. *Ramón del Valle-Inclán*, ed. Anthony Zahareas (New York, 1965), 35.

Chapter 2

GANIVET AND THE EMERGENCE
OF THE GENERATION

I. EARLY WRITINGS

Ángel Ganivet was born on 13 December 1865 in Granada. Although
he once referred to his origins as 'proletarian', it is clear that they
were really in the urban commercial lower-middle class. In 1875
when Ganivet was nine years old his father died. The family fortunes
do not seem to have been seriously affected, but Ángel left school at
twelve to work in a solicitor's office. Subsequently in 1879 he returned
to school and then, at nineteen, entered the University of Granada
as a student in both the Law and Arts Faculties. In 1888 he took his
degree in Arts and moved to Madrid in order to take his doctorate
and finish his Law degree at the same time. His first thesis, *España
filosófica contemporánea*, was rejected in 1889 and Ganivet was
forced to fudge up another, more conventional, academic exercise,
'Importancia de la lengua sánscrita', which was accepted in the
same year. In 1890 he completed his degree in Law and joined the
ranks of the *opositores*, young men like himself preparing for competitive entry into state employment. In 1891 he entered the com-
petition for a university chair of Greek and formed a friendship with
Unamuno who was likewise engaged. He was not appointed, but in
1892 came first on the list for the Consular Service and was posted to
Antwerp as vice-consul.

Meanwhile, probably in February 1892, he had met Amelia
Roldán, a young lady who was living in straitened circumstances in
Madrid. Ganivet took charge of her family and henceforth lived
with Amelia at intervals until his death. In 1893 Ganivet was
appointed consul in Helsinki, where he remained until mid-1898,
except for four months' summer leave in Spain in 1897. A few
months before his death he was transferred to Riga. Here symptoms
from which he had begun to suffer were diagnosed as pointing to progressive general paralysis and insanity, due to an earlier syphilitic
infection. On 29 November 1898 he drowned himself in the river
Dwina.

Ganivet's earliest known writings are his two theses of 1889, his
Prize Essay on the Concept of Causality, and an essay which is not

17

included in OC:[1] 'El mundo soy yo o el hombre de las dos caras'. They reveal voracious intellectual curiosity, chiefly orientated towards philosophy, and a remarkably powerful synthetic mind. They also show that Ganivet was already coming to grips with some of the general ideas and problems which were to condition his later work. One of these was the idea of national character, which he insisted on at the beginning of his thesis on Sanscrit. It was to acquire capital importance later. Equally crucial was the conflict, already discernible in his mind, between religious belief and critical rationalism. Though still deferential towards Christianity, Ganivet was demanding analysis and observation, scientific rigour and rejection of *a priori* assumptions. That he was already infected by that 'criticismo, que, dicho sea de paso, no es otra cosa que un escepticismo disfrazado' (I, 960) can be seen from 'El mundo soy yo . . .'.[2] This little piece describes the conflicting reactions of a young man during a walk through the centre of Madrid. At first what he sees fills him with furious disgust and misery. But on retracing his steps he finds that the selfsame spectacle produces in him completely opposite feelings of pride and contentment. The mechanical contrast shows Ganivet trying, without much success, to make light of the distressed state of mind described at the beginning of the article: one which was clearly his own.

What is interesting is the way in which the narrator's unhappiness is expressed, not in relation to himself, as we might expect from his description of its origin in scepticism, but in relation to Spain. How did Ganivet really envisage the problem of Spain at this time? We have already seen that he considered the root of the problem to be the lack of a united ideological outlook. In such a situation, both the individual and the nation suffer from what Ganivet later called *abulia.* That is to say: when 'una suma de ideas que se imponen a la voluntad' (II, 609) is lacking, the will itself becomes debilitated. Spain as a nation, Ganivet contended, lacked the necessary guiding ideas for concerted national action. Lack of *ideas madres* had produced national apathy. He saw the remedy at this stage in terms of an educational system specifically designed to reimpose ideological unity upon the nation. Teachers must operate consciously as agents of social cohesion. K. E. Shaw makes two unanswerable criticisms of Ganivet's standpoint.[3] First, Ganivet fails completely to define the content of the all-important *ideas madres* which the educational system is to reimpose on the collectivity; all we are offered are vague references to training pupils in the catechism and the introduction of philosophy as a school subject. Second, 'the idea of using teachers as moral policemen' rests on an astonishingly naïve view of the relations of teachers and pupils, especially when taken together with 'the casual assumption that because teachers are paid agents of the state and because their training is state supervised, they will absorb and teach with sincerity whatever the community regards as right'. The fact is that educational systems tend to reflect their social context. It is social change which brings about educational change rather than vice versa. The whole idea of using education as a means of social control is unsound.

We notice at this point a feature which is common to Ganivet and to all the Generation of 1898: their inability to see society as an ongoing creative process. While they recognize the fact of social conditioning, its influence on the individual was almost always seen as something negative and harmful. Correspondingly they saw intervention in the social process as a matter of individual initiative, by figures like Pío Cid, César Moncada, or San Manuel Bueno, rather than by organizations, political parties, or social groups. This naïve *personalismo* is unquestionably a weakness in their approach to the Spanish problem.

After these early writings two major themes preoccupied Ganivet for the rest of his life. The first is the need to combat the national prostration which he had described in *España filosófica contemporánea*. The second is his private struggle to escape from his own sceptical insight. Central to both was the hope of recovering a life-directing ideal.

II. THE SATIRIST

It was to the first of these themes that he now turned his attention. Between June and October 1893 he wrote most of his first novel, *La conquista del reino de Maya por el último conquistador español Pío Cid*. He almost finished it by December, but thereafter laid it aside until November 1895 when he revised and completed it before finally sending it to be printed at his own expense in Madrid, where it appeared in April 1897.

A deep sense of resentment at Spain's inability, because of her economic and military weakness, to compete with the other European powers who were pursuing territorial ambitions in Africa, and at the consequent frustration of what Ganivet regarded as her historic civilizing mission there, had taken hold of his mind. 'De aquí que no pudiendo intervenir, como no podemos materialmente', he wrote to Navarro Ledesma in October 1893, 'se me haya ocurrido a mí intervenir con la pluma'. (II, 928)

His object was clearly twofold: to satirize directly the kind of colonialism in which Belgium and other European powers were then engaged in Africa; and, at the same time, to satirize indirectly the state of Spain which his exile in Belgium had taught him to see with new eyes. It follows that *La conquista . . .* can be read in two ways:

first, in relation to the conquest of Africa; second, in relation to Spain. Jean Franco, in the only significant article on the novel,[4] develops the former approach, emphasizing Ganivet's intention to expose ironically, through parody, myth, and allegory, the fallacies which lay beneath the European powers' assumption of superior civilization. In this connection the two principal objects of Ganivet's attack are nineteenth-century Europe's naïve belief in progress, and its corollary: that to impose progress on more primitive peoples was a nobly humanitarian endeavour. A key passage occurs in his description in Chapter 7 of the history of Maya before Pío Cid's arrival (I, 394–6). The first part of it deals ironically with the aim of the Europeans and Arabs to 'meter por fuerza la felicidad en los países de África'. Ganivet affects to see in this aim a disinterested and consoling example of human compassion; but he goes on deftly to suggest that if the beneficiaries, the 'savages', understood such elevated motives and had ships available, they would in turn attempt to carry out the same humanitarian mission in Europe. The basis of the equivalence which Ganivet thus implies between 'advanced' and 'primitive' societies is his rejection of material progress, which appears in the second part of the passage. Like Unamuno, Ganivet resolutely affirmed that mere material improvements are largely irrelevant, since they do not affect the essence of man's lot. It is from this over-simple standpoint that Ganivet sets out to question satirically the presuppositions of the progressivists and of those who advocated the expansion of European civilization.

Pío Cid's barbaric behaviour, beginning with murder and ending with human sacrifice, caricatures their belief in white superiority. In his account of Maya religion Ganivet offers a grotesque parody of Darwinian theories and in particular of the utopian beliefs which accompanied contemporary faith in unlimited progress. All Pío Cid's experiments in social engineering and national administration can be easily recognized as satire of the élitist conception of government in vogue at the time. In the same way his authoritarian and large-scale approach, with its emphasis on conformity and collective advancement, can be seen as directed against the subordination of the individual to the aims and purposes of the state.

Most of all, however, Ganivet is concerned to challenge belief in material progress based on technology, industry, and the implantation of a money economy. He follows the usual satirical method of presenting as benefits what are easily perceived to be less than wholly beneficial novelties, and of commenting on them in terms which are usually the reverse of what the reader is intended to conclude. The whole process exposes capitalist exploitation of general economic advancement in order to produce profit for a few. But, like the industrialists Ganivet was satirizing, Pío Cid finds himself still thwarted by the low level of expectation of the Mayas, and the difficulty of imposing a market economy on a peasant society. In describing his arrangements to overcome this problem, Ganivet mounts his most ferocious attack on the economic progress-ideal of the late nineteenth century. A fundamental passage, which must of course be read to mean the opposite of what Pío Cid declares, is from chapter 8:

> En tanto que los individuos se consideran a sí mismos como hombres enteros, completos, y se mueven independientemente los unos de los otros, y no se asocian sino contra su voluntad y para lo más necesario – en lo que los mayas pueden servir de tipo perfecto –, el trabajo no progresa; todos los hombres son libres, pero la suma de sus libertades da la inestabilidad de la libertad general; ninguno es pobre, pero la reunión de sus mediocres fortunas da la pobreza colectiva. Si los individuos se transforman en fragmentos de hombres, en instrumentos especiales de trabajo, y se asocian de un modo permanente para producir la obra común, los resultados materiales son maravillosos, la obra es tanto más grande cuanto mayor es la humillación de los obreros, cuanto más completa es la abdicación de su personalidad. (I, 565–6)

Here we find the bedrock of some of Ganivet's most characteristic thinking. Industrialization means, in his opinion, wage-slavery. Individual liberty and dignity are traded away for material benefits (reaped chiefly by the directing class), men are reduced to mere 'fragmentos de hombres' unable to resist the power of the state, and tyranny is the outcome. The symbol of the material benefits obtained by the masses is, in the case of the Mayas, alcohol. The desire for alcohol having been created, the Mayas are compelled to work harder in order to obtain it; commerce is stimulated by the appearance of shops to sell it, and the whole process sets off a chain reaction designed to destroy the old subsistence-and-barter economy of the tribe. Culture and intellectual curiosity develop, but the kingdom ceases to accept isolation and the result is war with a neighbouring state. This war in its turn is revealed to be another Machiavellian arrangement to guarantee internal stability. Meanwhile the much-prized ideal of growing social mobility and evolution, thought to accompany industrialization and lead to the 'Open Society', is ridiculed by Ganivet's invention of a parasitic middle class of state functionaries obsessed with promotion by seniority.

Ganivet was clearly trying to induce his readers to rethink some of their basic presuppositions. But when we look beneath his critique of colonialism and the civilization it purported to transmit, to discover his underlying attitude, the story is different. What we perceive is Ganivet's nostalgia for an older, better, pre-industrial society which in his more reflective moments he must have known never existed. One wonders where in the Andalusia of Ganivet's experience, the *Andalucía trágica* of degrading poverty, unemployment, exploitation, disease, and ignorance which Azorín exposed in 1905, were the benefits of liberty, *mediocres fortunas,* and free association for mutual benefit which Ganivet writes about? Except, possibly, in his own class, which, much more than the masses, felt itself threatened by industrialization.

More particularly we perceive that Ganivet's general rejection of all material progress was not so much because it benefited the few more than the many, but because it did not fulfil his own spiritual aspiration. Ganivet was right to try and debunk his contemporaries' ingenuous faith in inevitable progress. But to deny that improvements in human welfare have any value, as Ganivet repeatedly does, because they do not provide an answer to ultimate why-questions, is worse than reactionary, it is simply silly. It would not be necessary to try the reader's patience with this commonplace if it were not that it is relevant to much of the outlook of the Generation as a whole, and particularly to that of Unamuno.

We notice with a certain surprise that the Mayas already possess before Pío Cid's arrival certain institutions which smack more of Europe than Africa: a standing army with uniforms, *esprit de corps,* and defined functions, a rudimentary parliament, political parties, a ministerial system, trial by jury, written records, a teaching profession, and so on. The purpose of these institutions is to provide Ganivet with the opportunity to ridicule their equivalents in Spain. The discontented followers of Lopo, excluded from power but dreaming of decentralization and land reform, correspond to the more extreme Spanish Liberals. The *nagangas,* whose activities include tongue exercises, crawling round in circles, and above all dancing an absurd fandango, travesty the Spanish parliamentary parties. We notice that the King, symbolizing real depositories of power and wealth, takes no notice of parliament, whose function is purely decorative, and that a major factor in maintaining political equilibrium is the army, which when not defending the country from exterior enemies engages in civil war. The triumph and subsequent collapse of Viaco in chapter 8 are probably to be read as relating to the Revolution of 1868 and the republican experiment which followed. The return of Pío Cid and King Mujanda thus represents the restoration of 1874. The 'regeneración nacional' (I, 433), which is then sketched out, begins with 'una honrosa transacción' among the parties, and the buying-off of the army, both in the classic Spanish tradition. It proceeds with 'una reforma orgánica' (I, 449) which vastly increases the army officer class, the civil administrative class, and the holders of political office: the three most prominent groups of drones in restoration Spain.

Ganivet alternates social with political satire. His tongue-in-cheek discussion of sexual customs in Maya, his description of the role of fashion, his quaint introduction of soap to the country, and his establishment of bullfighting, are each designed to reveal and ridicule a feature of Spanish life. Even the church as a central institution of Spanish society, is drolly represented by the new High Priest Asato and his embryo 'colegio cardenalicio', who propose to abolish adultery between sinners of different social classes by mass castration of men in the lower class.

The novel ends with an epilogue written two years after the rest of the novel, in quite a different tone. By this time Ganivet had added to his belief in the superiority of spiritual regeneration over material progress a curious obsession with the need for bloody conflict as the necessary source of new ideals. Hence the remark by Cortés in the epilogue itself:

> Yo amo a los hombres . . . pero no vacilaría en ponerme al frente de hordas amarillas o negras que por Oriente o por Mediodía, como invasores sin entrañas y pref'eticos verdugos, cayeran sobre los pueblos civilizados y los destruyeran en grandes masas, para ver cómo, entre los vapores de tanta sangre vertida, brotaban las nuevas flores del ideal humano. (I, 661)

Ganivet's letter of 12 April 1897 to Navarro Ledesma reveals conclusively that he was quite serious in this mystique of destruction as a means of recovering 'human ideals'. Not surprisingly he goes on to comment: 'Si yo espusiera mis ideas con claridad, me meterían en la cárcel' (I, 659).

Ganivet's correspondence contains more reference to *La conquista* . . . than to any other book. Two things are clear from his letters. One is that, although Ganivet was conscious of the originality of *La conquista* . . ., which he rightly says is like nothing else in Spanish literature, he was clear also that the stimulus to write the novel was an almost physiological need to get out of his system his disgust with humanity. This pressure prevented him from giving the book proper coherence and shape. 'No tengo idea exacta de él', he confessed (II, 922). He had written it 'a lo que salga' (II, 918) and the result was rather confused and chaotic, 'una sarta de incongruencias' (RO, 304).[5] The other point is that his view of what was essential in the novel was contradictory. Now he writes 'lo esencial son las reformas' (II, 920); now 'lo esencial es la mutación de Pío Cid' (RO, 305). *La conquista* . . . still awaits a detailed study which will evaluate these and other criticisms.

III. THE THINKER AND THEORIST

In 1896 Ganivet entered the main productive period of his short life. In the first weeks of that year he wrote the twelve articles first published in *El Defensor de Granada* which then appeared in a private edition in Helsinki, in the same year, as *Granada la bella*. By October he had finished the *Idearium español*. From October 1896 to March 1897 he was writing the first twenty *Cartas finlandesas*, published in the same newspaper and afterwards collected with two later ones and published under that title in Granada by public subscription in 1898. In summer 1897 he prepared eight contributions to the symposium of essays *El libro de Granada* published in 1899, and in December of that year began the sequel to *La conquista...*: *Los trabajos del infatigable creador Pío Cid*. At the same time, the first half of 1898, he was also writing a series of literary profiles of northern European writers for *El Defensor* which was published posthumously in 1905 as *Hombres del norte*. Later in 1898 he and Unamuno exchanged the series of public letters published in 1912 as *El porvenir de España*. In October 1898, a month before his death, he was writing his last major work, the play *El escultor de su alma*, performed in Granada in 1899 and published there in 1904. Thus six works, as well as major contributions to two others, were written in two years!

Ganivet wrote *Granada la bella*, which came between *La conquista...* and the *Idearium*, in order to urge, with regard to his native city, the same rather contradictory aspiration that he was expressing at the same time in the *Idearium* with regard to Spain as a whole. That is to say, he wished to see Granada and Spain preserved from modernization but at the same time inwardly regenerated. Poverty, he believed, was a prerequisite.

Already in the epilogue to *La conquista...* Cortés had associated national poverty with national grandeur (I, 656). In *Granada la bella*, Ganivet reiterated that 'Nuestra fuerza está en nuestro ideal con nuestra pobreza, no en la riqueza sin ideales' (I, 100). Granada, in his view, did not need, for example, running water in every household, still less what then passed for town-planning. What the city needed was 'la restauración de la vida comunal' (I, 117): the rediscovery and development of its municipal spirit. And above all, as always in Ganivet, ideas. For, he insists, 'las ideas no sirven sólo para componer libros, sino también para transformar las cosas reales' (I, 120). If Granada could somehow rediscover its spiritual heritage, that which makes it a city and not merely a *pueblo*, 'un espíritu que todo lo baña, lo modela y lo dignifica' (I, 120), it might recapture something of the heritage of the city states of Greece, Italy, and the Low Countries and perhaps create in Spain a pattern of municipal autonomy.

What is admirable about *Granada la bella* is Ganivet's desire to shake his native city out of its provincial sloth. What is less admirable is Ganivet's wilful failure to recognize that spiritual regeneration cannot be considered independently of, or in opposition to, material progress. Worse still is his failure to define adequately either what he meant by *espíritu* or what he meant by the 'ideas' to be associated with it. The same criticisms apply broadly to the *Idearium español*, of which chapter 6 of *Granada la bella*, 'Nuestro carácter', is a brief preview.

The *Idearium español*, written, as we have seen, almost exactly a year after Unamuno's fundamentally similar *En torno al casticismo*, is an attempt to explore in depth what Ganivet called indifferently *nuestra alma nacional, nuestro genio, la constitución ideal de España*, or *la autenticidad nacional*. The aim is to identify, through this exploration, the malady which had brought Spain to so low a point of national decline and thereafter to propose a therapy. The method, as Ramsden in his indispensable book on the *Idearium* convincingly demonstrates, is borrowed from Taine, whose work Ganivet devoured while living in Antwerp. But its remoter origins go back to the Romantics' mystique of national character and especially to Hegel. K. E. Shaw, in the article already mentioned, writes:

> Taking over from Luther the religious idea of *Geist* (spirit, pneuma), [Hegel] attributed to it a mystical quality which acted through men, and asserted that this activity could be detected by analysing their historical actions. The *Geist* is the real force in history. Once he has adopted this mystico-collectivist attitude, a writer has to adopt an exegetical approach to history. He has to see it teleologically as an evolving structure steadily making manifest its inner core of *Geist*. This is Ganivet's outlook in the *Idearium*.

The *Idearium* is in fact principally a heavily slanted interpretation of Spanish history in terms of its relationship to what Ganivet believed was Spain's national character. It has three sections. Section A attempts to isolate the basic forces whose interaction created the national character. These Ganivet reduces to two. The first is purely spiritual; it is the Senecan variety of stoicism combined with Christianity, tested and tempered by the reconquest of Spain from the Moors. The second is geographical; it is the 'territorial spirit' derived from the fact that Spain is a peninsula, as distinct from being an island or an integral part of a continent. The relationship between these two forces is not quite clear, for one thing because Ganivet relates them to different periods of Spanish history. But one feature common to both is the spirit of independence. While stoicism promotes personal independence, the territorial spirit of peninsulas is bound up with conserving their independence from adjacent areas. In contrast, that of continental countries (France, Russia) is bound up with resistance to aggression, while that of islands (Britain) is aggressive. The rest of section A is taken up with the examination of three fields of activity: military, legal, and artistic, which Ganivet discusses in relation to Spain's national character. Although he is more concerned to demonstrate the existence of a peculiarly Spanish reaction in each case than to apply his earlier postulates systematically to them, he extends and adds to his general picture of the national *modo de ser*. We perceive a general tendency to relate what is described to a single major feature: refractory individualism. It is relatively easy to link this in turn with personal independence and with the 'núcleo irreducible' of national character.

Section B is much more coherent. Faced with the difficulty of explaining Spain's aggressive imperial foreign policy from unification to the end of the Hapsburg era, bearing in mind that she is not an island, Ganivet had boldly asserted that it was an adventitious transformation of the true territorial spirit. He now examines Spain's historical expansion northward into Europe, westward into America, eastward to Italy and the Mediterranean, and southward to Africa. Approving of the last two, accepting the second, but regarding the first as a disaster, Ganivet goes on to consider their relevance to his own time. His conclusion is predictable. Spain must concentrate her energies inside her own territory. She must regenerate herself internally in anticipation of her new destiny.

Section C contains the kernel of Ganivet's entire ideology. It gathers together in a comprehensive synthesis the general convictions which he had been maturing since *España filosófica contemporánea*. In all his works and correspondence until this time it is as if he had been clearing the ground for this statement of belief. The starting-point is once more the conflict between the spiritual and the material. Spain finds herself divested of every shred of practical benefit from her past imperial enterprises; even the remaining colonies are a financial burden. Thus she has completed a stage of national development which some nations are still engaged in and others have not yet begun. More important, her material prostration leaves her free, detached, and open to spiritual renovation. The prerequisite for such renovation, we know already, is the recovery of a set of *ideas madres*, which Ganivet here calls 'ideas céntricas' (I, 297). These galvanize the will and lead to positive, fruitful action. At this point Ganivet develops his famous doctrine of national *abulia*, which, like that of the individual, is caused by the lack of guiding ideas. Its opposite is 'el sentido sintético' (I, 295). Nations which possess this sense of synthesis are able to formulate 'la idea clara, precisa, del interés común' (I, 299) and proceed to put it into effect.

But are we any nearer to knowing what the *ideas madres*, or *céntricas*, are, or where they come from, than we were in 1888? Hardly. For here Ganivet leaves us chiefly with inferences, optimistic statements, and declarations of faith. However, a few points are plain. The ideas will not arise spontaneously from the collective mind, but will 'aparecer concentradas en un reducido número de inteligencias' (I, 297) whose function is precisely that of formulating the ideas latent in the rest of society. This is a very important clarification. The regeneration of Spain will be, according to Ganivet, in the first instance the work of a small élite of intellectual *redentores* (II, 945) inspired by *patriotismo anónimo* (II, 934). The essential criterion of validity for any plan put forward by them is conformity with the national spirit, i.e., the territorial spirit of independence. Again, Ganivet does not develop the idea; the reader must scan afresh the *Idearium* as a whole to pick out examples of how the criterion can be used. A specific illustration is the case of Philip II, whose expansive European policy is said by Ganivet to have marked a major divergence from the country's true interests and illustrated a collapse of 'sentido sintético' (I, 235). Ganivet goes on from here to attack the politicians of his own day who similarly fail to recognize the need to integrate national policy with 'un punto de vista céntrico', and instead continue the policy of dispersing the country's energies. Logically to reverse such a policy would mean abandoning the colonies (Cuba and the Philippines) and concentrating on the reconstruction of the mother country. Though he avoids spelling out this conclusion here, this is in fact exactly what Ganivet later came to advocate in his letter to Navarro Ledesma of 17 May 1898 (*RO*, 311–13). What else indeed can 'la concentración de todas nuestras energías dentro de nuestro territorio' (I, 281) mean?

A second example concerns the vexed question of traditionalism versus *europeización*. Here once more Ganivet's criterion appears to offer guidance. While he recognizes that 'Cuanto en España se construya con carácter nacional debe estar sustentado sobre los sillares de la tradición' (I, 175), he makes it plain that he means by tradition only what can be reconciled to the territorial spirit of independence, or what he calls the 'spirit' of tradition (I, 278). Aims that conflict with this spirit, such as the colonization of Africa, however traditional they may have come to seem, are to be rejected. Similarly, while Ganivet wholeheartedly accepted traditional adherence to Catholicism as the national church, this did not preclude his suggestion that the genuinely Spanish form of it had been suffocated by the systematic use of force to impose a total religious conformity in Spain.

While Ganivet avoided the extremes of irresponsible traditionalism, on balance, his insistence on the need to 'españolizar nuestra obra' implies rejection of *europeización*. Believing as he did that Spain is embarking on a fresh stage of civilization, which other countries have not yet reached in their historical development, he tended to assume that their experience was likely to be irrelevant to Spain's new course. All Spain needed was ideas.

What kind of ideas? Here Ganivet made two points in addition to his insistence on the need to accommodate them to the national spirit. The first derives from his famous distinction between 'ideas picudas que incitan a la lucha' and 'ideas redondas que inspiran amor a la paz' (I, 302). A curious feature of *abulia* is a tendency to fanatical extremism. If the aboulic individual happens to be struck by a new idea, 'falto del contrapeso de obras, cae de la atonía en la exaltación, en la *idea fija* que le arrastra a la *impulsión violenta* (I, 292; italics Ganivet's). Such is the case, Ganivet believes, with Spaniards, who use ideas aggressively as weapons, in violent but sterile ideological conflicts. He offers the *Idearium* as a compendium of the opposite: 'ideas redondas' which 'se acomodan a vivir en sociedad'. His ideas, he asserts, admit of compromise. Above all their characteristic is not to stimulate bitter opposition, but to incite his readers to *trabajo individual* and the creation of *obras* (I, 303).

Finally, such ideas will tend towards the spiritual regeneration of Spain rather than fostering her material progress. The *Idearium* begins characteristically on one spiritual note, with a reference to the dogmas of the Immaculate Conception (which Ganivet unfortunately confuses with the Virgin Birth). It ends on another, with the assertion that Spain will be able to set the seal of her spirit upon a host of other peoples. The condition which must be fulfilled, however, before this last becomes possible, is that Spain herself must be transformed spiritually. Hence Ganivet states categorically 'el motivo céntrico de mis ideas es la restauración de la vida espiritual de España' (I, 300) and equally categorically declares his faith in 'el porvenir espiritual de España' (I, 305). The *Idearium* closes with the 'ideas céntricas' still undefined. By this stage we realize that Ganivet indeed could not define them. He believed in the inevitability of their appearance, given the right conditions, as a pure act of faith. An article published in *El Defensor de Granada* on 16 September 1898, less than three months before his suicide, entitled 'Nuestro espíritu misterioso' (not included in *OC*)[6] makes this quite plain.

By now the outline of Ganivet's belief is clear. It is a fundamentally nationalist mystique. Its presuppositions are simple. There exists a *Volksgeist*, an *alma de la raza* which Ganivet freely concedes is mysterious but recognizable. Determined partly by ethnic, partly by geographical, partly by cultural and religious forces, it is the perennial source of national ideals, and seen in proper perspective provides a guideline to the right direction of national development. Latent in the masses, its workings can be identified and interpreted by an intellectual minority (implicitly of writers) and embodied by them in brief manuals or *breviarios* of *ideas redondas* (such as the *Idearium* itself). The free play of such ideas, untrammelled by dogma, traditionalist prejudice, or undue reverence for foreign intellectual influences, ensures national progress and more especially the recovery of national grandeur when this has been lost. This grandeur is in the last resort always a form of spiritual superiority. Spain has diverged from the direction indicated by her territorial spirit and has stifled its manifestations. But disaster will bring her back to self-insight and lead to a spiritual revival. The result of this will be the exercise of an international influence far greater and more durable than her former imperial grandeur. It will be achieved through the spreading of Hispanic ideals.

The *Idearium*, the central manifesto of Ganivet's outlook, is an easy target for attack. All the more intellectually responsible of Ganivet's many critics have questioned major aspects of his reasoning. Ramsden, in particular, has both analysed and criticized the *Idearium* with rare impartiality.[7] He finds the *Idearium* undocumented, unsubtle, and sadly indifferent to fact. It is a simplification of reality, governed by a belief in a simple process of determinism, which is at once dogmatic, all-embracing, and naïve.

A feature of Ramsden's book is his failure to question the whole basis of Ganivet's approach. An attempt to deal with a country's problems which takes as its starting-point the national character is beginning from an unverifiable concept. We do not know what agencies combine to produce national character; we do not know whether such a character if it exists is static or evolutionary; we do not know how it operates: whether it determines historical developments, is determined by them, or interacts with them. To attempt to interpret any historical situation or happening in terms of such a concept is not merely a simplification or an example of naïve determinism, it is an attempt to explain one mystery in terms of another.

Three other issues are important in relation to the rest of Ganivet's work. The first is Ganivet's constant tendency to slip from talking about ideas to talking about ideals; to shift his mental viewpoint from the beginning of action to the end at which it aims.

Secondly, while we have seen that Ganivet never defines which *ideas madres* Spain needs, we now also perceive that he is unclear about their origins as well. Let us accept the existence of an engrained national outlook which is in part at least of racial origin. Is it from this 'conciencia colectiva' (I, 247) that the all-important guiding ideas spring? Apparently it is, for Ganivet goes on to refer to the ideas of the individual as the manifestation of *ideas colectivas*. But how does this square with Ganivet's insistence in his letter to Navarro Ledesma of 27 November 1893 that the idea of the people as a single living organism is a fiction, that the *conciencia colectiva* cannot rise above attachment to the soil, and that 'geniuses' are needed to lead peoples onward (II, 942), or with his obsessive insistence on individual effort. If a collective conscience exists, why does it not operate collectively?

Finally, in criticizing the *Idearium* note must be taken of Ganivet's ambiguous attitude to the practical aspect of his proposals. Since he had asserted, in *España filosófica contemporánea*, that abstract philosophical ideas were paradoxically the most practical ones, he probably believed that material advance would automatically accompany its spiritual counterpart. This is, however, nowhere explicitly stated. Instead material renovation is grudgingly granted only a minor place in Ganivet's scheme. He clung obstinately to a 'peasant and artisan' model of social organization, believing it to be the only safeguard against the dehumanizing effects of working merely for cash-benefits. The fact that Ganivet allowed himself to believe that artisan-made shoes, for example, could possibly be cheaper than the factory-made product reveals his utter contempt for economic facts. Thus Ganivet's errors of perspective in the *Idearium* come full circle. For if national character exists and plays any part of the role Ganivet assigns to it, the forces which can be most readily employed to alter it positively are the very ones Ganivet despised and belittled: economico-social ones.

A pendant to the *Idearium* appeared in 1898. It took the form of an exchange of open letters with Unamuno which was published in *El Defensor de Granada,* and later (1912) as a book under the title *El porvenir de España.* In his contributions Ganivet repeated the gist of his earlier book with a few modifications. In contrast to the timid *europeización* formerly advocated by Unamuno, Ganivet reaffirmed even more absolutely his conviction that Spain must retire into herself. But he went on to reveal significantly that the 'fuerza ideal y material' – the order of the adjectives is inevitable – accumulated during this retreat might well be used in conjunction with the Arab nations for a neo-colonial venture (defined only as 'algo original') in Africa. The ambivalence perceived by Ramsden in the *Idearium* is thus fully confirmed. What is really significant in *El porvenir de España,* however, is Unamuno's extremely penetrating criticism of Ganivet's faith in ideas, and of his confidence in Spain's ability to retreat into herself with positive results. Unamuno quite rightly pointed out that ideas are very often results, and not causes. He himself emphasized that social and economic changes can provoke ideological changes (though he was careful to make an exception for religion), a fact which Ganivet never took sufficiently into account. Moreover, Unamuno prophesied that a withdrawal of Spain into herself, rather than solving problems, would bring to light new ones, in particular the acute problem of regionalism in Spain, and 'el problema económico-social'. Time has shown that he was entirely correct.

Between finishing the *Idearium* and beginning *Los trabajos...* Ganivet wrote most of his *Cartas finlandesas.* His point of departure is inevitably 'el espíritu del país' manifested in Finland's sense of nationality, her literature, and her political institutions. The yard-stick is that of the *Idearium*. Of major importance are the third and fourth letters, which provide Ganivet with the opportunity to develop his political ideas, and the sixth letter, on the familiar topic of material progress. If we look for Ganivet's answer to the ideal of *europeización*, it is in *Cartas finlandesas* that we find it.

Successively Ganivet proposed to carry on the work of the older Spanish novelist Emilia Pardo Bazán, who had been prominent in publicizing the Russian novel in Spain, by sending to *El Defensor* a series of articles on Scandinavian writers. The collection appeared as a book in Granada in 1905 as *Hombres del norte*. Earlier in his career Ganivet had vacillated between the view that literature should aim at formal beauty, and the view that literature was an instrument for exploring reality in all its aspects and for propagating ideas.

By 1898 he had come down firmly on the side of ideas. His articles on Scandinavian writers in every case examine the ideological content of their work, virtually ignoring formal considerations. The end of the Hamsun article contains one of the main tenets of Ganivet's literary creed. Describing Hamsun's 'decandentism' as a reaction against naturalism, he wrote, probably in August 1898:

> Hay en el decadentismo un lado bueno, el de ser una protesta contra el positivismo dominante; pero esta protesta hay dos modos de formularla; quejándose como mujeres, que es lo que hacen los decandentistas, o luch-ando como hombres para afirmar nuevos ideales. El decadentismo es cansancio, es duda, es tristeza, y lo hace falta es fuerza, resolución y fe en algo, aunque sea en nuestro instinto; que, cuando nos impulsa, a alguna parte nos llevará.[8]

IV. A NEW FORMULA FOR FICTION

He was already trying to illustrate his attitude in a new novel. On 1 December 1897 he began to write the sequel to *La conquista . . .*, *Los trabajos del infatigable creador Pío Cid*. Originally intended to contain twelve labours, like those of Hercules, it remained unfinished when Ganivet killed himself. But the publication of the first six, on 12 October 1898, marks a turning-point in modern Spanish fiction, for two reasons. First, Pío Cid, as he now reappears, is the first fully-fledged fictional hero of the Generation of 1898. Second, the form of the work marks a major break with the structural conventions of the novel as they had formerly been understood. The basic feature of Pío Cid is his analytical intelligence. Like all the major novelistic heroes of the Generation he is essentially an intellectual, a man of thought and insight, dogged by an intense and anxious awareness of himself and his relationship with life and society. He is a man with a problem, but a different kind of problem from those which the novel had been exploring since 1868. It is the spiritual dilemma created by the collapse of belief in life-directing absolutes, guiding ideas (whether religious, rational, or humanistic), which Ganivet had attempted to analyse in 1888. We shall meet the syndrome repeatedly in later chapters of this work; it is a unifying characteristic of the major fictional characters of the Generation of 1898. Three others may be mentioned along with it. The first is implicit in Pío Cid's resort to action: henceforth an important question with regard to the Generation's fictional heroes concerns their ability or otherwise to escape from the dilemma into action.[9] The second is that love does not provide a cure. None of the Generation of 1898's major heroes succeeds in achieving fulfilment through emotion. They remain cut off, isolated by their insight, not only from lasting happiness achieved through love and marriage, but also from any real social integration. The third is a more general failure to find a life-directing ideal and a consequent tendency to relapse into anguish and occasionally suicide. This last characteristic gives rise to a criticism of Ganivet's conception of Pío Cid which can also be levelled at the Generation of 1898 as a whole. The group tended to write about the need to rediscover *ideas madres* as if it were common to all humanity. Unamuno even went to the extreme of questioning the sincerity or the sanity of anyone who claimed that he was happy to live in a world which offered no answers to the kind of question which plagued the Generation. It is arguable that nowadays the need for a system of absolute values is no longer so commonly felt.

Structurally *Los trabajos* is just as much a new departure. A generation before, Valera had once defined the novel as 'acción contada'. Though there were exceptions, his definition is generally valid for novels written in the thirty years prior to 1898. There was, as the word *acción* implies, an engrained respect for plot: for happenings, conflict of personalities, dramatic and emotional climaxes. Together with them went consciousness of the need for variety elements, that is for sub-plots, for picturesque descriptions, for balance of characterization, for strongly emphasized love-interest, and in general for reader-appeal.

Ganivet ignores most of these conventions. *Los trabajos* has no organized story-line; the novel is deliberately episodic, even fragmentary. There are no dramatic events; there is no developed love-interest; there is no conflict of personalities, no suspense, little description of places, and no autonomous characters apart from Pío Cid himself. It is a book which stands the previous conception of the novel on its head, reversing its entire approach. The two main structural features are the total domination of the narrative by a single central character and the displacement of dramatic interest, love-interest, and events generally by dialogue, which occupies some 60 per cent of the text. It is clear in retrospect that these departures from tradition constitute an important turning-point in the history of modern fictional technique in Spain. Eugenio de Nora's failure to include Ganivet in his *La novela española contemporánea* (Madrid, 1958) was a gaffe of the first magnitude.

The whole book is constructed around Pío Cid. His aim supplies the book's theme; his experiences are its episodes; his ideas are voiced in the conversations and provide an equivalent to the psychological or social commentary in the fiction of the earlier generation in Spain. He is always on stage. Everything that happens either happens to him or happens through his agency. Every other character exists in relation to him. He is, we must notice, a very different Pío Cid from that of *La conquista*. . . . Like his fellow novelists of the Generation of 1898 Ganivet is now using a transparently autobiographically-inspired figure to explore, and in this case act out, his own attitudes, problems, and aspirations.

In a letter reproduced by N. María López in *La Cofradía del Avellano* (Granada 1936), Ganivet explained that his aim had been to use the pattern of 'una de novela de costumbres contemporáneas' in order to describe 'la transformación social y humana por medio de inventos, lo mismo que en *La conquista*, sólo que ahora la nación es España y los inventos son originales'. As usual when Ganivet writes about his own work this statement has to be interpreted before it can be accepted. The transformation in question is, of course, that which Ganivet had prophesied in the *Idearium*: the spiritual transformation of the country, or what he refers to in the fifth *trabajo* as 'el renacimiento ideal de España' (II, 495). In the book as it stands Pío Cid assists this transformation not by inventions, but by his personal example and influence on a group of representative individuals. Pío Cid acts like a benevolent antibody in the bloodstream of society, stimulating healthy reactions at all levels. The lowest level, that of the common people, is represented by Purilla, the maid-servant of the Madrid *pensión* where the novel begins. She is taught to read and write by Pío Cid and through her love for him evolves rapidly into something like a *señorita* and at length becomes a hospital nun. Purilla more than all the others symbolizes Spain. Redeemed from ignorance, she discovers a spiritual vocation which has a practical application. The middle class is represented by Pablo del Valle who is converted from being a drone to becoming a working functionary and future editor. He is thereby also enabled to marry; indeed Ganivet shows an almost mystical devotion in this novel to the institution of marriage. At the top of the social scale, Pío Cid advises a duchess on the education of her son, and implicitly on a positive role for the aristocracy, as well as setting her on the road to personal fulfilment.

Not all Pío Cid's interventions are directly social. Culture and religion are not forgotten. Finally, in the longest *trabajo*, Pío Cid takes a hand in politics, putting a brake on a particularly flagrant example of local despotism. Pío Cid's own position in all this is clearly explained in two crucial passages. The first, in a conversation between Pío Cid and the Duchess of Almadura in the sixth *trabajo*, contrasts, in true Ganivetian fashion, that inventiveness which produces power and wealth by contributing to merely material progress, with true creativity:

> Estas invenciones dan dinero y poder, dominio material; pero esto ¿qué vale? ... Si yo supiera crear fuego en todos los corazones e ideas nobles y generosas en todos los cerebros, ¡esta sí que sería una invención maravillosa! Los inventos materiales, desprécielos usted. (II, 530–1)

The second is in the very kernel of the book, the 'Ecco Homo' which Pío Cid reads to his friends at the Fuente del Avellano in the fifth *trabajo*, and which in his last declaration he referred to as containing his 'ideas prácticas sobre la vida' (*RO*, 321). Here he takes issue afresh with materialism, this time with the idea of more equitable distribution of wealth as a social panacea. Pensions and social justice he describes flatly as *componendas inútiles* and insists:

> Lo bello sería obrar sobre el espíritu de los hombres. Los héroes del porvenir triunfarán en secreto, dominando invidiblemente el espíritu y suscitando en cada espíritu un mundo ideal. (II, 445)

This, then, is what Pío Cid means when he tells Gandaria 'hay que trabajar para que España se levante' (II, 192). Not to struggle for political change: this is symbolized by Pío Cid's retirement from the political arena after winning his election; not to aim at economic progress or social reform; but to trust to ideas, 'ideas que influyen con el tiempo para cambiar los rumbas de la sociedad' (II, 233), implanted by individual contact and spread by example.

If this were the whole story of Pío Cid's position, *Los trabajos . . .* would stand as a work of noble, if somewhat utopian, optimism. But practically every critic of the novel and of Ganivet's work in general has noticed the fundamental duality which emerges in Pío Cid himself and which cannot be divorced from Ganivet's own outlook.[10]

The *locus classicus* of the 'Ecce Homo' which Pío Cid reads to his friends at the *Fuente del Avellano* is the famous passage on the power of ideas:

> La transformación de la humanidad se opera mediante invenciones intelectuales, que más tarde se convierten en hechos reales. Se inicia una nueva

idea, y esta idea, que al principio pugna con la realidad, comienza a florecer y a fructificar y a crear un nuevo concepto de la vida. Y al cabo de algún tiempo la idea está humanizada, triunfa, impera y destruye de rechazo la que le precedió. (II, 449)

This oracular statement is, like all its fellows in Ganivet's work, a declaration of faith. On what does this faith rest? A page or two later we are given a clue. It is Pío Cid's reference to 'la ley primitiva y perenne de la creación ... una ley nueva, que, más que ley, es aspiración permanente del universo' (II, 452). The basis of Pío Cid's doctrine of regeneration of his country and ultimately of mankind is the effort and sacrifice of superior individuals 'que llegan a conocer con su espíritu el espíritu que llena todo el universo'. It is from communion with this spirit that they draw the ideas, the strength of will, the spirit of sacrifice, the 'idealismo y fuerza', and above all the love which make them what they are. Only when Ganivet's last declaration before his suicide, addressed to Navarro Ledesma, was published in full in 1965 was it possible to understand that this 'spirit' was in fact a process:

la ley fundamental del universo no es la atracción, es la *psicofanía* o sea la manifestación gradual del espíritu. (*RO*, 321)

The end of the process, Ganivet asserted, was the evolutionary transformation of man into a new type of being (which he christened the *psícope*) whose only developed organ would be his brain, converted into an organ of transcendental spiritual vision. Every effort by individuals to ennoble man spiritually was part of this evolutionary process.

We are now able to situate Pío Cid's activities in their total perspective of a universal evolution, to which the spiritual progress stimulated in each individual is a contribution. We can also interpret the most enigmatic point in the text: the reference to 'la visión blanca que tanto debía influir en su vida' (II, 384), of which Pío Cid has a presentiment on the mountain top in the fourth *trabajo*. To interpret the passage, it must be connected with Ganivet's postulate that man's destiny is to evolve spiritually, and hence physically, from his present form to that of the *psícope*. that is, to achieve total spiritual insight. The *visión blanca* would seem to symbolize the possible realization of such insight, the eventual fulfilment of Ganivet's ideal for humanity.

Did Ganivet actually succeed in resolving the spiritual problem out of which the *visión blanca* emerges? The evidence provided by Pío Cid together with that of parts of Ganivet's correspondence suggests a negative answer. From the earliest pages of *Los trabajos* ... the reader is startled by references to Pío Cid's total absence of ideal, his fundamental scepticism, his pessimism, his habitual 'humor sombrío, tétrico', his constant sense of pain, bitterness, and suffering, and finally to his disgust with life.

His dialogue with Consuelo in the third *trabajo* is of capital importance. Consuelo makes two separate points. One concerns Pío Cid's scepticism: '[Usted] debe tener en su alma un vació inmenso que asusta . . . me parece ver en usted el hombre de menos fe que existe en el mundo . . . además de no tener fe no tiene tampoco alegría de vivir, ni esperanzas, ni ilusiones ni ambición' (II, 226). The other suggests that all Pío Cid's activity is performed merely to beguile his sceptical insight: 'Quizás la pena que usted tiene por vivir sin creencias le inspire ese deseo de fortificarlas en los demás' (ibid.). Pío Cid makes no serious attempt to deny either of these points. He replies with three statements of his own. First, lack of fixed ideas and submission to contradictory impulses are no bar to possessing a high and permanent ideal. Second, 'la muerte es fecunda y crea la vida' (I, 227): from the death of the ideal in the individual, there can emerge a higher ideal relevant to humanity as a whole. Finally, if existence is to be conceived as a period of free endeavour bound in on both sides by *la nada*, effort on behalf of universal human ideals is preferable to the cultivation of merely personal ones. None of these statements is easy to accept. If life is a mere parenthesis bounded on all sides by nothingness, then all types of ideals are mere mockeries, and all endeavour is futile.

v. *El escultor de su alma*

That the scene between Pío Cid and Consuelo reflects Ganivet's personal dilemma is beyond question. The evidence which has accumulated since Jeschke's perceptive case-study of his personality in 1928,[11] especially the published correspondence, confirms the German critic's view that he was a personality in crisis. The originality of Herrero's *Ángel Ganivet, un iluminado* (Madrid, 1966) lies in the author's argument that the crisis in Ganivet's spiritual evolution came to a head in 1895–96 and eventually resolved itself into a renewal of existential confidence. The central problem here is the interpretation of Ganivet's last work, *El escultor de su alma*. The ambiguity and contradictions which confuse the interpretation of Pío Cid's character and symbolism re-emerge even more prominently in its hero, Pedro Mártir. In consequence critics remain divided about its meaning.[12] One thing is certainly clear. In this final work, Ganivet set out to explore his own personal dilemma in the light of what he declared was 'la tragedia invariable de la vida'. The play has three brief acts: 'Auto de la fe', 'Auto del Amor', and 'Auto de la Muerte', each of which examines a different aspect of Pedro

Mártir's spiritual struggle. The key-lines occur in a speech of Pedro Mártir in the last *auto*:

> Un sueño agitó mi vida
> y este sueño fue mi Dios,
> y tras de este sueño en pos
> se lanzó el alma atrevida . . .
> Ser de mi alma creador,
> Crear un alma inmortal
> en mi alma terrenal,
> ser yo mi propio escultor
> con el cincel del dolor;
> solo, sin Dios, esto fue
> lo que en mis sueños soñé. (III, 100–17)

These lines enunciate Ganivet's personal ideal: to achieve self-transcendence through one's own efforts and suffering, independently of any divine intervention. The idea is clearly akin to Unamuno's aspiration to the personal conquest of immortality which we shall meet in the next chapter. In the first *auto* Ganivet confronts Pedro Mártir's aspiration with the orthodox religious faith of Cecilia, the future mother of his child. Pedro Mártir, after a struggle with himself, rejects both the ideals which Cecilia offers him: that of human love and happiness and that of the orthodox religious faith she begs him to reaffirm. He must follow instead the 'imperious force' inside him which impels him onwards. But whither? This is the crucial problem to which neither Pedro Mártir himself nor Ganivet critics can furnish a convincing answer: the problem of finality.

The second *auto* is by far the weakest of the three. In it Pedro Mártir develops the thought which concludes the 'Ecce Homo' in *Los trabajos . . .*: that there is a form of redemption by love which is higher and nobler than the conventional one. He attempts to wean Alma, now no longer a symbolic sculpture but his daughter by Cecilia, away from the human and carnal love-ideal represented by her fiancé Aurelio, to his own ideal of *psicofanía*:

> . . . una verdad
> ¡ la sola que hay que saber!
> ¡ verdad que yo he descubierto! (II, 802–3)

To turn his daughter into a further link in the chain of being, at the end of which is total spirituality, offers a simulacrum of finality, which could console Pedro Mártir for the inevitability of death. The diamond which he gives to Alma symbolizes his own soul. Its light is the light of his ideal of spiritual progress and forms part of the light-darkness imagery which conveys much of the play's general symbolism. Alma feels the attraction of this 'destello divino', but at length rejects both it and her father, refusing to forsake religion for satanic pride.

The last *auto* is, of course, crucial. In it Pedro Mártir, revealing himself to Alma as her father, reveals at the same time that his passion for her is incestuous rather than paternal. Of what then follows no critic has been able to give a convincing interpretation. A shot is fired off-stage, but it is not clear why. Alma holds her father at bay with a dagger. Pedro Mártir sees in her action a symbol of his own struggle with himself and proclaims that he has now broken the last chain (his love for her) which prevented him from attaining his ideal. He kisses her, and she is transformed into a stone statue. After Pedro Mártir has once more, with blasphemous violence, rejected Cecilia's appeal to him to accept Christianity, Alma reappears in the guise of a statue of the Virgin Mary. Her father, happily adoring her, is in turn converted into stone. Two explanations of this ending are possible, according to the reader's decision as to which of Ganivet's conflicting aspects of character was uppermost. One is his repressed desire for religious faith, fed by his yearning for immortality and by his anguished desire to escape from his conviction of life's ultimate pointlessness. This is the view taken by Herrero, who asserts that 'la escena final representa la conversión de Pedro Mártir a la fe católica', but accepts that this should not be read as applying to Ganivet personally. His conclusion seems to me to overlook a fundamental objection to Ganivet's attitude. It is that no act of will can do the work of faith. Alma's re-emergence as the Virgin certainly symbolizes the possibility of a religious solution. But it does not apply to Pedro Mártir. The other explanation of the play's ending relates the petrification first of Alma and then of her father to Ganivet's revulsion against the human condition caused by his inability to solve rationally the interrogations which it poses. It symbolizes his recognition, like that of Darío in the famous poem 'Lo fatal', that existence as inanimate matter is preferable to the struggle against the unknowable.

In retrospect it can be seen that all Ganivet's thought and work is dominated by four simple postulates: that Western society's preoccupation with material progress is an error, with dehumanizing consequences; that the true law of progress for Spain in particular and for other nations in general is dictated by man's spiritual evolution; that the source of such progress is personal sacrifice and effort by individuals who are capable of formulating new guiding ideas for themselves and the collectivity; and that such individuals can be recognized by their ability to intervene positively in their own spiritual evolution and model their own souls by acts of will. However, Ganivet was never able to formulate clearly the new pattern of *ideas madres* which he regarded as the essential basis for individual and national regeneration. At the same time the evidence of his own deep spiritual disorientation and its manifestation in the ambiguity of both Pío Cid and Pedro Mártir, necessarily cast doubt on the degree of certainty which he was able to attach to the above-mentioned postulates. In any case their relevance to the contemporary situation is doubtful. The history of Spain and Europe has not hitherto borne out Ganivet's hopes. The renovation of ideals and beliefs he hoped for has not taken place; instead we have become used to plurality of attitudes inside any given society. The regeneration of Spain has not arisen from the peasant/artisan economy which Ganivet advocated, but since the 1950s has been the product of industrialization, tourism, and foreign investment. Collective, not individual, effort has been the mainspring. Ganivet's cultural reformism was based on the missionary zeal and faith of the few leading to the individual conversion of the many. It was borrowed from a Christian model of progress, at the centre of which was a set of ultimate beliefs that Ganivet himself had rejected. It was more than an anachronism, it was a paradox.

NOTES

1. All bracketed references are to Ángel Ganivet, *Obras completas*, 2nd ed. (Madrid, 1951).
2. Published by H. Jeschke in *La Gaceta Literaria*, 15 November 1928 and reproduced by J. Herrero in *Ángel Ganivet, un iluminado* (Madrid, 1966).
3. K. E. Shaw, 'Ángel Ganivet: a Sociological Interpretation', *Revista de Estudios Hispánicos* (Alabama), II (1968), 1–17.
4. Jean Franco, 'Ganivet and the Technique of Satire in *La conquista del reino de Maya*, *BHS*, XLII (1965), 34–44.
5. *Revista de Occidente*, III, no. 33 (1965), the Ganivet memorial number.
6. Published by L. Seco de Lucerna, *Juicio de Ángel Ganivet sobre su obra literaria* (Granada, 1962), 148–53. Apart from this article and the one referred to in note 2, eight other articles published by Ganivet between 1892 are also missing from *OC*. They are: 'Un festival literario en Amberes', *El Defensor de Granada*, 21 August 1892; 'Lecturas extranjeras', ibid., 4 October 1895; 'Arte gótico', ibid., 17 November 1895; 'Socialismo y música', ibid., 23 November 1895; 'Cau Ferrat', ibid., 12 September 1897; 'Una idea', ibid., 26 October 1898; 'Nañññ', *Vida Nueva*, 16 October 1898; and 'Mis inventos', ibid., 1 January 1899.
7. H. Ramsden, *Ángel Ganivet's Idearium español: a Critical Study* (Manchester, 1967). This indispensable book includes a full account of earlier criticism of the *Idearium*.
8. Seco de Lucerna, op cit., 144. *OC* has only three of the originally six literary profiles contained in *Hombres del norte*. The others are on Arne Garborg, Vilhelm Krag, and Knut Hamsun and are reproduced by Seco.
9. Cf., e.g., Doris King Arjona, '*La voluntad* and *abulia* in Contemporary Spanish Ideology', *RHi*, LXXIV (1928) 573–672, and D. H. Bollinger, 'Heroes and Hamlets: the Protagonists of Baroja's Novels', *Hisp*, XXIV (1941), 91–4.
10. See especially (among many others) M. Fernández Almagro, *Vida y obra de Ángel Ganivet*, 2nd ed. (Madrid, 1952), 260, and S. J. Arbó, 'La lección de Pío Cid', *Ateneo*, XXXV (1953), 12.
11. H. Jeschke, 'Ángel Ganivet. Seine Persönlichkeit und Hauptwerke', *RHi*, LXXII (1928), 102–246. The most perceptive article since then is D.

Castro Villacañas, 'Ángel Ganivet, su contradicción', *Clavileño*, XXV (1954) 49–54.

12. F. Seco de Lucerna in his prologue to the first edition (Granada, 1904) launched the positive interpretation of the play: 'obrar sobre sí mismo para su propio perfeccionamiento', which has since been broadly followed by Bonilla, Almagro, and Herrero. M. Olmedo Moreno, *El pensamiento de Ganivet* (Madrid, 1965), 99 and I ('Ganivet's *El escultor de su alma*: An Interpretation', *Orbis litterarum*, XX (1965), 297–306) have taken the opposite view. Norma Hutman, '*El escultor de su alma*', *PSA*, CXX (1966), 265–84 avoids expressing a clear opinion.

Chapter 3

UNAMUNO:
THE GIANT OF THE GENERATION

J. Herrero states categorically that Ganivet was 'el primero entre los hombres de su generación en adoptar una actitud que caracterizará a los componentes de lo que llamamos la Generación del 98'.[1] This is in one way strictly true. The key-year for Ganivet was 1888, the year of *España filosófica contemporánea*, from which so much of the rest of his work stems. But this thesis was not published. Apart from one minor item, Ganivet did not break his silence until October 1895 when he began to send articles home from Antwerp. He only emerged as a national figure in 1897 with the publication of *La conquista...* (April) and the *Idearium* (August). By this time Unamuno had already published, with much else, his earliest short stories ('Ver con los ojos', 1886; 'Solitaña', 1889) and the articles later collected as *Recuerdos de niñez y mocedad*. More especially he had brought out *En torno al casticismo* (February–June 1895) and had completed in 1896 his first novel, *Paz en la Guerra*, published like *La conquista...* in 1897. Unamuno bitterly resented the fact that Ganivet was regarded as a precursor of his ideas. The assertion of Gallego y Burín[2] that Unamuno admitted having borrowed ideas from the *Idearium* for *En torno al casticismo* is the exact opposite of what Unamuno actually wrote. Ganivet's fame as a forerunner of the Generation of 1898 derives from the efforts of devoted friends to publicize his work after 1897 and from the fact that most of that work appeared in the short period between 1896 and 1898. This was what allowed Maeztu in his article 'El alma de 1898' to refer to Ganivet as 'nuestro predecesor inmediato'.[3]

Miguel de Unamuno y Jugo was born on 29 September 1864 in Bilbao. He lived there, through the siege of the city in 1874 during the Second Carlist War, until 1880 when at sixteen he left for Madrid to begin his Arts Degree course. He left behind not only the girl he was to marry in 1891, Concha Lizárraga, but also the world of his childhood with its serene acceptance of life and faith, a world he afterwards longed for desperately, but was never fully able to recover. Like Ganivet he was an outstanding student, graduating brilliantly in 1883 and achieving his doctorate the next year at the age of twenty. The rest of the decade was spent in Bilbao teaching, writing for local newspapers, and publishing learned articles. In

41

1891 after spending his savings on a trip to France and Italy, Unamuno returned to Madrid to the dreary grind of *oposiciones*. A fellow competitor was Ganivet, who is said to have modelled on Unamuno the character of Orellana in *Los trabajos*. . . . In January 1891 he married Concha and in June was awarded the Chair of Greek at Salamanca, where most of the rest of his life was spent.

In 1900 in spite of his reputation as a stormy petrel and left-wing intellectual, he was made rector of the university. Henceforth he became a public figure of growing importance and by 1906 was being spoken of for a ministerial appointment. But although he took part in political activities, he refused to sit as Senator for the university. He also refused a high appointment in the Education Ministry and remained outside Ortega's *Liga de Educación Política Española*, which in 1914 had among its members Maeztu, Antonio Machado, Pérez de Ayala, Madariaga, Azaña, Salinas, and Américo Castro. What really consecrated him as a public personality was his arbitrary dismissal from the Rectorship of Salamanca in August 1914. The reasons have never been fully explained, but Maeztu in 1920 declared categorically that it was 'por una cuestión electoral'.[4]

Unamuno emerged as the martyr-figure of the Liberal-opposition intelligentsia. His support for the Allies in the First World War accelerated the polarization of public opinion into pro- and anti-Unamuno factions. Though clear of party affiliations, he could write in 1917: 'tengo la convicción de influir en la política – en el más alto sentido de esta palabra – española más que la inmensa mayoría de los diputados y senadores'.[5] Another official reaction became inevitable and in 1920 Unamuno was condemned to sixteen years imprisonment for allegedly insulting the king. The sentence was not carried out, but his prestige as the leading intellectual figure of the opposition was reinforced. Unamuno's hostility to the political role of the monarchy persisted and became even more outspoken under the dictatorship of Primo de Rivera. On 20 February 1924 he was dismissed from his teaching post and exiled to Fuerteventura in the Atlantic. The official reason given was 'la activa campaña contra el Directorio Militar y contra el Rey'. On 9 July, unaware that he had been pardoned, Unamuno secretly left Fuerteventura and took up voluntary exile in France. From now on he was the living symbol of opposition to the regime. His return to Spain in 1930 after the fall of the dictator was a personal triumph. He lost no time in adding his voice to those calling for the abdication of Alfonso XIII and for a republic. Restored to his rectorship, he was elected to the Constituent Assembly when the Republic was declared, and made president of the National Council for Public Education. Disillusionment soon followed, and by the end of 1933 he was back at work in Salamanca.

A year later he was made Citizen of Honour of the nation, Oxford awarded him a doctorate, and the Nobel Prize was spoken of. But dark clouds were gathering. After the outbreak of the Civil War Unamuno, disgusted with parliamentary anarchy, briefly supported the rebels; but on 12 October 1936 he crowned a long political career with a noble rejection of their mentality. On 31 December he died suddenly in the house at Salamanca which is now his museum.

I. HIS EVOLUTION AND THE CRISIS OF 1897

The two cardinal facts of Unamuno's formative years were his loss of religious faith as a student in Madrid and his temporary acceptance of Marxist socialism. The origins of his religious problem are clearly documented in *Recuerdos de niñez y mocedad*, originally published as articles in 1891–92 before appearing, with modifications, as a book in 1908. They are also described indirectly in *Paz en la guerra*. Of the former work Unamuno later wrote that there was an 'íntima relación entre mis *Recuerdos*, mi *Vida de Don Quijote* y mi *Senti-miento trágico*, tres actos de la misma tragedia íntima'.[6] Up to the age of fourteen he had enjoyed the unquestioning certainty of childhood. But his experiences as secretary of a Catholic youth organization, the *Congregación de S. Luis Gonzaga*, together with the discovery in his father's bookcase of the works of Donoso Cortés and especially Balmes, opened his eyes to the conflict of faith and reason. The first stage of his spiritual development ended when as an undergraduate in the capital he ceased religious observance (spring 1881). Once back with his family and Concha in 1884, he returned to Mass, but 'la intuición serena de los primeros años' (I, 325) was gone for ever. In 1886 he again ceased to practise, but the period until the beginning of his major crisis in the middle 1890s was characterized by intervals of severe spiritual distress.

Among the intellectual influences operating on his evolution three stand out: Kant, Hegel, and Spencer. The latter's positivistic and organicist (for its time 'scientific') vision of social progress interpreted in a Hegelian sense may have served as a bridge leading the young Unamuno towards a growing interest in the objective problems of society. This ran parallel with his spiritual preoccupations, his pro-fessional philological interests, and his attraction towards creative writing. At all events, by 1892 he was ready to declare to a correspon-dent: 'Yo hago propaganda francamente socialista desde un periódico de aquí [i.e. Salamanca]'[7] and had moved on from Proudhon to Marx. In October 1894 the new Socialist weekly *La Lucha de Clases* of Bilbao invited him to be a contributor. He accepted with enthusiasm, bought a few shares in the paper, and joined the Bilbao branch of the Socialist Party. In the years following he sent the paper more than two hundred articles. At this time he both read and admired Marx and was strongly influenced by his thought and that of other Socialist writers on social and economic questions. For a time he was convinced of the inevitable triumph of Marxian socialism. However, he resolutely refused to accept the dogmatism of the hard-line Marxists who refused to countenance any brand of socialism but their own; more especially he rejected their insistence on atheism and materialism, along with their view that socialism and religion were incompatible. On the contrary, he wrote to Clarín: 'Sueño con que el socialismo sea una verdadera reforma religiosa cuando se marchite el dogmatismo marxiano'.[8] These views led him to leave the party at the end of 1896. Soon, though he was still re-reading Marx and regarded himself as a Socialist as late as 1898, he was to take up a radically anti-Socialist position, although (as with Azorín) a certain residual reformism remained.

The importance of this phase in Unamuno's intellectual evolution lies chiefly in the fact that it was during an interval in writing for *La Lucha de Clases* that he wrote his first really famous work, *En torno al casticismo*, which came out in 1895 in what was then Spain's most respected intellectual review: *La España Moderna*. Here Unamuno swerved suddenly away from his developing Marxist-orientated approach to the problem of Spain. In a book which revealed a wholly un-Marxist order of priorities he turned to the consideration of national character. Going back via Taine to Hegel and accepting, like Ganivet, the latter's belief in a *Volksgeist* determining the historical evolution of each people, Unamuno reached the conclusion that any economico-social method of regenerating Spain could only succeed if it were adapted to 'la personalidad nacional'. This was to be the main theme of his essay 'De regeneración en lo justo' in 1898. An exploration of the *Volksgeist* was a prior necessity. Again like Ganivet, Unamuno began from history, seen as a process which revealed the workings of a national spirit. In his interpretation, the unification of Spain under the Catholic Kings, the prelude to the nation's greatness, was the work of Castile. It proved that the true national spirit was that of Castile, operating as a recognizable historical force. Having identified it, Unamuno proceeded to analyse it, though in a curiously ambivalent way. Its origins remain undefined, though some play is made with influences of landscape and climate (a point to be taken up repeatedly by Azorín). Unamuno preferred to shift his angle of vision nimbly from the past to the present in order to return momentarily to the most important postulate in the entire book. It was that beneath, and concealed by, external historical events, there exists a 'fondo eterno' and an 'intrahistoria castellana', still very much alive and operating under the surface. This reservation having been made, Unamuno was free to criticize sharply sundry prominent aspects of the Castilian spirit, notwithstanding his recognition of its impressive historical and artistic achievements. His chief criticism is a variant of the idea of 'mediterranean clarity' of thought. Rather in the manner in which Ganivet was to describe Spanish ideas as *picudas*, Unamuno declared them to be lacking in 'nimbus'. They were too stark, too simplistic, too clearly defined; their very form was an obstacle to conciliation, compromise, and creative synthesis. Hence the Castilian spirit as revealed in its literary and spiritual manifestations is 'dualista y polarizador', dissociative, rigid, and categoric. Combined with the impulsive voluntarism of the Castilian mind, it can be observed in the characteristic heroes of the Golden Age *comedia* and in real life in the *conquistador*. Socially its effect is disgregatory. It produces a community of exacerbated individualists restrained by repressive, authoritarian laws and customs: 'anarquismo moral bajo el peso de absolutismo social' (III, 248). Once more like Ganivet, and in the *Krausista* tradition of seeing a nation's literature as a guide to its national spirit, Unamuno pursues his interpretation through Golden Age drama and mystical writing, contrasting along the way Calderón with Shakespeare and the Mystics with Fray Luis de León. Just as the *hidalgos* and *conquistadores* of secular Golden Age society despised manual work and patient intellectual effort, so the Mystics sought the conquest and possession of unity with God not by the hard, slow road of meditation and rational inquiry, but in a single effortless upward swoop of the soul. To all this Fray Luis is the exception. His ideal is 'la modesta ciencia del trabajo' (268), the search for the 'elementos espirituales' which are 'ideas madres' (269) productive of peace, harmony, and synthesis.

The conclusion is predictable. With the defeat of Spain's imperial policy and the onset of national decadence, the old Castilian spirit, which for all its defects had been a source of national grandeur both material and spiritual, became fossilized. It survived, Unamuno declared, in the dead, reactionary traditionalism of his own day, mistakenly thought to be genuinely *castizo*. It had become the platform of a blinkered nationalistic *casta histórica* who not only resisted *europeización* and progress, but also perpetuated all the negative characteristics of the Castilian spirit. These Unamuno tabulates afresh in the final essay, which attributes the nation's sorry state to their survival and prestige. Happily, the reservation made earlier remains. Alive in the hearts of the common (implicitly rural) people of Spain is *la intrahistoria, la tradición eterna*, which is 'la sustancia del progreso' (185). The role of the intellectual is to study this 'eternal tradition', 'haciendo conciente lo que en el pueblo es inconciente' (187), and to fertilize it as it had often been fertilized in the past by incorporating anew into the nation's life a process of *europeización*. 'Europeizándonos para hacer España y chapuzándonos en pueblo, regeneraremos esta estepa moral' (302), Unamuno concluded.

En torno al casticismo is open to the same criticisms that were levelled in the previous chapter at the *Idearium* of Ganivet. Historicism; the idea that there are abstract forces working themselves out in history; the idea of the *Volksgeist*, just as mysterious and unverifiable in its origins and operations here as in Ganivet; indifference to other historical forces in all their immense complexity, simple deterministic assumptions about national evolution; selection of evidence; determination to interpret rather than to observe and study; lack of definition of 'lo intrahistórico'; they are all here as rampant as ever. More grave in Unamuno's case, given his acquaintance with Marxist thought, is the bland way in which he too applies abstract considerations to concrete social problems.

Yet a feature of the book is Unamuno's specific statement: 'La pobreza económica explica nuestra anemia mental' (290) and his remark in a footnote to the page: 'Es un punto que merecería estudiarse el de la influencia de nuestra pobreza económica en nuestra cultura'. A wholly different and more direct approach to *regeneración* is suggested in these sentences. To his credit, Unamuno did not entirely ignore it. He was, like Maeztu, a critic of Spain's agrarian situation, then the root of her economic problem. But while from 1899 ('La dehesa española' and 'La conquista de las mesetas') to 1914 ('Campaña agraria') he attacked the policies of the capitalists and the large landowners, his writings on this reveal by their fewness and repetitiveness the total inadequacy of the economic thinking which Unamuno, in common with the Generation of 1898 as a whole, brought to the practical problem of regenerating Spain.

The articles and political activity of 1914 reveal Unamuno's continuing commitment to the most basic of all concrete reforms in Spain, land reform, but they were by this time marginal to his real preoccupations. One reason was his confidence in an undefined 'virtus medicatrix societatis', because of which regeneration would just happen anyway.[9] The real reason, however, is to be found in the very acute spiritual crisis he underwent in 1897. It brought him also face to face with the problem which Ganivet finally failed to resolve: that of finality. In a letter to Costa of the following year he confessed that 'la idea, indesarraigable de mi espíritu de que es inútil que nos propongamos fin alguno si el universo no lo tiene' had turned his mind completely away from social and economic questions.[10]

Unamuno's crisis of 1897 was a turning-point in his life. His terrible experience of the previous year, when an attack of meningitis had dreadfully handicapped his infant son Raimundín, probably helped to bring it on, but as Zubizarreta has shown,[11] it was already incubating even before then. In March 1897 Unamuno awoke from his restless and unhappy agnosticism to a dreadful awareness of living 'al borde de la nada', to fear of 'la muerte y total acabamiento', and to an intense and irrepressible yearning for immortality. He seems to have experienced a moment of simple belief, but it did not last. What his position then became is a subject of deep controversy. Lacy has excellently summarized in English the divergencies of opinion, especially as between Zubizarreta and Sánchez Barbudo.[12] The reader's conclusion is likely to depend on his views about whether any firm dividing-line exists between belief and unbelief. Both the extreme clerical and atheistic critics from their respective positions class Unamuno as an unbeliever. As such he was condemned by the Catholic Holy Office in 1957. *Del sentimiento trágico de la vida* and *La agonía del cristianismo* were placed on the Index. Other critics, including Lacy, avoid this dogmatic stance and plead that all faith is to some extent ambiguous and even sporadic. While admitting Unamuno's *unorthodoxy*, they accept that he achieved some degree of faith or leave the matter open.

That Unamuno never achieved serene belief is beyond doubt; but that does not automatically make him an atheist. If he could not totally reconcile himself to believing in God's existence or in the promise of eternal life, neither could he reconcile himself to rejecting such beliefs. His desperate will to believe is, even to the unbeliever, just as apparent as the rational obstacles which it encountered. If the absolute sincerity of that will to believe is sometimes to be questioned in the light of Sánchez Barbudo's cogent arguments, at other times it shines forth so brightly as to be indistinguishable from faith itself. No poem as deeply moving as *El Cristo de Velázquez*, which has been insufficiently studied in this connection, can be the product of insincerity. Unamuno's religious position must not be judged by narrow criteria which are applicable only to a small minority of intellectually aware Christians. On the contrary, much of the extra-literary appeal of his work is due to the fact that it centres on problems of belief which many who unhesitatingly profess themselves to be Christians share.

The fruits of his crisis and travail were not long in appearing. Foremost was a radical deviation from his earlier preoccupation with progress and the *europeización* of Spain.[13] 'Cada día me siento menos progresista', he wrote to Ganivet on 20 November 1898. He dis-associated himself from the 1901 manifesto of Azorín, Baroja, and Maeztu. His last major statement in which we can recognize his earlier allegiances was his 'Discurso en el Ateneo de Valencia' of 24 April 1902. Already it was slightly anachronistic in his development. By

1914 the view he had expressed to Costa, which he reiterated to his friend Ilundaín and incorporated into his important essay 'La vida es sueño' (1898), had become a fixation. 'Es su idea fija monomaníaca', he wrote of himself in the prologue to his novel *Niebla*, 'de que si su alma no es inmortal, y no lo son las almas de los demás hombres y aun de todas las cosas . . . si no es así, nada vale ni hay esfuerzo que merezca la pena'. There is no obvious or necessary connection between recognizing the absence of ultimate transcendental finality and refusing to accept an immanent finality, even of a material-progressive kind. Yet it was in the name of this arbitrary association of ideas that Unamuno turned his back on the regeneration movement. His erstwhile Socialist comrades, including Maeztu, did not spare him their criticisms for so doing.

His spiritual trajectory at this time can be followed through a series of writings beginning with *Nicodemo el fariseo* (1899) and *Tres ensayos* (1900). The former has come to be seen as the key to Unamuno's future development. While still recognizing economic factors as the 'efficient cause' of human progress, he now (as in his play *La esfinge* of the previous year) shifts the emphasis firmly to religious aspiration as its 'final cause'. Acceptance of an intemporal transcendental finality for all life is now seen as the indispensable condition of genuine progress, which thus comes in the end to be spiritual progress. The need is now not for collective regeneration but for personal salvation; not for the nation to escape from underdevelopment but for the individual to escape from 'eterno hastío, ansia y terror a la vez de la nada' (III, 141). This is to be achieved by releasing from the 'dura costra mundana' in which it is encapsulated the 'hombre interior', first in oneself, then in others, and finally stimulating in all men 'hambre de eternidad' (134, 142–3). Among the chief obstacles to this process of discovery and release of the hidden self Unamuno identified two: dogmatic rationalized belief (*creencia*, gnosis) which displaces faith (*fe*, pistis) and dogmatic intellectual doctrines which displace 'living' truth and imprison the mind in rigid formulae. The third of the *Tres ensayos*, 'Adentro', is an epistle of encouragement to those who are prepared to follow Unamuno in his new-found direction. The task of the intelligentsia, he now proclaimed, was no longer that of conciliating *europeización* with the *tradición eterna* of Spain, but that of spreading spiritual awareness.

II. *Agonismo* AND THE TRAGIC SENSE OF LIFE

A major development of the lines of thought contained in these early essays appeared in 1905 as *Vida de Don Quijote y Sancho*. Using *Don Quixote* as a framework and interpreting the characters and episodes symbolically, Unamuno extensively re-explored the human and national problems. Reversing the hostility to Don Quixote which he had shown in *En torno al casticismo*, he now adopts the knight as the 'símbolo vivo de lo superior del alma castellana' (III, 385). Don Quixote's quest for undying fame, his struggle to impose his vision of life by force of will on the rationalistic world, and his detachment from worldly self-interest are presented as symbolizing the Spanish people's 'culto a la inmortalidad' (the spiritual essence of the race) in action. Don Quixote is seen throughout the book as the prophet of 'cristianismo quijotesco', of 'fe quijotesca y quijotizante', which Unamuno passionately commends. Though still attacking wealth and property (IV, 361), he now resolutely condemns 'todo eso que llamen soluciones concretas' (132) and ridicules as cheapjack nostrums 'el cocimiento regenerativo, el bálsamo católico, el revulsivo anticlerical, el emplasto aduanero o el vejigatorio hidráulico' (132). Priority is firmly accorded to spiritual regeneration; 'Nuestra patria no tendrá agricultura, ni industria, ni comercio, ni habrá aquí caminos que lleven a parte adonde merezca irse mientras no encendamos en el corazón de nuestro pueblo el fuego de las eternas inquietudes' (206). Since this is an individual question, emphasis was now and always henceforth primarily on the individual problem.

In regard to this the note of confidence sounded in the writings of 1899–1900 was not sustained. What makes the *Vida* Unamuno's first fully mature ideological statement and the direct antecedent of his central work as a thinker, *Del sentimiento trágico de la vida*, is the perceptible difference of tone compared with the *Tres ensayos* (especially with 'La fe'). It is here in the *Vida* that the most famous reference to Unamuno's *angustia* occurs. In chapter 58 he expresses his central intuition: that the thought, not of death, but of total non-existence after death, annihilation, *anonadamiento*, is something at once unbearably anguishing and at the same time, by that very fact, the point of breakthrough to ultimate, 'substantial' truth. The encounter with anguish, Unamuno held, is a positive experience, the birth of existential awareness: 'La congoja del espíritu es la puerta de la verdad substancial' (314). It releases the mind and the spirit from the rational 'aparential' truth of 'logic', whose inevitable message is the negation of all finality, and it leads them to accept the affirmations of 'la cardíaca': the truth of the heart, the truth of faith. In the other two fundamentally important chapters of the book, 54 and 57, Don Quixote is exalted as the prototype of all seekers after immortality in the teeth of reason, while the contribution of Spain to Western civilization is asserted to be that of keeping alive his spiritual quest and upholding the notion of the spiritual nature of man in a world increasingly committed to values based only on his material appetites.

In 'Plenitud de plenitudes' (1904) and 'El secreto de la vida' (1906) followed by *Mi religión y otros ensayos* (1913) Unamuno continued to expound his position. But it was above all in *Del sentimiento trágico de la vida* (1913) that he expressed what is in many respects his final view of the human situation. It is chiefly around the latter work that controversy persists. The best that can be attempted here, amid conflicting interpretations, is a summary of the main points of interest. All Unamuno's thought is founded on two irreducible facts which the experience of anguish forces man to face: his consciousness of his own personal existence and his fear of non-existence. It is impossible either to think of ourselves as non-existent or to contemplate total annihilation. It follows that man's deepest experience is 'terror a la nada', and his deepest aspiration is to continue to exist eternally as himself. Knowledge of the existence of the outside world is inseparable from consciousness of the existence of self, and vice versa. Thus personal immortality involves the immortality of all creation. The orthodox Christian response to this state of awareness invokes the concept of sin as its cause and grace as the means of escape from its consequences. Neither of these concepts occupies a significant place in Unamuno's thinking; hence much, though not all, of his unorthodoxy. Hence too his main difference from Kierkegaard. Without grace, faith is problematic. For Unamuno, it is not a state, but a dynamic creative effort, a struggle: 'fe agónica'. Identifying man's religious impulse, 'las ganas de Dios', an instinctive, irrational, visceral need, with man's longing for immortality, and this in turn with the essence of life itself, Unamuno presents the vital impulse along with the will and agonic faith as allies in a struggle to impose themselves on reason, 'obligándola a que sirva de apoyo a sus anhelos' (XVI, 243). For it is reason which affirms 'que la inmortalidad del alma individual es un contrasentido lógico, es algo no sólo irracional, sino contrarracional' (245).

Chapter 9 of *Del sentimiento* amplifies Unamuno's conception of faith not as a gift from God, but as a continuous process by which we create God in ourselves. It carries with it the implications that our power to develop this process is an indication of the fact that God already exists within us, and that our creation and personalization of Him in our image is simply a form of His creation of us in His image. Any other faith than this, whether it is the unquestioning *foi du charbonnier* or the dogmatically structured belief of the professional theologian, Unamuno rejects as unhesitatingly (and perhaps as uncharitably) as he rejects the rational alternatives to faith as well as all forms of agnosticism.

Unamuno's view of truth, which found comfort in William James's pragmatism, is determined by the foregoing view of faith. Truth is what is genuinely believed, the test of this being action. Truth is what contributes to living meaningfully, not just being right. The truth which can be perceived by logical processes of reason is for Unamuno anti-vital in the sense that it contradicts the yearning for immortality which he believed was indistinguishable from the vital impulse itself. Yet the only faith which could support him was a faith not based on reason, but nevertheless supplemented and aided by reason. Although, for him, truth is experienced rather than known, over and over again in *Del sentimiento trágico* he insists on the fact that 'la fe necesita algo en que ejercerse' and on the need for 'guarantees'. These he attempted to find in the postulate of a higher kind of truth, the product not of the rational mind but of the heart and the inmost being: 'lo cardíaco', 'lo biótico', of man's almost physiological religious instinct. His writings on the religious question constitute a desperate attempt to evolve a rationally persuasive structure of support for the overriding dictates of *cordialismo*. This was what Unamuno meant when he wrote of the need to 'vitalizar la razón'.

It is when Unamuno comes to the problem of combining his concepts of faith and truth and transmitting intelligibly the discoveries of his faith's cognitive element that he leaves behind not only orthodoxy but also the bulk of his readers. For while he is discussing the nature of spiritual experience and its attendant difficulties, he is handling a matter of universal interest. But the conclusions he appeared to reach by means of 'agonic faith' expressing itself via 'vitalized reason' are very much more personal and less generally acceptable. What is the transcendental process to which agonic effort contributes? What is its goal? For Unamuno being is personal consciousness, *ser* is *serse*; but also in an active, dynamic sense, *ser* is *hacerse*. Desire for immortality is painful desire for the continuity of consciousness. God, too, is consciousness: 'conciencia del mundo', as Unamuno repeatedly called Him. Hence it is not surprising to find that finality is also consciousness: 'conciencia y finalidad son la misma cosa en el fondo' (139). In what sense? The answer lies in Unamuno's belief in the expansiveness of consciousness: 'La conciencia tiende a ser más conciencia cada vez' (338). The thrust of consciousness operates in two directions: outwardly as 'el impulso de serlo todo, a ser también los demás sin dejar de ser lo que somos' (275); and inwardly as the ceaseless *hacerse* of our inner personality, which Unamuno in an important essay, 'El individualismo español' (III, 617–32), distinguished from our individuality. The goal of life is thus to be ever more consciously oneself, and ever more all things: to stretch the self to infinite dimensions by means of a dolorous effort of love and compassion aimed at absorbing all creation into consciousness: 'ser cada uno lo que es, siendo a la vez todo lo que es'

(XVI, 334). This process, which Unamuno identifies with 'la divinización de todo', leads to the discovery of God's being as personal consciousness also, while at the same time making 'la fe creadora' an integral part of authentic existence. Logically the end would be the absorption of all things into God's consciousness. But here, in chapter 10 of *Del sentimiento trágico*, Unamuno characteristically calls a halt: 'el alma, mi alma al menos, anhela otra cosa, no absorción, no quietud, no paz, no apagamiento, sino eterno acerarse sin llegar nunca, inacabable anhelo, eterna esperanza... Un eterno Purgatorio, pues, más que una Gloria' (381). For only thus can personal consciousness, 'inmortalidad de bulto', survive beyond the grave. The difficulties implicit in these notions are too complex and numerous to warrant discussion here. They centre above all on the fact that while objectively speaking Unamuno's position was broadly pantheistic or panentheistic, with God presented as immanent, in his intention and desire God was 'el Dios vivo, el Dios-Hombre'. All attempts to interpret Unamuno's God-talk come to grief on this point.

Finally, Unamuno asserts, in the thrust of consciousness towards personal immortality we find a basis for moral action: 'Obra de modo que merezcas a tu propio juicio y a juicio de los demás la eternidad, que te hagas insustituíble, que no merezcas morir' (387). Without the help of grace, without the fear of hell, the responsibility for conduct rests squarely on the individual and is attested by his intention alone. The moral imperative is to act in such a way as to make any ultimate annihilation an injustice.

Del sentimiento trágico de la vida was not to be Unamuno's final formulation of his agonic *credo*. Another deep and anguishing spiritual crisis can be discerned in his life during the early years of exile. The two main works of this period, *Cómo se hace una novela*,[14] begun in 1924, and *La agonía del cristianismo* (1925), reveal that the state of 'feliz incertidumbre' or 'resignación activa', which Unamuno seemed to have achieved in middle life, proved fragile. Separation from Spain and from Concha who, as he was to write:

> desde el seno mismo de mi nada
> me hiló el hilillo de una fe escondida

together with a deep sense of the failure of his political role and perhaps some feeling of guilt for his flight to France, provoked in him an acute need to reassess his life and beliefs. Perhaps now he finally lost his struggle to believe in personal immortality. Equally there seems to have come to him an awareness of the threat presented by private vanity which had played such an obvious part in motivating both his public activities and the exhibition of his spiritual intimacy to the reading public. His play *El otro* (1926) expresses symbolically the fear that the role he had accepted for himself since 1898 and the public image surrounding it had destroyed another, more intimate, self with a greater chance of achieving serene faith. So near the end of his life the growing suspicion that there existed an 'el que pudo ser' which had been stifled by his 'querer ser' led to his last great creative work, *San Manuel Bueno, mártir, y tres historias más* (1933), in which he approached 'el pavoroso problema de la personalidad'.

III. UNAMUNO THE NOVELIST:
THE INVENTION OF THE *Nivola*

There is indeed no firm frontier between Unamuno's broadly philosophical books and his creative writings. He himself asserted in the *prólogo-epílogo* to his second novel, *Amor y pedagogía* (1902): 'el sentimiento, no la concepción racional del Universo y de la vida, se refleja, mejor que en un sistema filosófico, en un poema en prosa o verso, en una novela ... ante todo y sobre todo la filosofía es, en rigor, novela o leyenda' (II, 431). Thus when we turn to his novels and poetry it is with the double intention of relating them to his general outlook and examining their intrinsic literary quality.

A feature of criticism of Unamuno's fiction is a tendency to exaggerate his originality. There was no sudden change in the Spanish novel at the turn of the century; rather we perceive a transition from the later novels of Galdós to the fictional manner of the '98. In so far as there was a shift, it was marked by the appearance of Ganivet's *Los trabajos de Pío Cid* in 1898, at a time when Unamuno was still writing in the 'oviparous' realist manner. The salient characteristics of the '98 novel were introduced, as we have seen, not by Unamuno or Baroja, but by Ganivet. What Unamuno's fictional practice does mark in the history of the Spanish novel is the emergence (especially in *Niebla*) of interior monologue as a major feature of the narrative technique. In retrospect we can see that this was the beginning of stream-of-consciousness literature in Spanish.

We may none the less agree with Batchelor that 'Unamuno is undoubtedly one of the first writers to have seen the novelistic possibilities pertaining to the existential condition'.[15] Certainly this is what lifts his first novel, *Paz en la guerra*, above the level of a mere chronicle of episodes in the Second Carlist War. Outwardly the story concerns the siege of Bilbao and the campaigns near it in 1874. A series of parallelisms runs from end to end of the text, linking the figures of Pedro Antonio Iturriondo and his family, who are of peasant origin, to the common people, the countryside, Carlism, simple faith, Spain's 'tradición eterna', and the placid serenity of *intrahistoria*. In contrast it links the Aranas and Pachico Zabalbide, who are lower-middle-class townsfolk, with the educated classes, the city, liberalism, rational and class influences on faith, and ultimately with modernity. A second structural element is, as it were, horizontal. It divides the historical events of the setting from the 'intrahistorical' (to Unamuno more real) pattern of life which goes on inside them. The design is intended to convey in fictional terms the conflict which Unamuno had explored in *En torno al casticismo* between *historia* and *intrahistoria*, Spain's *casta eterna* and modern influences, and in the autobiographical figure of Pachico, the corresponding spiritual conflict in the individual who is caught between the nation's heritage of traditional ideas and beliefs which conditions his upbringing, and the discovery of modern thought. We must notice that Unamuno worked backwards from Pachico's vision at the end, incorporating earlier work, refurbished, into the fabric of the narrative.

Unamuno's aim was to express, through the balance he achieved between the various opposing elements in the novel, the notion of fruitful conflict. Pachico's discovery of this ongoing dialectical process in himself and in the nation at large, reveals an Unamuno whose outlook was already agonic but not yet tragic. This more than the sometimes uneasy mixture of conventional realist observation and unconventional interpretative commentary accounts for the mixed impression the reader receives. While the balance of the narrative is mentally and aesthetically satisfying, it simplifies the complexity of experience. Unamuno's vision of a fecund cosmic struggle, extrapolated from the one supposed to take place in Nature, seems to a later generation naïve and oracular.

After *Paz en la guerra* Unamuno turned sharply away from what he later called 'el engañoso realismo de lo aparencial' (II, 430) to what he saw as true realism: 'la realidad íntima' (IX, 418), the inner, noumenal, reality of his characters. It led him to a marked change of fictional technique. He described it in 'Escritor ovíparo' (1902; X, 106–9) followed by 'A lo que salga' (1904; III, 789–805) as a change from 'oviparous' writing, based on observation, documentation, and preliminary sketches (i.e., the method he had followed in *Paz en la guerra*), to 'viviparous' writing in which the creative imagination is paramount. This produced the *nivola*, whose technique is described in chapter 17 of *Niebla*. It has four main characteristics. First, as we have just seen, the shift from painstaking preparation of notes, files, and drafts to writing 'a lo que salga': 'ir disertando de todo lo que se presenta bajo unidad de tono que es la íntima' (V, 276). It would be quite misleading to identify this with the relative indifference to form that we find in Baroja; *Niebla* and *San Manuel Bueno, mártir* in particular are very cunningly constructed. What

Unamuno was rejecting was *a priori* attachment to formal principles. Second, elimination of descriptions and settings: where the background does reappear, as in 'Una historia de amor' and *San Manuel Bueno, mártir*, it is symbolic. Third, a shift of emphasis from the realist conception of the central character as 'antagonista', i.e., struggling with external reality, to the conception of him as 'agonista', i.e., struggling with his own sense of existential contingency. Fourth, the promotion of dialogue to first place of importance in the narrative. In 1934 Unamuno defined the *nivolas* retrospectively as 'relatos dramáticos acezantes, de realidades íntimas, entrañadas, sin bambalinas ni realismos en que suele faltar la verdadera, la eterna realidad, la realidad de la personalidad' (II, 429).

A first experiment, *Nuevo mundo* (1896?) has been lost. *Amor y pedagogía* (1902) marks the transition to the new manner. It is a satirical account of a failed experiment aimed at producing a genius by controlled choice of parents and upbringing. Life refuses to fit the formula. Unamuno was here caricaturing the *cientificismo* of the late nineteenth century. Chapter 4 introduces Don Fulgencio de Entrambasmares, partly a self-satire by Unamuno. After his appearance, which marks an articulation in its structure, the novel acquires a deeper level of meaning. The contrast between Fulgencio and Avito, the originator of the experiment, developed in the next four chapters, shows the narrative growing away from its original theme and turning into a fully-fledged philosophical novel. By chapter 8 the boy genius Apolodoro is old enough to play his role. The rest of the book chronicles his unsuccessful struggle to break out of the oppressive world of conscious existence to which his father and Fulgencio in their different ways have both condemned him. At first only sleep, 'que es vivir sin saberlo', releases him. But soon his creative imagination adds its liberating force and almost at the same time love opens his eyes to 'la substancialidad de las cosas', to a sense of the infinite and eternal. The crushing world of determinism, whether that of his father or of Fulgencio (who sees life as a stage where each human being merely acts a preordained part, with God as author and producer), splits open to reveal the intoxicating possibility of true spiritual autonomy. But, with a brusque transition in chapter 11, one of the book's technical defects, Apolodoro is compelled to face failure as a writer and humiliation as a lover. Resorting to Fulgencio for comfort, he is brutally introduced instead to 'la perspectiva de la nada de ultratumba'. The impact of this discovery, combined with his own sources of despair, drive him to suicide, but not before he has taken one step to ensure himself temporary immortality. He leaves behind a child.

Amor y pedagogía illustrates the main features of the *nivola*, what Unamuno called 'el propósito de dar a mis novelas la mayor intensidad y el mayor carácter dramáticos possibles, reduciéndoles, en cuanto quepa, a diálogos y relato de acción y sentimientos' (I, 602).

Dialogue actually constitutes more than half the text of the novel. In addition Apolodoro's evolution through a phase of failure with the other sex to the acquisition of tragic insight is not untypical of the Generation of 1898's fictional heroes generally. More particularly, with *Amor y pedagogía*, Unamuno overtakes Ganivet in the reaction against old-style realism. Not the least important aspect of this reaction is Unamuno's insistence in the prologue on the need (also emphasized by Ganivet, Baroja, and Azorín) not merely for a new fictional method, but also for a new, more precise and concrete, anti-rhetorical style.

Since 1886 Unamuno had been writing short stories. A collection of them, *El espejo de la muerte*, appeared in 1913, and altogether he eventually wrote more than sixty. Except for those which can be directly related to his personal outlook (e.g., 'Una visita al viejo poeta') or to his other works (e.g., 'Artemio, heautontimoroumenos' to *Abel Sánchez* or 'El Maestro de Carrasqueda' to *San Manuel Bueno, mártir*) they still await adequate critical attention. The most developed of the earlier short stories is 'Una historia de amor' (1911). It reveals the main anti-Romantic feature of the Generation of 1898's fictional practice: its consistent tendency to avoid presenting human love as a source of ultimate satisfaction and fulfilment.

Niebla (1914), Unamuno's most popular novel, harks back to *Amor y pedagogía* in several ways. The most important of these is the analogy between life and the theatre, originally expounded by Fulgencio de Entrambasmares, which now provides the basis for *Niebla*'s highly original climax. Once more the novel deals with the awakening of insight; once more love plays a major part in the process; once more the tone is *humorístico*: not comic, but *bufotrágico*, reflecting the author's inner spiritual stress. Unamuno defined his aim in writing *Niebla* in chapter 30 as that of shaking his readers' faith in their own reality. In order to do so he had to create a hero who was sufficiently self-aware to recognize the problem – Augusto Pérez, like all the major heroes of '98 fiction, is pre-eminently an intellectual – yet passive, i.e., able to be manipulated in the course of the narrative. We feel intuitively that a convincing link between these two characteristics, virtually his only ones until late in the novel, is missing. We are fobbed off with a pseudo-explanation in chapter 5 in terms of maternal over-protection. Because of this initial failure to present Augusto as a character 'de carne y hueso', the reader finds it difficult to identify with him to the full and until the powerful final scene follows his evolution with an amused and curious, but detached, attention.

Ribbans convincingly divides the novel structurally into three parts: chapters 1–7; 8–24; and 25–33; the two main turning-points in the narrative being Augusto's first achievement of clearer insight into existence, and the intervention in the narrative by Unamuno writing in the first person.[16] The essential facts of the opening section are Augusto's chance meeting with Eugenia and his attraction to her. These, he asserts, give his life a finality, releasing him from his initial aboulia and forcing on him a decisive choice of courses of action. But as with Apolodoro, this emotionally determined finality triggers off, in chapter 7, a train of reflections concerned with life's ultimate finality. The 'niebla de la existencia' (which symbolizes unawareness and envelopment in the vision-obscuring details of daily life) clears away under love's influence. But it is only to reveal 'el abismo pavoroso de la eternidad' (II, 836). The act of falling in love with Eugenia (literally 'happy birth') opens the door to authentic existence – 'Amo, ergo sum' – but love does not provide a solid basis for ultimately meaningful existence. Augusto's courtship turns into a philosophic quest for 'el enjullo a que se arrolla la tela de nuestra existencia' (837).

The central section of *Niebla* illustrates the danger of misunderstanding Goti's statement: 'Mi novela no tiene argumento o mejor dicho será el que vaya saliendo' (894–5). This represents what Unamuno wanted the *nivola* to *look* like. But as Livingstone and Stevens in particular have elucidated,[17] the series of intercalated anecdotes which begins with Avito's reappearance from *Amor y pedagogía* in chaper 13 is a cleverly arranged set of variations on the theme of marriage designed to display the options open to Augusto. In the event none of them is taken up. All that has changed in Augusto is his level of awareness, not his capacity for self-affirmation; the 'alma de bulto' which he discovered in himself in the first moment of love fails to withstand the test of introspection and the doubts cast on it by Goti in chapter 10. The latter's assertion: 'Tu mismo no eres sino una pura idea, un ente de ficción' (853) is an important step forward in the narrative. Henceforth the 'verdadera vida' to which Eugenia had awaked Augusto takes on an increasingly threatening aspect. In proportion as Augusto enmeshes himself in the complexities of his emotional problem, his confidence in his own substantiality fades. Successive stages are marked by the ends of chapters 14 and 16, until by chapter 20 both external reality and his own sense of himself as real have dissolved into mere appearances symbolized by his fear of looking at himself in the mirror.

Thus, even before Eugenia dashes his feeble hope of achieving some degree of self-authenticity through marriage to her, Augusto is in growing spiritual distress, his contingent problem having been displaced by his transcendental one. His decision to kill himself is therefore not wholly paradoxical, nor is it entirely the consequence of his having been jilted. The paradox lies, if anywhere, in the fact that this is his only really autonomous decision in the book. Now Unamuno steps in to try to deny him even that small measure of freedom and authenticity, only to provoke Augusto's speech, as it were, from the scaffold:

> ¡ también Vd. se morirá, también Vd, y se volverá a la nada de que salido . . . ! Dios dejara de soñarle . . . ¡ Se morirá Vd y se morirán todos los que lean mi historia, todos, todos, todos, sin quedar uno! Porque Vd, mi creador, mi don Miguel, no es Vd más que otro ente *nivolesco*, y entes *nivolescos* sus lectores . . (982)

With this outburst, the fictional character, his author, and the reader are forced to confront each other in the same existential situation. Augusto's preoccupation with his own reality and the ultimate finality of life emerges into the wider question of man's free will. The novel ends ambiguously, leaving Unamuno and Goti contradicting each other about whether Augusto in fact succeeded in killing himself, i.e., in asserting his own (and man's) freedom.

In both Apolodoro and Augusto weakness of volition is directly associated, as in Ganivet's thinking, with lack of life-directing convictions. With *Nada menos que todo un hombre* (1916) Unamuno turned to exploring the opposite phenomenon: brutal strength of will and personality. By comparison with Baroja's, Unamuno's voluntarists are monsters of egotism. In removing them from a well-defined social context he removed part of their justification: the 'struggle for life' against the grand collective adversary. Alejandro Gómez in *Nada menos que todo un hombre*, Raquel in *Dos madres* (1920), Carolina in *El Marqués de Lumbría* (1920), and Tula in *La tía Tula* (1921) pit themselves, not against society, but against pathetically vulnerable fellow human beings. These are studies, Unamuno suggested, which probe beneath the complexities of individual psychology to lay bare an essence: 'el personaje de verdad, el que es de veras real' (IX, 420) which he identified with the character's *querer ser*. Nora criticizes such a view as a wilful simplification,[18] and so it is. When, too, this inmost essence is not simply revealed at the end of the story but consistently emphasized throughout, and when it turns out to be selfish and cruel, the tragic effect Unamuno thought he was achieving threatens to give way to melodrama.

La tía Tula is partially saved from this threat by its greater length and complexity as compared with the *Tres novelas ejemplares* mentioned above; but like them it suffers from the absence of real conflict of character. Tula is surrounded by weaklings. This absence of other opposing wills is a consistent feature of Unamuno's novels and emphasizes his aim of keeping all conflict inside the individual character. The defect of the *Tres novelas ejemplares* is that in them even this interior conflict is lacking. Tula, on the other hand, comes alive because of her ambiguity. The *querer ser* of Alejandro, Raquel, and Carolina may destroy the happiness of others, but it is always positive self-assertion; whereas behind the *querer ser* of *Tula* – her 'maternidad espiritual' – lurks something negative: fear and disgust at the thought of normal sexuality.[19] True to his inescapably religious vision of life, Unamuno presents this fear and disgust not as a neurotic state, but as a form of sin. What makes Tula's life tragically heroic, attenuating – but not obscuring – the more inhuman and distasteful aspects of her character, is her sporadic awareness of guilt and her acceptance of inner solitude. Batchelor associates the theme of maternity here and in *Dos madres* implicitly with the ontological avidity which Unamuno displays in *Del sentimiento trágico*. Logically this ought to make Tula's doubt and guilt lead her to insecurity about her own essence, but this is not a feature of the book.

This is what makes *Abel Sánchez* (1917) the better novel. Joaquín Monegro is, like Tula and the main characters of the *Tres novelas ejemplares*, possessed. His innermost being is soiled with envy and hatred of his rival in love and fame, Abel Sánchez. But unlike Tula and the others, whose moments of self-scrutiny are rare and inadequate, Joaquín is almost morbidly introspective. The reflective interior life, which impeded action and decision in Augusto Pérez and which gave place to them almost too consistently in Tula, coexists in Joaquín on equal terms with a force of volition which, though still intense, is diminished to more credible proportions. Though implacable with himself, Joaquín is unable coldly to dominate and instrumentalize others. Unamuno's statement in the prologue to the second edition that Joaquín's envy is 'una envidia trágica, una envidia que se defiende, una envidia que podrá llamarse angélica' is thereby fully justified. The essence of tragedy is pathos, calling forth compassion from the spectator. We feel compassion for Tula only momentarily, as our understanding of her reaches and even overtakes her own obscure understanding of the self that hides behind the face she shows to the world. But for Joaquín our compassion grows progressively because his character evolves, not lineally like Tula's, but conflictively, through struggle and frustration to insight.

This evolution is brought out by the contrast between Joaquín and Abel. The latter, though an artist of some merit, has not learned the gospel of art according to Víctor Goti of *Niebla*: that true art 'liberates' those who understand it by inducing them to question their own existence. Abel is incapable of doubting his 'realidad de bulto'. He lives a life devoid of spiritual complexity, symbolized by the fact that when he paints a picture of Cain and Abel (the myth which is the starting-point of the book), it is the soul of Abel which he is unable to express. As his art is unreflective, so his personality is passive and his actions instinctively egotistical and at times casually immoral. Joaquín, in contrast, is initiated into conscious existence, like Apolodoro and Augusto Pérez, by unrequited love and shame. The process of self-discovery set in motion by losing Helena to Abel gradually reveals a deepening split in his personality between his moral self (with which in contrast to figures in the *Tres novelas ejemplares* his will-power is now associated), and a demonic instinctive self striving to possess him. Joaquín's rivalry with Abel is thus in the end totally subordinated to his struggle with himself.

Behind most tragedies lies an implicit criticism of the design of things, the recognition of an arbitrary, mysterious source of suffering in existence other than human error. It is through the resistance he puts up to this force that the hero acquires authentic stature. So it is with Joaquín. His life attains tragic significance in that it is spent in a basically noble, anguished, struggle against an unjust fate to which he has been condemned through no fault of his own, ' ¿Qué hice yo para que Dios me hiciera así?', he asks vainly (II, 1055) and again: ' ¿Por qué he sido tan envidioso, tan malo?' (1117). Part of the pathos of the book lies in the fact that Joaquín dies with his questions unanswered. But this is only one of the ways in which, here and in other novels, Unamuno makes self-awareness merely an intermediate stage in a process of evolving existential awareness. Like Augusto Pérez, Joaquín is drawn by emotional distress to question his own existence. At the wedding of Helena and Abel, he writes, 'Me sentí como si no existiera ... ¿Yo soy Yo? me dije' (1023). In chapter 12 the frightful suspicion grows upon him that it is his alternative demonic personality, free of volitional or ethical constraints, which is the 'substantial', immortal part of him. In Paul Ilie's interpretation,[20] the existence of this hated, demonic self stands between Joaquín and substantiality. Joaquín is forced to reject his innermost *querer ser* because it is evil. He thus remains in the state of existential suspense implied in his question: ' ¿Dónde estoy yo?' (1069), and in his daughter's reference to the 'niebla oscura' and 'tinieblas espirituales' which emanate from him. At the end of the novel Joaquín's question ' ¿Quién quiero ser?' (1091) is answered when he attempts to throttle Abel, but not before Unamuno has added a final note of ambiguity to his character with the suggestion (1099) that Joaquín had half-consciously imposed his sufferings on himself in order to maintain his belief that he was 'un espíritu de excepción y como tal torturado'. The reader is left to decide whether his hatred of Abel was part of a dream of self-aggrandizement or a reality which, by combating it, he overcame as he heard his pardon pronounced at last, with the wisdom of innocence, by his grandchild.

In its narrative method, as in its theme (of liberty versus predestination), *Abel Sánchez* looks back to *Niebla*. This is especially the case in its use of symbolism: this time sunshine and icy cold instead of mist and clarity, and in the employment once more of stories within the story, not now to present Joaquín with options, but to provoke reflections in his mind (the woman patient in chapter 8) or to present parallel cases of hatred (the disinherited Aragonese, Federico Cuadrado). This method of narration, which reaches a peak of creative ingenuity in the intricate interior reduplication of *Cómo se hace una novela*, penetratingly analysed by Inés Azar,[21] emphasizes the technical subtlety which is typical of the *nivolas*. But their claim to genuine modernity of technique is compromised by Unamuno's general fidelity to third-person narrative and authorial omniscience, as well as by his occasionally intrusive interventions as commentator on his characters' psychology.

The clumsiest aspect of the technique in *Abel Sánchez* is the way in which Unamuno, in his anxiety to extend the commentary, accumulated direct authorial intervention, brief interior monologues by Joaquín, and long quotations from the latter's *Confesión*. When in 1930 he wrote *San Manuel Bueno, mártir, La novela de don Sandalio, jugador de ajedrez*, and *Un pobre hombre rico*, the narratives were stripped of such devices. *Don Sandalio* is the most enigmatic of Unamuno's fictional works. Its hidden theme is the diversity underlying the apparent unity of individual personality. A series of clues alerts the careful reader to the fact that the narrator, whose letters tell the story, the recipient of them, and Don Sandalio himself are in fact one and the same, that is, Unamuno, and in a sense Everyman. The game of chess represents life. The other players at the club do not take it seriously. Don Sandalio is totally absorbed in it, but refuses to consider problems not related to the actual game; we presume, that is, that he ignores transcendental problems. The narrator, a lonely figure whose symbols are a hollow, but living, oak covered with bright ivy and a ruined house, symbols perhaps of Unamuno's inner spiritual life and his public life as he had come to see it, needs Sandalio, with his family, home, and absorbing but contingent interest, in order to complete himself. But he recognizes in him an 'other' self whom he does not fully understand or wish to investigate. Sandalio's problems, which are hinted at, remain mysterious. Only his death in prison is clear. The prison is again life, from which Sandalio has no escape into transcendence. *Un pobre hombre rico* is by comparison a trivial story, *bufo* without being *trágico*.

San Manuel Bueno, mártir is the story of a rural parish priest who has lost his faith, but who continues to minister to his flock. On its first appearance it was at once hailed as a masterpiece and ever since then it has been seen by critics both as Unamuno's spiritual testament and his most artistically successful fictional work. Its tone, like that of *Cómo se hace una novela*, is both far removed from *bufo-trágico* and markedly different from that of *Abel Sánchez*. It is possible that this change of tone is to be related to the resurgence of acute spiritual malaise in Unamuno during his exile. But the novel is too subtle and ambiguous to be read simply as Unamuno's final confession of atheism.

The original source of ambiguity is the form. Abandoning the straight third person, Unamuno presents the story as a memoir by a friend and parishioner of Don Manuel's, Ángela Carballino. At first sight Ángela appears to enjoy the untroubled 'intra-historic' faith of Joaquín Monegro's wife or his grandchild; and as the latter had absolved Joaquín, so she absolves Don Manuel. We shall see presently what we are to make of her question: ' ¿Y yo, creo?'. The fact that the story is told by her, a far-from-impartial witness, and not by Unamuno directly, still less by Don Manuel, combined with the fact that the essence of her narrative consists of her memories of reported conversation between Lázaro (her brother) and Don Manuel, deliberately places the reader at a considerable remove from the actual events. Doubt is even cast on these when Ángela finally asks herself ' ¿Es que esto que estoy aquí contando ha pasado, y ha pasado tal y como lo cuento?' (XVI, 626).

The theme of the novel is truth in relation to life, at two distinct levels. The first is that of Don Manuel himself, Lázaro, and – subsequently perhaps – Ángela: the level of intellectual awareness. Here truth is the opposite of belief. The kernel of the novel at this level is Don Manuel's statement: 'La verdad, Lázaro, es acaso algo terrible, algo intolerable, algo mortal' (605). It is the truth of reason, the realization that death is the end and belief in transcendental values an illusion. All the Generation of 1898 shared this vision of the truth. For Ganivet it was revealed by 'el escepticismo científico'. Azorín awoke to it in *Diario de un enfermo*. Machado expressed it in the phrase:

> Ya estamos en el secreto
> todo es nada.

Baroja, most explicitly of all, declared roundly: 'la verdad en bloque es mala para la vida'. His priest, Don Javier in *El cura de Monleón*, finding his faith collapse, leaves the ministry. Don Manuel chooses to stay. Why? One of his motives is that of comforting and supporting the faith of his flock, protecting them against 'torturas de lujo'. This is the second level at which the theme of truth and life operates: that of the peasants, for whom truth and belief coincide. Don Manuel's attitude to his parishioners is simply that 'Con mi verdad no vivirían' (605) and more explicitly: 'No hay más vida eterna que ésta ... que

la sueñen eterna' (614). Yet Ángela denies equally explicitly that the
common people of the parish would understand the problem even if
it were spelled out to them, and Unamuno made it plain elsewhere
that he agreed with her. Is Don Manuel's first motive, then, the result
of self-deception? His second motive is more complex and personal.
By unceasing pastoral work he distracts himself from the painful
contemplation of his own disbelief; but also, Ángela suggests, by
remaining in loving contact with the faith of the common people, he
reserves for himself the possibility that their faith, which he has
protected and fostered, will somehow help his unbelief. Taking up
an idea already formulated by Joaquín's wife in *Abel Sánchez*, she
declares that both Don Manuel and her brother Lázaro, who had
abandoned his former materialist and progressive ideas in order to
help Don Manuel in his 'engaño', 'murieron creyendo no creer lo
que más nos interesa, pero sin creerlo, creyéndolo' (624–5).

A glance at the story's symbolism is now required. That of the
characters is suggested by their names. Ángela's suggests a divine
messenger. She tells most of the story from the standpoint of faith.
But Unamuno recognized that by choosing a believer as his narrator
he ran the risk of making the reader jump to the conclusion that her
interpretation of Don Manuel's position was in fact the author's.
So he introduces, later in the story, an element of doubt in her mind.
Lázaro is raised from the dead (i.e., from preoccupation with merely
material progress) to the life of the spirit – but not to belief. His
symbolism remains highly ambiguous. Don Manuel (Emmanuel:
God with us) is firmly associated with Christ; but, we must note,
with the suffering, doubting Christ of Unamuno's *El Cristo de
Velázquez*. He cures the sick; he raises Lazarus; he refuses to judge;
he feels the full force of Christ's 'Dios mío, Dios mío, ¿por qué me
has abandonado?' The meaning of his heroic self-sacrifice is but-
tressed by that of the clown: ethical behaviour is the ultimate refuge;
we must deserve immortality, whether or not we are destined to have
it. Blasillo – the name is intended to recall Pascal's 'Cela vous
abêtira' – stands at the opposite extreme from Don Manuel. His
mindless faith contrasts with the priest's rational awareness and
disbelief. Their deaths, hand in hand, symbolize the inseparability
and interdependence of faith and doubt. Finally the *zagala* on the
hillside symbolizes the unchanging 'intra-historic' life of the peasants.
Oddly, Unamuno attributes to them here a 'tedio de vivir' which
leads to the death-wish. It is not clear how this can be reconciled
with the need to safeguard their traditional faith.[22]

The flower in Don Manuel's breviary stands for his lost faith;
hence the cross and date. The nut-tree from which he cuts planks for
his coffin represents his childhood faith. Hence the strange adjective
'matriarcal' applied to it: Unamuno identified spiritual comfort

with return to his mother's arms. The lake and the mountain are more difficult. Don Manuel is inextricably associated with both. Yet they appear to symbolize works of God indicating His existence: the lake reflects the heavens above it, the mountain rises towards them. Equally the lake reflects the placid faith of the villagers; the church bells which can sometimes be heard ringing beneath its waters symbolize Spain's timeless religious tradition. Ángela transposes this symbolism to Don Manuel implying that faith is alive, submerged, in him; but for him the lake seems to symbolize *la nada*. The cold wind and snow on the hilltop appear to represent freezing (but temporary and superficial) doubt, such as even Ángela later feels. The lake, we notice, simply absorbs it and is unchanged. Don Manuel uses the lake's water to wash away sin and sickness, but for him its calm is that of illusion. Through the lake runs a river (time) carrying its waters away to the bitter sea of death – for Don Manuel, of annihilation. But Ángela, protected by her faith, can ignore it: 'no sentía pasar el agua del lago' (624); besides, she believes that the 'alma del lago', a changeless residue of pure faith and confidence, remains. Finally, the snow which falls as Ángela writes her final words symbolizes once more rational doubt, with its deceitful crystalline clarity and luminosity, falling over the world around her, blotting out the memory of the past and even her trust in what she writes. But only briefly.

IV. UNAMUNO THE POET
THE REJECTION OF *Modernismo*

The ambiguity which thus persists to the very end of Unamuno's fictional work is not wholly resolved in his poetry, though some critics have regarded the latter as containing the most reliable evidence about his true spiritual position. Although he did not publish his first book of poems (*Poesías*, 1907) until he was in his forties, he had been writing and publishing poems piecemeal since his early twenties. Because of his deep-seated conviction that only what the creative unconscious, the emotions, 'lo biótico' contributed to literature was really valid, and associating this chiefly with poetry, he yearned to be remembered above all as a poet. *Poesías* was followed by *Rosario de sonetos líricos* (1911), *El Cristo de Velázquez* (1920), the poems in *Andanzas y visiones españolas* (1922), *Rimas de dentro* (1923), *Teresa* (1924), *De Fuerteventura a París* (1925), *Romancero del destierro* (1928), and the vast posthumous *Cancionero* (1953) together with the uncollected poems gathered up and published by García Blanco in the *Obras completas*. The sheer volume of Unamuno's poetry production has daunted critics and large areas of it remain relatively unexplored. But while the popularity of his novels has fluctuated, that of his poetry has grown steadily.

Although Darío could write in 'La dulzura del Ángelus' and 'Lo fatal' poems respectively of nostalgia for faith and of spiritual anguish almost as deep as Unamuno's, only sporadic comparisons can be made between the work of the two poets. What is true of the two men, is true of the movements they represent. *Modernista* poetry was not exploratory of the human condition in the way the poetry of Unamuno and Machado is. For these two poets of the '98, art was not a refuge but an instrument for scrutinizing and expressing the inner reality of the spirit. So Unamuno, in his 'Credo poético':

> El lenguaje es ante todo pensamiento
> y es pensada su belleza
> Sujetemos en verdades del espíritu
> las entrañas de las formas pasajeras. (XIII, 201)

Nor are the influences acting on Unamuno those we associate with *modernismo*. Quevedo and Luis de León, Leopardi and Carducci, Wordsworth, Coleridge, and Browning are as far remote from the *modernistas* as Poe, Baudelaire, Verlaine, and D'Annunzio are from Unamuno. Only Bécquer is a major influence in common.

In contrast, then, to *modernismo* which, he wrote contemptuously, was 'poesía de pura sensación' (XIII, 25) and which he accused both of making out of art 'una religión y un remedio para el mal metafísico' (XVI, 179) and of lack of passion and excessive preoccupation with novelties of form and diction (91–2), Unamuno advocated what he called 'poesía nouménica' (24): poetry of naked human statement. His definition of the poet in *Teresa* is 'El que desnuda con el lenguaje rítmico su alma' (XIV, 295). Rejecting, too, the oratorical tone of Spanish poetry from Quintana to Nuñez de Arce, he repeatedly praised the musing, meditative tone discernible in English poets such as Gray and Browning. As he had called for the overthrow of the older Spanish prose style, calling, like Baroja, for 'más ligereza y más precisión a la vez' ('Sintaxis macánica', XI, 778) so he insisted that the Spanish ear for poetry should be reattuned. He preferred traditional metres, particularly sonnets and, in longer poems, unrhymed hendecasyllables. At first we perceive a search for freedom and flexibility typified by his use of a new form of *silva* with five-syllable lines as well as the usual eleven- and seven-syllable ones. In his earlier verse, too, rhyme tended to be dropped as if it were an obstacle to the free flow of poetry from the inner fount of creativeness. But later Unamuno came to realize that rhymes themselves can at times suggest ideas. He lacked musical sensibility and rejected poetry of acoustical incantation on the characteristic grounds that he wanted his poetry to awaken, not to lull, the reader. But this did not prevent his achieving superbly solemn effects in some descriptions, especially of churches, or a charming melodiousness in his cradle-songs and poems for children.

The bulk of his poetry is inspired by his spiritual alarm, tension, and aspiration. It is metaphysical poetry of a quality which Spain had not seen since the time of Quevedo and Calderón. Its stark and vibrant sincerity contrasted completely with the superficially similar poetry of doubt we associate with Revilla, Bartrina, and most of all Nuñez de Arce, who made his name with it. We sense the mental involvement, but not that 'grito de congoja' of the whole personality so audible in Unamuno's verse. He himself emphasized the difference between true philosophic poetry and their 'simple mezcla de la poesía y filosofía . . . versos conceptuales en que el esqueleto lógico asoma sus apofisis y costillas por entre la carne flaca poética' (XIII, 64).

Poetry of thought, of meditative awareness, is inevitably for Unamuno poetry of pain. For consciousness was for him pre-eminently suffering consciousness. The presence of pain and the poet's reaction to it is thus a consistent feature of his poetic work.

> ¿Qué es tu vida, alma mía?, ¿cuál tu pago?
> . . . pesar la sombra sin ningun consuelo
> y lluvia y viento y sombra hacen la vida. (XIV, 651)

he wrote when exile from Spain had been added to exile from her faith. The inner recess of this pain is dread: the pain of the soul and spirit generated by God's silence:

> una sola pena
> una sola, infinita, soberana
> la pena de vivir llevando al Todo
> temblando ante la nada. (XIII, 329)

Two of the principal expressions of this pain are the poet's torment-ing consciousness of time and his awareness of the insidious approach of death. A striking image from *Teresa*:

> Una clepsidra es mi pecho
> por donde la sangre fluye (XIV, 323)

introduced a characteristic network of antithetical concepts suggest-ing alternatively that life is mere illusion, and the kindred illusion that death is an awakening into real reality. Fear of that awakening inspired some of Unamuno's best-known poems: the unforgettably dramatic 'Es de noche, en mi estudio' (XIII, 434–5), the anguished 'Vendrá de noche' (XIV, 610–11), and perhaps most pathetic of all 'Si caigo aquí' (XIV, 607–9).

More clearly than in his prose we perceive in Unamuno's poetry his divided reactions to the anguish of unknowing. His poems explore manifold possibilities of comfort and escape. In the sestet of his sonnet 'El ángel negro' his wife's unfailing support in moments of despair is tenderly attested. The lost serenity of childhood draws a prayer for its recovery in 'Mi cielo':

> ... hacia un eterno ayer haz que mi vuelo
> emprenda sin llegar a la partida.   (XIII, 565)

Beauty, too, tempts momentarily with an offer of release from insight in 'Hermosura':

> ¡Santa hermosura
> solución del enigma!
> Tu matarás a la Esfinge (XIII, 235)

but the end of the poem says otherwise. In reality, only a sign from on high could afford release:

> Una señal, Señor, una tan sólo
> una que acabe
> con todos los ateos de la tierra.   (XIII, 282)

In the absence of a sign suffering itself reassumes its role as the criterion of authentic existence. In his adaptations of the myth of Prometheus, 'El buitre de Prometeo' and the sonnet 'A mi buitre', the torment inflicted by the bird is no punishment:

> el dolor de pensar es ya un remedio
> mejor tus picotazos que no el tedio (XIII, 315)

for with the ending of pain comes the threat of annihilation.

The link between Prometheus, for whom suffering is the alternative to non-existence, and Christ, whose suffering is redemptive, is provided by the reference to the former in Part II of *El Cristo de Velázquez* and in 'Ecco Homo', in which the vulture's prey, eternally renewing itself, becomes the Eucharist: Christ's flesh eternally re-created as 'pan de inmortalidad a los mortales'. In this poem Unamuno shakes off almost totally the ambiguities and contradictions of the rest of his work. Even when the symbolic whiteness of Christ is momentarily obscured by the equally symbolic darkness of His hair:

> la sombra del ala sin perfiles
> del ángel de la nada negadora (XIII, 678-9)

no anguish supervenes. Symbols, particularly that of the river running into the sea, elsewhere negative, have become positive. The *enjullo* which Augusto Pérez had vainly sought in *Niebla*, reappears triumphantly in Part I, fragment 34:

> Tu cruz es el enjullo a que se arrolla
> la tela humana del dolor ...

and the *clepsidra* which in *Teresa* recorded, in anguished heartbeats, Time's rapid passage, in line 1880 confidently measures eternity.

The 'Dios tenebroso' of 'Aldebarán' (1908), Unamuno's most consistently interrogative philosophical poem, is not entirely absent from *El Cristo de Velázquez*. In lines 2048–9 the image of Him is that of

> mar caliginoso
> donde el alma se ahoga.

But the predominant image for God is that of the sun, whose blinding light is more bearable to human eyes when reflected by Christ who is symbolized by the moon. Sin and grace now take their conventional places in Unamuno's outlook, though the church as the living body of Christ is not prominently mentioned. The entire work being a meditation in richly symbolic language on the biblical names and physical attributes of Christ, one of its limitations is the lack of a narrative element. Unamuno does not wholly escape the dangers of monotony and repetition in a purely descriptive poem of 2,539 hendecasyllables. But passages of great lyrical beauty, different in their serenity from anything else he wrote in verse, stand out. A fine example occurs at the end of Part I, fragment 15:

> es música tu cuerpo
> divino, y ese cántico callado
> – música de los ojos su blancura –
> como arpa de David da refrigerio
> a nuestras almas cuando ya el espíritu
> del Malo las tortura, y a las notas
> de la armonía de tu pecho santo
> se aduermen nuestras penas hechizadas
> en los nichos de nuestros corazones
> abrigados. Y entonces la pobre alma,
> hecha antes un ovillo por la tétrica
> mano del Tentador, que nos la estruja
> y engurruñe, al sentir la sinfonía
> de tu cuerpo, como un retoño ajado
> a que la savia vuelve, se endereza
> y en postura de marcha se recobra.
>   El canto eres sin fin y sin confines;
> eres, Señor, la soledad sonora
> y del concierto que a los seres liga
> la epifanía. Cantan las esferas
> por tu cuerpo, que es arpa universal.

The faint echoes of Fray Luis de León's poem to Salinas which we hear in these lines only enhance our perception of their nobility and beauty. These are the result of a single dominant image (cuerpo = música – cántico – arpa – armonía) unfolding triumphantly and enveloping a subordinate image complementing its meaning (el alma hecho un ovillo – se endereza y se recobra) and culminating in a climax of carefully graduated intensity (canto sin fin – soledad sonora – cantan las esferas – arpa universal).

A feature of Unamuno's poetry, related to its volume, is the speed at which much of it was written. The dates appended to the sonnets of the *Rosario* . . ., and to later poems, reveal that he was frequently capable of writing several poems in a day. We know that in the case of *El Cristo de Velázquez*, whose composition occupied him at intervals for six years, he tirelessly polished the text. Elsewhere he published poems in what for other poets would be their raw state, as they had spontaneously taken shape, increasing the peril by his readiness to print all he wrote, refusing either to select himself or allow editorial selection. The inevitable result is inequality. This is the defect of all prolific poets. But in individual poems we sometimes see great beauty seriously compromised. An example already noticed by Blanco Aguinaga is the unhappy moment of distraction which intervenes between the first two lines of 'Dulce silencioso pensamiento' and the last sentence of the octet, to spoil one of Unamuno's otherwise most moving sonnets. His rhyme-schemes, especially those in *esdrújulos*, and his attempts at innovations of diction are sometimes infelicitous, and critics have complained that he abuses *encabalgamiento*. An examination of writings about his poetry reveals how often it has been used as a source of information about his personality and how seldom it has been studied for its own sake. Thus while the brilliant inventiveness displayed in the plot-structure and the intricate symbolism of his novels have received due need of praise, the seemingly endless outpouring of imagery which sustained his poetry has not been so fully recognized. The greatest service to Unamuno's reputation as a poet has been rendered less by critics than by discriminating anthologizers, such as Vivanco.

The nature-imagery and symbolism which Unamuno applies to Christ in the early part of *El Cristo de Velázquez* form a link between his poetry and an important part of his prose: that which expresses his view of nature. The title of one of his collections of essays, *Paisajes del alma*, indicates the standpoint from which he saw the countryside. His writings about it convey a vision rather than a description, and one which is not always serenely contemplative. An adjective which he frequently applies is *trágico*, and there were moments when nature exacerbated rather than mitigated his spiritual distress. Referring to one such occasion he wrote in *Andanzas y visiones españolas*: 'nunca comprendí mejor su metáfora. Hubo momentos en que creí que me iba a parar el corazón o a estallárseme o cuajárseme la sangre. Y a la angustia física se me unió le angustia moral, la angustia religiosa, más aun la angustia metafísica' (I, 843). More commonly, however, the spiritual impact of the Spanish countryside, its 'metaphor', is a source of comfort, of unity with the hidden spiritual reality of the *madre patria*. Of the Gredos mountains, Unamuno wrote:

> Que es en tu cima donde al fin me encuentro
> siéntome soberano
> Y en mi España me adentro
> tocándome persona
> hijo de siglos de pasión cristiana
>   y cristiano español. (XIII, 836)

The countryside Unamuno presents to his readers is a countryside of 'pequeños rincones' seen subjectively with his 'vista espiritual' whether in poems ('Camposanto junto al río', 'El padrenuestro en el campo', 'Casa con tejado rojo') or in the evocative essays of *Por Tierras de Portugal y España*, for example. Ledesma, Yuste, Sepúlveda, Salamanca itself, the *meseta* of Castile, the green mountains of Vizcaya, the sea he 'discovered' in Fuerteventura, draw from Unamuno descriptions less of what they look like than of what they mean: tranquillity and permanence.[23] In their atmosphere he heard at intervals the music which in *El Cristo de Velázquez* inspired the soul to stand erect, so that he associated lakes and hills with the Christ of the poem. Momentarily even God seemed to break that silence which at the end of *La agonía del cristianismo* and elsewhere had led Unamuno to accuse Him of atheism.

V. UNAMUNO'S THEATRE

Unamuno's theatre is the least-known part of his work. Of his eleven original plays only eight were staged in his lifetime and of those only one, *El otro*, could be called a success. Until 1959 when García Blanco published his edition of the *Teatro completo* it was impossible even for scholars to examine the full range of Unamuno's dramatic work without having recourse to manuscripts. Hence critical comment has been rather sparse. Before turning to the stage himself, Unamuno had published in 1896 a curious essay, 'La regeneración del teatro español', condemning the triviality of the contemporary Spanish theatre and advocating from his, at that time, Marxist standpoint, a return to 'el espíritu popular'. How far his political, and with it his artistic, outlook changed is illustrated by his eventual practice as a dramatist. Nothing is further from the spirit of Dicenta's *Juan José* or Hauptmann's *The Weavers*, which Unamuno initially regarded as plays which pointed the path to follow, than that of his own theatre which, like most of his other works, is essentially concerned with the mind and the spirit, and not with social conflicts. This is plain from his earliest play, *La esfinge* (1898), which specifically subordinates collective social regeneration to the individual's spiritual quest. The affinity between the hero, Ángel, and Ganivet's Pío Cid, who attempts to solve a similar dilemma by importing spirituality into social endeavour, has been overlooked by critics. It reveals once more the consistent ambivalence of the Generation of 1898 in regard to the national problem. *La venda* (1899) offers points of comparison with *San Manuel Bueno, mártir* in its postulate of faith as a *mentira vital*. It stands as a warning to those who would see in that novel a quite new development in Unamuno's religious thinking.

The theatre was by far the most profitable branch of the arts to cultivate in Spain. A short run of a play would bring the author in as much money as two or three moderately successful books. This, as well as his desire to reach a wider public and to stimulate a revival of serious theatre in Spain, may have been a factor influencing Unamuno to try his luck afresh, in spite of constant disappointments, at different stages of his career. His later plays were written in three main periods. The first, when he was in his middle forties, saw his two one-act *bufo-trágico* farces *La Princesa doña Lambra* (1909) and *La difunta* (1909), together with *El pasado que vuelve* (1910) and *Fedra* (1911). The second, in 1921, saw *Soledad*, a reworking of *La esfinge*, and *Raquel encadenada*. The third, during his exile in France, saw *Sombras de sueño* (1926), *El otro* (1926), and *El hermano Juan* (1927?). Finally, after his triumphant return to Spain, his translation of Seneca's *Medea* was staged briefly in 1933. To Unamuno's chagrin, a dramatist of slight talent, Julio de Hoyos, adapted in 1925 *Nada menos que todo un hombre* for the stage, with such success that it was even performed by Pirandello's company in Italy. It was, unfortunately, the nearest Unamuno ever came to popularity with theatregoers in his lifetime. As stage-artifacts Unamuno's plays are too static, abstract, and cavalier in their treatment of everyday reality to be commercially successful. Nor was the technical skill evidenced in other parts of his work carried over into his theatre. It remains, as Iris Zavala in her lucid critique of it asserts, 'un teatro metafísico, con intereses extraescénicos'.[24]

VI. CONCLUSION

Within the Generation of 1898 Unamuno occupies a special position. His view that the Spanish problem was inseparable from the universal problems of ultimate values, objective knowledge, and the finality of human existence generally, was shared in one way or another by the other members of the group. But the questions: has life a recognizable aim?, is the mind equipped to know ultimate truths?, is there a valid system of moral absolutes? belong in a different category, however closely related, from the question: can I, Miguel de Unamuno, be certain of my own immortality as a creature of flesh and blood?

To this extent his preoccupations must be classed as theological rather than philosophic in origin. Until 1959 the Unamuno who was extensively studied was the Unamuno *agónico*, dramatically torn between rationalism and the will to believe in the afterlife. Then Blanco Aguinaga added a new dimension to the discussion by uncovering the Unamuno *contemplativo*, a different and less anguished figure. In enigmatic contrast to both of these there was also the Unamuno *histórico*, the public figure, the one member of the Generation of 1898 apart from Maeztu who remained during the whole of his life involved in the political struggle. Except for his early Marxist period, this last Unamuno has been the least systematically studied. Both the religious and political overtones in his work and the complex interaction of the different facets of his personality and outlook conspire to prevent a balanced judgement of his work.

In Spain he contributed more than any other single figure to the task of attempting to break up the hollow consensus of passively accepted religious and nationalistic ideals and beliefs which lay like a carapace over the country. Unfortunately, despite his political activity, he does not seem to have recognized fully the interdependence of those aspects of the Spanish mentality which he chiefly detested and the social order obtaining around him. For this reason much of his effort in the role of *excitador Hispaniae* was expended in an unprofitable direction. The remark of Felipe in *La esfinge* Act I, scene vi: 'Regénerese cada cual y nos regeneraremos todos', which contains in a nutshell Unamuno's views on regeneration after 1898, reveals the wilful onesidedness of his approach. It presented no threat at all to the *status quo*.

As a creative writer his achievement was undoubtedly greatest in the novel. The *nivolas* remain a landmark in modern Spanish fiction, and to some extent in that of Europe as a whole. This is not only because of their intrinsic artistic merit and originality, but also because in a striking way they mark a shift from reported reality, in the high realist tradition, to created reality; a shift from observation to intuition as the main force guiding the novelist, and to open-endedness in construction rather than closed patterns of plot. We recognize all these as important parts of the process of change taking place in the early twentieth-century novel in Europe. Unamuno's poetry attempted to break equally radically with the manner of an earlier generation of poets, though not always with as much success. At its best it expresses a vision of the spiritual life of man, in serenity and anguish, unparalleled in Spanish verse since the Golden Age. Though his more conventional love-poetry (in *Teresa*) was unsuccessful, the appeal of his intimate poems of family life can be appreciated best by comparing them to Querol's *Poesías familiares* from which they partly derive. Though Machado surpassed him in the evocation of the Spanish countryside, it is with a narrower range of vision. Unamuno's immense confidence in his creative originality played him false only in the theatre.

His position as a thinker is clearly vulnerable. The 'leap' which his thought necessitates from the need for God to the existence of God, requires, as Huertas Jordá points out,[25] just as much an act of faith as traditional theological assumptions. To the committed Christian it is unnecessary: to the unbeliever, gratuitous. In the same way Unamuno's attempt to transfer value from the possession of faith to the struggle for its attainment, from confidence to doubt and dread, and from serenity to spiritual unrest as the test of authentic life, is apt to provoke resistance in the reader's mind. Maeztu's critique of it in 'Sobre el egotismo' (1909) is still one of the best correctives.[26] Above all it is fair to ask the question directly: does the quest for immortality, either bodily or in any other sense, possess the primordial existential importance which Unamuno attributes to it?

Granting all this, the relevance of Unamuno remains. For whether we consciously belong to those for whom ambiguity and contradiction are part of the essence of being, or to those who indignantly deny such an assertion, some degree of existential anxiety persists. It is to this that Unamuno cunningly and successfully directs his appeal in most of his work. His own intense consciousness of it, and his ability to express it in dramatic and disturbing ways, constitute his unique originality. To some an irritant, to others a stimulus, his writings fulfil their author's intention of inducing the reader to question and re-examine his presuppositions about the nature of life and reality.

NOTES

1. *Correspondencia familiar de Ángel Ganivet, 1888–1897*, ed. J. Herrero (Granada, 1967), 20.

2. A. Gallego y Burín, *Ganivet* (Granada, 1921), 19.

3. Reproduced in Granjel, op. cit.

4. 'La influencia de los intelectuales' in *Los intelectuales y un epílogo para estudiantes*, 16.

5. Letter to Pedro Corominas of 2 May 1917, cited by E. Salcedo, *Vida de Don Miguel* (Madrid, 1964), 210.

6. Letter to G. Beccari, cited M. García Blanco, *Miguel de Unamuno: Obras completas* (Madrid, 1959–64), I, 19. All subsequent bracketed references are to this edition.

7. Cited C. Blanco Aguinaga, *Juventud del 98* (Madrid, 1970), 55.

8. Letter of 31 May 1895 in *Epistolario a Clarín* (Madrid, 1941), 53.

9. On this point see the very useful articles of J. W. Butt, 'Determinism and the Inadequacy of Unamuno's Radicalism, 1886–97', *BHS*, XLVI (1969), 226–40, and Pedro Ribas, 'El *Volksgeist* de Hegel y la intrahistoria de Unamuno', *CCMU*, XXI (1971), 23–33.

10. Cited R. Pérez de la Dehesa, *Política y sociedad en el primer Unamuno 1894–1904* (Madrid, 1966), 127.

11. A. F. Zubizarreta, 'Desconocida antesala de la crisis de Unamuno: 1895–96' *In*, 142 (1958), 1.

12. A. Lacy, *Miguel de Unamuno: the Rhetoric of Existence* (The Hague and Paris, 1967), 240–84. The most convincing critique of Sánchez Barbudo's interpretation is C. Blanco Aguinaga's *El Unamuno contemplativo* (Mexico, 1959), 36 note 6 and 39 note 11.

13. See G. Ribbans, 'Unamuno en 1899: su separación definitiva de la ideología progresista', *CCMU*, XII (1962), 15–30, included in *Niebla y soledad* (Madrid, 1971), 17–44.

14. Readers should note that *Cómo se hace una novela* appears in *OC* in so heavily censored a form as to be utterly useless to scholars and readers alike. Only the Buenos Aires (1927) edition is complete. Good discussions of it are to be found in Zubizarreta's *Unamuno en su nivola* (Madrid, 1960), and Sánchez Barbudo's *Unamuno y Machado* (Madrid, 1959) and the article of Inés Azar mentioned below in note 21.

15. R. E. Batchelor, *Unamuno Novelist* (Oxford, 1972), 33.

16. G. Ribbans, 'Estructura y significado de *Niebla*', *Rev. de la Universidad de Madrid*, XIII (1965), 211–40. Included in *Niebla y soledad*, 108–42.

17. Leon Livingstone, 'Interior Duplication and the Problem of Form in the Modern Spanish Novel', *PMLA*, XXIV (1941), 442–50. H. Stevens, 'Las novelitas intercaladas en *Niebla*', *In*, 170 (1961), I.

18. E. de Nora, *La novela española contemporánea 1898–1960* (Madrid, 1968), I, 26–7.

19. D. G. Hannan's interpretation in '*La tía Tula* como expresión novelesca del ensayo "Sobre la soberbia" '. *RoN*, XII (1971), 296–301 unwisely ignores the sexual aspect and hence distorts the meaning of the novel.

20. Paul Ilie, 'Unamuno, Gorki and the Cain Myth', *HR*, XXIX (1961), 310–23.

21. Inés Azar, 'La estructura novelesca de *Cómo se hace una novela*', *MLN*, LXXXV (1970), 184–206.

22. M. Nozick, *Miguel de Unamuno* (New York, 1971), 102 says plainly: 'Unamuno's reverence for the masses, it may be said, alternated with fear and contempt'. This was the case both at the political level and, as C. Blanco Aguinaga showed (*El Unamuno contemplativo*,190), even at the spiritual level!

23. Hence Unamuno's criticism of Pereda in 'El sentimiento de la naturaleza' (*Por tierras de Portugal y España*) for his inability to convert 'sus estados de conciencia en paisaje, y los paisajes en estados de conciencia'. Cf. Azorín's desire in *La voluntad* to 'interpretar la emoción del paisaje'. The poem 'Cáceres' (*OC* XIV, 776–7) is, however, an important exception because of its unusual tone of almost Machadian disgust with provincial sloth and triviality.

24. Iris M. Zavala, *Unamuno y su teatro de conciencia* (Salamanca, 1963), 138.

25. J. Huertas Jordá, *The Existentialism of Miguel de Unamuno* (Gainesville, 1963), 54. This is the best short introduction in English to Unamuno's thought.

26. Included in *Los intelectuales y un epílogo para estudiantes*, 163–98.

Chapter 4

MAEZTU: FROM LEFT TO RIGHT

I. THE YOUNG SOCIALIST

Among those who were initially most critical of Unamuno's drift away from socialism and the economic approach to *regeneración* was Ramiro de Maeztu. The very first article he managed to publish in Madrid: 'El socialismo bilbaíno', in the progressive magazine *Germinal* on 16 July 1897, reproached Unamuno for leaving behind the 'carácter científico' of the movement (i.e., its Marxist orthodoxy) and veering off in a religious direction. The attack was repeated in *El País* in January of the following year.[1] Ironically Maeztu's own about-face, when it came, was to be much more spectacular. He was born on 4 May 1874 in the Basque town of Vitoria, his father being a well-off Cuban slave-holding sugar-planter and his mother English (née Whitney). Though the latter was and remained a Protestant, Maeztu's upbringing was strongly traditional and Catholic. A sharp decline in the family's fortunes largely caused by the abolition of slavery in 1886 prevented him from taking a university course. Instead, he emigrated to Cuba in 1891 and for three years had to accept a variety of unskilled jobs. But he began to read widely, discovering Sudermann and Ibsen and more especially Schopenhauer, Kropotkin, and Marx. His return to Spain in 1894 coincided with the death of his father and the final collapse of the family economy. So he turned to journalism on the local paper *El Porvenir Vascongado*, where his articles on the Cuban question in 1895–96, using his first-hand knowledge, were reproduced in Madrid newspapers and laid the basis for his future reputation.

In 1897 Maeztu moved to Madrid and joined the group of writers connected with *Germinal* and *El País*, where he met Azorín and Baroja. Thus the friendship of 'Los tres' came into being. At that time the doctrinaire extreme Left in Spain was divided between the Anarchists and the (Marxist) Socialists under Pablo Iglesias. The latter repelled middle-class intellectual sympathizers by their rigid dogmatism, by their insistence on party discipline and orthodoxy, and by their grimly materialistic hostility to any higher spiritual ideals. Thus the group to which Maeztu gravitated, which also included Benavente and Valle-Inclán, though calling itself Republican-Socialist, remained outside real party affiliations. Its members wrote

75

impartially for Anarchist publications as well as for *El Socialista* and *La Lucha de Clases*, and maintained personal hostilities from the columns of their own rival newspapers. Azorín and Unamuno attacked Dicenta and the *Germinal* group in *El Progreso*, Maeztu defended them in *El País*.

For the moment Unamuno ignored him. But when in 1899 Maeztu collected some of his articles into his first book, *Hacia otra España*, Unamuno was stirred to reply forcibly. The divergence between the two on the regeneration issue and Maeztu's later move towards (and even beyond) Unamuno's position offer the clearest possible illustration of the Generation's failure to evolve an adequate economico-social platform and its tendency to take refuge in mystiques. After the turn of the century Maeztu also began to move away from commitment to the Left, beginning in 1901 with a series of articles in the top Madrid daily *El Imparcial* (which later sacked Azorín for his exposure of rural famine and oppression in Andalusia), attacking Anarchism and its policy of organizing strikes and industrial unrest. By 1904, like Azorín (see his *OC*, I, 948), he had become convinced that Marxist doctrines of simple economic determinism, as they were then interpreted by Iglesias and his party, did not fit the facts. Even before this time he had, like Baroja (see below, p. 97), come under the influence of Nietzsche and was gravitating rapidly towards an élitist solution to Spain's problems. ' " ¡Hombres superiores!" Lo que España necesitaba es lo mismo que Nietzsche había predicado',[2] he was to write thirty years later, after advocating, like Ortega, 'una aristocracia directora'.[3]

A bohemian turbulent figure at this time, Maeztu took an active part in the famous affair of Galdós's *Electra*, came to blows with Azorín amongst others, and was under threat of court proceedings for a serious assault on a fellow journalist when *La Prensa*, the prominent Buenos Aires daily, offered him the post of London correspondent in 1905. In Edwardian England Maeztu became actively interested in Guild Socialism, whose founding father, A. J. Pentry, published his pioneering book *The Restoration of the Guild System* in 1906. Maeztu's book *Authority, Liberty and Function* (London, 1916) is still mentioned by the *Encyclopaedia Britannica* as a major work on the subject, along with those of Hobson, G. D. H. Cole, Tawney, Bertrand Russell, and Orage. In the latter's paper, *The New Age*, which popularized Guild Socialism, articles by Maeztu soon began to appear beside those of the other founders of the movement and by literary figures of the stature of Wells and Maugham and T. S. Eliot. The influence of Sidney Webb and the Fabians (illustrated by Maeztu's articles 'El socialismo de corbata' and 'La Fabian Society', *La Correspondencia de España* 24 and 28 March 1907)[4] completed Maeztu's awareness of the insufficiency of

Marx's analysis of socio-economic conditions and drew him towards the British brand of non-Marxist State Socialism. But his instinctive, Spanish distrust of the State, which he saw in terms of an inefficient, parasitic bureaucracy presiding over an immensely uneconomic administrative machine, led him to seek within the British movement a more functional theory, which he found in the *New Age* group. Unfortunately, as subsequent events were to prove, especially in Mussolini's Italy and Perón's Argentina, the guild or corporative idea was all too readily detachable from democratic socialism and formed a natural bridge – which Maeztu was ready to cross – to the authoritarian conception of state organization.

Maeztu's association with the intellectuals of the new British Left presented him with a golden opportunity: the chance to elaborate and redefine the naïve and insufficient socio-economic theories he had absorbed from hasty acquaintance with Marx, Kropotkin, and Costa into a solid, comprehensive, firmly-found methodology on which to base practical reforms in Spain. In a word, the opportunity to become a Spanish Sidney Webb. He had set his foot on the path, he had a large and secure captive audience of readers, and he had the basic blueprint. But at that precise moment, in 1911, he veered off, like Ganivet, Unamuno, and Azorín, towards the abstract and went to Marburg to study Kant. Among his primary aims was that of developing a philosophic basis for his socialist ideals, but in the process he soon left practical reformism behind. By now two submerged tendencies in his mind were coming to the surface: his latent spiritual aspiration and, allied to it, his instinctive belief in historical determinism.

On 14 December 1916 Maeztu married, like his father, an Englishwoman. The next year a General Strike inaugurated a new era in Spanish political and social life. Into the new era the Maeztus returned in 1919. For four years, as correspondent of the Madrid daily *El Sol*, he watched the death agony of the political system inaugurated by Martínez Campos and Cánovas in 1874. Slowly he came to see in the dictatorship of Primo de Rivera after the *coup d'état* of September 1923 a hopeful alternative. But while his political stance was shifting he wrote his most successful book: *Don Quijote, Don Juan y la Celestina* (1926). A year later he stepped definitively to the right, leaving *El Sol*, and joining *La Nación*, which openly supported the new regime. In late 1922 he also joined Primo de Rivera's *Unión Patriótica* party. There the unhappy discovery awaited him that the old-style Conservative political groups found their *raison d'être* almost exclusively in the protection of class interests. They had no social programme capable of offering any kind of alternative to the myth of the Left, and no understanding of the need for one. Before long he was isolated.

At the end of 1927 Maeztu accepted the appointment of ambassador to Argentina and took up his post in February 1928. Two years later, after the resignation of Primo de Rivera in January 1930, he gave up the post and returned to Spain. Foreseeing the triumph of radical left-wing republicanism and a return to the disorders of the early 1920s, he called for authoritarian political reforms supported by the monarchy and the armed forces. Six years later, his evolution complete, he was openly demanding a powerful dictatorship to head 'a counter-revolutionary steamroller'. It came, with the consequences we know. They did not include the reforms Maeztu anticipated. Meanwhile he founded a counter-revolutionary magazine, *Acción Española*, which divided Spain's intellectual readership with the two great progressive cultural magazines of the period: *La Revista de Occidente* and *Cruz y Raya*. In *Acción Española* he published in instalments his last major work, *Defensa de la Hispanidad* (1934). After his imprisonment by the Republican government during a purge of opposition figures in 1932 he was a marked man. He was still more under threat after he became a right-wing deputy in the *Cortes* of 1934. In the disturbed days of 1936 he was aware of the danger, but refused to flee. In July he was arrested and after 28 October no certain news was heard of him. Then, or soon after, he was summarily shot. Part of his brief post-war reputation was due to his being one of the intellectual martyrs of the victors of the Civil War.

What strikes the reader of *Hacia otra España* at once is the book's ideological inconsistencies. Maeztu lacked in 1899 a unified, thought-out approach to the Spanish problem. The book is in fact an agglomeration of articles written usually in great haste under the immediate impact of events, together with a specially written prologue and concluding section. Maeztu himself, in a sentence which is of key importance, referred to:

las dos tendencias que han ejercido influjo sobre el alma nacional; la tendencia histórica, guerrera y heroica; y la tendencia contemporánea, conservadora y positivista, hija de cierto mejoramiento, operado últimamente, en nuestra vida económica.[5]

The fluctuation in his outlook which Maeztu attributed to the conflicting influence of these two tendencies: the historist-nationalistic one with its emphasis on ideals and the 'spirit of the race', versus the economico-social one with its stress on the primacy of Spain's poverty and underdevelopment, is basic not only to his own evolution, but also to that of the Generation of 1898 as a whole. In the end the former influence largely prevailed: the importance of *Hacia otra España* lies in the fact that it was the one major book of the '98 which unequivocally emphasized the latter.

In the opening section, 'Páginas sueltas', however, this emphasis is only sporadic. Of the fourteen short articles which Maeztu collected here, only five are really relevant to the book's aim,[6] the others have little contemporary interest. Maeztu's thesis in the five was not a strictly economic one. His argument dealt primarily with the human factor: the lack of trained technical personnel, of entrepreneurs, of industrialists, agriculturalists, and businessmen with a modern, competitive mentality: in a phrase, the lack of 'hombres que conocen su oficio' (45). Although in the opening 'Dos palabras' he identified the basic issue in his statement 'A mi juicio se encuentra España en los comienzos de una grande y necesaria lucha económica' (27), and demanded in 'El desarme' the replacement of traditional mental categories by a practical pragmatic approach, he continued to think of the problem as one of the Spanish middle-class *mentality* rather than as one of resources. A very clear indication of this is to be found in the fact that, conversely, he instinctively identified economic progress with 'la fuerza moral' and the power to reach 'la alegre aceptación de la existencia, el sí a la vida' (33).

The sixteen essays of the second section of *Hacia otra España*: 'De las guerras', which include those recording Maeztu's immediate reaction to the military crisis of 1898 and to the subsequent disaster, emphasize the dichotomy within his outlook in much plainer terms. Though he was completely aware of the tragic inferiority of the Spanish war-machine, and pessimistic of the outcome, the military climax of 1898 brought from Maeztu the decision to join the army, albeit for the briefest of periods, and an outburst of patriotic rhetoric. 'La marcha del regimiento', 'Sobre el discurso de Lord Salisbury', and especially the key-parts of 'Frente al conflicto' reveal a Maeztu as possessed momentarily by war-fever and as ready to exalt his race above that of the Anglo-Saxons as the most bigoted traditionalist. The future Maeztu of *Defensa de la Hispanidad* is already recognizable here. For the moment, however, learned values prevailed over gut-reactions. In his calmer moments Maeztu recognized that Spain must come to terms with her obvious weakness. 'Busquemos', he wrote, after the disaster, 'tras el fenómeno político el subsuelo económico' (135). His denunciation of the scientific, industrial, and agricultural underdevelopment of Spain in the central article of Section I, 'Las quejas de Raventós', re-emerged in the picture of Spain presented in 'Un suicidio'. On the one hand he saw 'esas yermas sin árboles, de suelo arenoso, en el que apenas si se destacan cabañas de barro donde viven vida animal doce millones de gusanos, que doblan el cuerpo, al surcar la tierra con aquel arado, que importaron los árabes'; on the other, he saw 'esas fábricas catalanas, edificadas en el aire, sin materia prima, sin máquinas inventadas por nosotros, sostenidas merced al artificio de protectores aracelas' (101). Instead of seeking like Unamuno a mythical 'eternal tradition' to offset the imperial tradition which now lay in ruins (though there is a hint of this attitude in his reply to Lord Salisbury), Maeztu insisted on the direct approach he had learned from Costa: 'Necesitamos mejores alimentos, mejores viviendas, regar la tierra seca, inventar máquinas, crear obras bellas, mejorar la instrucción, aprender toda la ciencia de la vida' (142). If the war had produced the Sedan which he had forecast in November 1897, let it serve, as in France, to stimulate economic growth.

The general survey of the state of the Nation at the opening of the final section of *Hacia otra España* (which gives the book its title) contained both a restatement of Maeztu's practical approach to *regeneración* and an awareness of the difficulties and countervailing forces which led the other members of the Generation of 1898 to retreat from an economic solution and take refuge in less effective but more tractable attitudes. Economic take-off requires not only long-term investment and technical know-how, but also an adequate substructure of communications, ports, transport networks, modern banking methods, and labour resources which Spain simply did not possess and was not equipped to provide. Faced with this bleak fact Maeztu was compelled to postulate in 'Lo que nos queda' an interim period, a phase of transition, in which a foreign-trained entrepreneurial class with a defined policy could be built up, while 'un Estado-Empresa que construya carreteras, levante puentes y tienda vías férreas' (171) came into being. This postulate, which in the absence of economic incentives was just as much a pipe-dream as Unamuno's hopes of spiritual regeneration, revealed the hopeless frustration to which Spanish intellectuals were condemned in the years between the 1890s and the 1950s.

With – in retrospect – pathetic hopefulness Maeztu turned his attention none the less to the problem of breaking the vicious circle created by a lack of home markets for manufactured products, which held back industrial expansion, thus in turn necessitating protective trade-barriers, which increased costs to the consumers and hence restricted the home market. His solution was investment in the primary sector of the economy, agriculture: 'industrialización del suelo castellano', as he called it in his famous essay 'La meseta castellana'. Land reform, tax reform, irrigation, the breaking-down of internal trade-barriers and negative commercial practices, the appearance of an efficient, reorganized civil service, but above all the mobilization of investment capital, were other objectives Maeztu hoped to see achieved in which he called 'el período burgués que ahora se está incubando'. The difficulties he perceived were inertia, lack of organization and unity in the industrial and commercial classes, bureaucracy, failure on the part of the press and the influential intellectuals (notably Unamuno) to influence public opinion in the right direction, and finally the plague of unemployable university graduates in the professional disciplines scrambling for state jobs which ought to go to technocrats. The end of the book, like the beginning, called for united efforts on the part of the 'hombres de negocio' and recognition that '¡el oro *vil* irá haciendo la otra España!'

Unamuno was nettled by the attack on him in 'El separatismo peninsular' as 'ese bilbaíno colosal aunque atropellado, confundido, sin valor eficiente' (the reference was to his recent turn-about on the issue of economico-social renovation, after abandoning his Marxist phase). In 1899 he replied tartly with 'La conquista de las mesetas' and 'La tiranía de las ideas', which followed up his more famous 'La vida es sueño' and 'Doctores en industrias' of the previous year. In the last-mentioned article he had already suggested that 'Es inútil querer industriales sin industrias correspondientes'. In 'La conquista de las mesetas' he pointed out to 'el joven escritor Maeztu, inteligencia brillante e impetuosa, envuelta en un yanquismo tan generoso como poco maduro aun' some of the hard economic reasons (infertility, world over-productions, short-term leases, artificial overpricing of land, excessive agricultural population, lack of fertilizer, and above all the entire system of landownership) which made it utterly uneconomic to invest heavily in the *meseta*. A careful reading shows, however, that Unamuno was not the expert economist that Inman Fox and Blanco Aguinaga suggest.[7] His approach was in fact as defective in its way as Maeztu's, since it was wholly theoretic and avoided the basic questions of land- and tax-reform which the latter assumed as an integral part of his case. However naïve Maeztu's opinions seem, they emphasized the need for change, while Unamuno's defended the old oppressive *status quo*.

Few of Maeztu's other articles belonging to the period before he left for England have been collected, but it is clear from *Debemos a Costa* (1911)[8] that he gradually came to recognize that Costa's ideal of 'escuela y despensa', cultural and economic reform, did not constitute a full enough blueprint for national progress. Similarly the slogan-word *europeización* needed to be given a precise meaning. He found this last in an early pronouncement of Ortega, who took over from him after 1905 as the leader of the *Europeizantes*, that Europe meant precision and exactitude, logic and mathematics, in contrast to Spanish improvisation and disdain for the exact sciences. Thereafter Maeztu frequently repeated this. In 1900 and again in 1903 and 1905 he formulated his once-famous accusation against *Don Quixote* as a characteristic expression of Spain's decadence, an accusation which brought him suddenly into the middle of the literary-critical scene. As Inman Fox has shown, he kept up the running fight with Unamuno which had begun in 1897 with fresh outbreaks in 1901, 1903, 1904, and culminating in 1907 with a polemic in *La correspondencia de España* on one of Maeztu's chief hobby-horses at this time: Spain's excessive and anti-progressive individualist tendency, which atomized society. The most revealing articles of this early period are 'Cómo muere un superhombre' (1902) and the better-known 'Juventud menguante' (1904).[9] Both are autobiographical. They paint a picture of a young journalist writing, by his own confession, in a state bordering on frenzy. Possessed with patriotic indignation, he was ready, as Beser has shown,[10] to believe in a Jesuit conspiracy to split the intellectual Left, as well as to attack his closest friends, to engage in duels with his opponents, and to sacrifice his chances of advancement to his violent critique of social conditions. His motto was 'Había que reedificar de nueva planta todo el edifico social español'.[11] His mentor was Nietzsche; his chief preoccupation the cause of the oppressed classes. Beneath it all, however, both articles reveal an unhappy young man, intellectually and spiritually confused, desperately seeking, like his friends Baroja and Azorín, to 'recobrar de alguna manera la unidad de su espíritu'.[12] When he left for England it was to look for his real self as well as to study a different socio-political environment.

At the time Maeztu arrived in London the traditional role of the British Trade Union movement, which had been restricted to the sphere of industrial bargaining, was under challenge from the 'direct action' movement aimed at using strikes as political weapons to overthrow the whole state apparatus. This situation polarized Maeztu's thought around the trade union aspect of political reformism and led to the view that some method of integrating workers' organizations into the power-structure of government had to be worked out. He set out to elaborate a political system in which each individual could be represented both narrowly as a worker and broadly as a citizen. The evolution of Maeztu's ideas can be followed in the articles collected as *Un ideal sindicalista* (Madrid, 1961) and in *Authority, Liberty and Function in the Light of War* (London, 1916), translated as *La crisis del humanismo* (Barcelona, 1919). We can group his ideas briefly around three critiques.

First, his critique of the State. Maeztu believed that the institution of the State was threatened by a loss of dynamism and energy on the part of the traditional governing class, coinciding with a growth of political consciousness among the governed. Political principles had in consequence given place to class interests. The state political leadership, Maeztu argued, had progressively lost its powers to big business on the one hand, and to a huge and intolerably expensive civil service on the other. Loss of confidence, loss of effective power, and loss of economic efficiency, he believed, were bringing the state apparatuses of parliamentary democracy in western Europe to their knees.

Second, his critique of the Socialist alternative. At that time Socialists in Britain advocated nationalization of major industries and land, as a logical step following the municipalization of certain services which had already taken place. Maeztu criticized both the means and the ends. If the State were, as Socialists asserted, a bourgeois conspiracy against the workers, it was futile to work for a peaceful takeover by a workers' party. Even if such a takeover were achieved, state control would merely expand and enrich to an even greater degree the parasite administrative bureaucracy without corresponding benefit to the proletariat.

Third, his critique of French-type radical syndicalism. Here Maeztu made his primary distinction between the State as guarantor of individual civil rights and liberties ('la communidad legal') and the State as depository of political and economic power ('el que manda'). The syndicalists saw only the latter and demanded the devolution of this power to associations of workers in the various spheres of production and distribution. But in attempting to free the economic producer they failed to make provision for the citizen. Their ideal of 'una Sociedad sin Estado' was, like their mystique of the General Strike, a myth. Maeztu, still a Socialist, fully accepted the ideal of 'la organización del proletariado para la abolición del proletariado mismo'.[13] But he firmly believed that state organization was the safeguard of liberty and had to be maintained indivisible; and he resolutely rejected the simplification of social categories into bourgeois exploiters and proletarian victims. Logically therefore he insisted on the retention of the parliamentary system. But from as early as 1906 he advocated a bicameral arrangement, in which one House represented the voter as citizen, and one House the worker from the point of view of his economic function. For, he wrote in 'Clase y partido' (1913), 'La causa de las actuales incertidumbres consiste en que en los Estados modernos no tiene representación directa el principio sindicalista'.[14]

II. THE ESSAYIST AND CRITIC

Hitherto we have seen in Maeztu the would-be practical thinker. But by the time he came to write *Authority, Liberty and Function* a change was coming over his entire outlook. Instead of looking ever more closely at the political and economic facts he now increasingly began to theorize, like Unamuno, about the imponderables which he persuaded himself underlay and determined these facts. From considerations of society he moved to considerations connected with the spiritual nature of man. 1911 was the critical year. At the old Café Royal in London he had formed a friendship with the poet and philosopher T. E. Hulme, who like himself was a contributor to the *New Age*. Hulme, he wrote, 'me mostraba la inmensa trascendencia de la doctrina del pecado original',[15] and thereby began to wean him from the liberal, humanistic, and optimistic interpretation of human possibilities and potential for progress which he had until then as a Socialist largely taken for granted. From here it was but a step to a dawning religious preoccupation. Under Hulme's influence Maeztu came to see that if humanist presuppositions were false, the only force which would draw men to sacrifice themselves for the collectivity, or for the future, would be religion. Hence, when he went to Germany he was anxious to find a way to 'espiritualizar el socialismo', as he wrote in a letter to his friend Plá Cárceles in December 1911.

In the same letter he wrote the sentence which perhaps more than any other epitomizes not only his own fundamental outlook but that of the Generation of 1898 as a whole. The British, he asserted, had solved their political problems 'por pura experiencia, por polémica práctica y cotidiana'. For Spaniards this approach was impossible because of their abstractivating anti-pragmatical cast of mind. 'Para nosotros, no cabe más camino que el de meternos en la cabeza los principios y transformar las cosas con los principios'.[16] It was, alas, Ganivet's postulate of the need for 'ideas madres' all over again. It led Maeztu, as it had led Ganivet and Unamuno, straight into a blind alley.

Maeztu returned to Spain in 1919 a very different man from the bohemian journalist who had left the country in 1905; and he found a very different Spain. He was still, as he had always been, an admirer of Costa and a believer in economic regeneration. But although he continued to advocate what he was to call 'el sentido reverencial del dinero', which harked back to his assertion in 1899 that 'el oro vil irá haciendo la otra España', he allowed himself to think that the regeneration was now successfully in progress. What now began to preoccupy him more directly was the crisis in values and ideals, which the other members of the Generation had long been asserting. This crisis had progressively taken possession of his mind after his trip to Marburg and during his attack on humanism's hedonistic values, as he saw them, in *Authority, Liberty and Function*. For a time during the 1920s he was able to conciliate his advocacy of economic progress with his advocacy of moral regeneration,[17] but the balance was shifting all the time towards the latter. The triumph of the Republic in 1931, which he (having now abandoned socialism) regarded as a catastrophe from the outset, completed his evolution. 'La revolución de 1931', he wrote in July 1932, 'ha nacido de ese sobreexceso de actividades económicas. Nuestras clases directivas han desdeñado las actividades espirituales'.[18] Already the ideas of *Defensa de la Hispanidad* had germinated in his mind. We must now examine the process by which they came to prevail.

Time had taught Maeztu that not all industrialization brought social and economic benefits: 'Hay buenas fábricas y malas fábricas, porque hay fabricantes creadores y fabricantes especuladores'.[19] Faced with the need to analyse and study in detail the forms of economico-social progress, Maeztu had found himself unprepared and turned his attention instead to elaborating the theory of politico-social organization formulated in *Authority, Liberty and Function*. The next stage of his evolution was marked by his essay 'La reconciliación' (1922) and by a trip to North America in 1925. Here what he had begun in London took definite shape. He came to believe that the emphasis placed by the Catholic church on the primacy of the soul's salvation had led to a state of conflict between material and spiritual progress. In 'La reconciliación' he argued that the theological doctrine which proclaimed the unity of body and soul implied that 'este mundo es parte esencial del otro'.[20] In consequence, material progress pursued not for selfish aims or for its own sake (i.e., with what he was to call the 'sentido sensual del dinero'), but ultimately for the good of all (i.e., with 'el sentido reverencial del dinero'), was inseparably allied to spiritual progress. North America seemed to him the perfect illustration of his ideal in practice.

Maeztu returned to Spain believing that he had found in North America first the true point of union between spiritual principles and the creation of wealth, and second an economic system in which men could enrich themselves without impoverishing their fellows. He set himself at once the role of communicating his discoveries to the Spanish reading public. His aim was now to harness the inherently spiritual incentive, which his generation had argued almost with one voice was ultimately the only operative one in Spain, to material advance. Having decided that in Britain, Germany, and the United States 'los hombres fueron persuadidos de que su oficio o profesión era también, y al mismo tiempo, su vocación y tarea espiritual',[21] his task became that of converting Spanish workers of all classes to this outlook. At the same time he advocated the creation of wealth, not for unproductive expenditure, in what he saw as the Latin tradition, but for socially responsible investment. The years following his return to Spain, and especially his trip to America, removed the last vestiges of his former socialist ideas. Now, in contrast, he presented as an additional advantage of his proposals the fact that enlightened capitalism in the United States had proved an effective antidote to socialism. Nevertheless Maeztu was immediately attacked and misrepresented on all sides by the traditionalists, for whom he was at last providing a sensible rationale. He was accused by Julio Camba, Giménez Caballero, and even by Gómez de la Serna of propagating Jewish and Protestant principles and of being the agent of Anglo-Saxon cultural colonization.

He was, of course, merely ahead of his time. His vision of the Protestant ethic of capitalism and its benefits was, like all his ideas, simplified and naïve. He failed for instance to recognize that some of the wealth of the United States came from the exploitation of the resources of underdeveloped countries, whose relative poverty was thereby increased, or to understand that not all the wealth produced was responsibly reinvested or distributed. There is no sign in his work that he understood the problems of negro and urban poverty in the wealthy and meritocratic America he thought he was observing. But the history of Spain since the late 1950s is the history of a country in which industrial take-off has begun to modify traditional attitudes to work and wealth in ways of which Maeztu would have approved. What he could not foresee, any more than Ganivet or Unamuno, was that the economic transformation would be financed largely from outside Spain, and would precede and accompany, instead of following, a change of social outlook which is still by no means complete.

Maeztu's campaign in favour of the creation and socially responsible use of capital was the last major effort he made to influence the Spanish public in a practical direction. Already he had embarked, like Ganivet and Unamuno previously, on a scrutiny of aspects of Spanish literature with the aim of identifying the major national myths underlying the country's history and discussing the issues of principles they raised. The result, which was *Don Quijote, Don Juan y La Celestina* (1926), raises afresh all the difficulties connected with the historical-determinist, *alma de la raza*, approach. Ironically Maeztu had been the only member of the Generation of 1898 to question seriously the existence of a national character imposing its pattern on the country's development.[22] Needless to say, he was at the time attacking Unamuno. But by 1927 ('Las ideas dominadoras') he too had come to believe in 'un fondo impreciso en los pueblos' (i.e., a sort of *intra-historia*) which theorists seeking to launch new dominating ideas (Ganivet's *ideas directoras* with a new name) ignored at their peril.[23] His praise of Costa in 1911 for breaking deliberately with the past[24] gave way now to the bald assertion 'en los pueblos, su ser moral se identifica con su historia'.[25] *Don Quijote, Don Juan y La Celestina* was a foray into cultural history in search of Spain's 'ser moral'.

The book is therefore in no real sense a work of literary criticism; it is interpretation pure and simple. We have mentioned that as early as 1900 Maeztu raised a storm in the *Ateneo* by presenting

Cervantes's *Don Quixote* as a work of Spain's decadence. He returned to the idea repeatedly afterwards, even linking it in a curious way to his ideal of strengthening the economy in the 1920s with his slogan 'Don Quijote con dinero'. But the definitive treatment came in the first essay of *Don Quijote, Don Juan y La Celestina*. While waiting for the book to be presented, Maeztu explained his intentions in a short essay: 'En la barra'.[26] He was, he asserted, analysing the three works as myths, for 'En los mitos literarios representativos hemos de encontrar no ya la historia, sino algo mejor: los sentimientos que la mueven'. The thought-pattern is familiar to every reader of Ganivet and Unamuno, from whom Maeztu borrowed it: national character gives rise to representative myths which are reflected in literary works. These myths condition the historical development of the nations in question. To analyse them is to identify the limiting factors governing any solution of national problems. However, when we turn to the consideration of *Don Quixote* in *Don Quijote, Don Juan y La Celestina* this is not quite what we find.

Maeztu's argument is, as usual, suspiciously simple. When *Don Quixote* first appeared Spain had exhausted herself in the attempts to 'conquistar al mismo tiempo el mundo de la acción y el del espíritu',[27] the threefold struggle for imperial expansion, political supremacy in Europe, and defence of the Catholic faith. Cervantes's own life had mirrored Spain's desperate fight. Both writer and nation were weary and disillusioned. Despite its eternal and universal significance *Don Quixote* was the product, then, of a particular negative moment of Spanish history: that in which 'el ideal se muestra superior a los medios para realizarlo' (19). In contrast to *Hamlet*, also the product of a particular, but positive, moment of British history, and to the *Luisíadas* in Portuguese history, *Don Quixote* preaches a doctrine of rest and disengagement. The chivalric ideal which Cervantes laughs away, is in reality the ideal which Spain had been draining her energies to pursue for centuries, 'porque toda España ha sido Don Quijote' (55). The consequences of learning the lesson of *Don Quixote* too well, had been three centuries of national repose. But the fact 'that the nation's exhaustion had rendered its fulfilment impracticable did not make the original ideal itself wholly false; nor did it preclude the eventual recovery of a new national ideal. This was Maeztu's affirmation now. The resignation and repose appropriate for 1605 were not appropriate for 1926. 'Comprendemos que [el Quijote] había que desengañar, por su propio bien, a los españoles de aquel tiempo. Y advertiremos, a la vez, que lo que el nuestro necesita no es desencantarse y desilusionarse, sino, al contrario, volver a sentir un ideal' (67). Following Ganivet afresh, Maeztu insisted that 'la abulia española' was merely the result of 'la falta de ideal'. To recover an ideal would be to recover the national will and hence what Maeztu called 'la iniciativa histórica' which Spain had long since lost. But, he insisted, in conformity with his personal belief in the need to 'sacramentalize' work and wealth: 'el ansia de dinero [for its own sake, that is] es insuficiente para hacer recobrar a una nación la iniciativa histórica' (69).

In contrast to Don Quixote, who possesses the ideal without possessing the strength to realize it, stands Don Juan, who is endowed with powers before which normal obstacles seem to fall aside almost instantly. But Don Juan has no ideal other than the satisfaction of his caprices. He has unbounded energy, but no directing concept of duty. Underlying his lack of a moral value-system is his lack of religious belief: 'Es el jugador, porque la vida carece de sentido' (93). In Zorrilla's version of the legend, however, Don Juan recovers, through love, a fleeting intuition of the 'posibilidad de un universo en que hombre e instituciones colaboran en el servicio de Dios' (101). For Maeztu, Don Juan represented modern man, and in particular the modern Spaniard, for whom it had become possible to live selfishly and hedonistically without a guiding ideal. But the possibility of new insight and redemption remained, if collective faith could be recovered in a God-ordained absolute pattern of values: a 'patrón absoluto' to offset Don Juan's 'capricho absoluto'.

The weakest of the book's three sections concerns La Celestina. Maeztu interprets the actions and outlooks of Celestina herself in terms which do not differ significantly from the terms applied to Don Juan. Her hedonism, materialism, and utilitarian attitudes derive once more from absence of religious faith, denial of a Providential pattern in events, and a consequent vision of life as a blind struggle against arbitrary unknown forces. By a natural extension of his argument Maeztu connects Celestina with his idea of the 'sentido sensual del dinero' predominant in Spain. This enables him to dedicate the climax of the book to a further impassioned plea to reject the church's traditional hostility to the pursuit of wealth by the individual, and to replace it with a sacramental sense of temporal occupations.

Maeztu's writings as a literary critic in the strict sense of the word are negligible. He firmly believed and repeated tirelessly even in the 1930s that 'La generación a que Palacio Valdés pertenece, la de Galdós, Pereda, Valera, Menéndez y Pelayo, Campoamor y Nuñez de Arce no ha encontrado sucesores de su altura'.[28] He considered Peñas arriba by Pereda the greatest Spanish novel after Don Quixote, while at the same time systematically ignoring the creative work of the Generation of 1898 and failing to notice the emergence of the poetic Generation of 1927. Characteristic of Don Quijote, Don Juan y La Celestina and of all Maeztu's literary criticism is his almost total disregard of formal considerations in the works discussed. From start to finish of his career as a writer Maeztu remained uncompromisingly hostile to the idea of pure art, or 'Art for Art's sake'. He attacked it in 'Autorretrato' in 1904, in *Authority, Liberty and Function*, in the opening pages of *Don Quijote, Don Juan y La Celestina* itself, and most specifically of all in his 1932 address to the *Academia de Ciencias Morales y Políticas*: 'El arte y la moral'. He came gradually, but inevitably in the light of his other ideas, to associate the doctrine of Art for Art's sake with the generalized loss of ideals (other than that of hedonism) which he saw as the great problem confronting Western civilization. As part of that process 'la técnia artística se ha separado de los ideales humanos todo lo que ha podido'.[29] But he himself remained firmly attached to the view that 'la función del arte es religiosa: revelarnos un valor o crearlo'.[30] In this he was completely at one with the mainstream outlook of the Generation of 1898.

III. THE THEORIST OF *Hispanidad*

Don Quixote, Maeztu believed, had destroyed Spain's faith in her historical ideal, *El burlador de Sevilla* and *La Celestina* had confirmed Spaniards in the belief that they could manage without such an ideal. But the collapse of 1898 had revealed the consequences of that belief, and the time was ripe for the discovery of a new collective value-pattern and national direction. Earlier, just as he had questioned the existence of an 'espíritu nacional', Maeztu had also dared for one exciting moment to question whether even in the climactic moment of her history, the sixteenth century, Spain had really been conquering and creating at the behest of a national ideal.[31] But the instant of lucidity remained unique. Now he consciously sought and found the new *idea dominadora*, like Ganivet and Unamuno, in Spain's tradition, setting alongside 'el espíritu territorial' and 'la tradición eterna' his own conception of *Hispanidad*.

The best introduction to *Defensa de la Hispanidad* (1934) is Maeztu's essay of the same year 'La nueva filosofía de la historia y el problema de la Hispanidad' which synthesizes its main ideas and discusses them in relation to Nicolai Hartmann's *Das Problem des geistigen Seins* (1933) where, as in his old Marburg professor's earlier work, Maeztu believed he found independent confirmation of his own ideas. The theses of his *Defensa*, Maeztu declares, are:

Que la Hispanidad es un espíritu, que hay un espíritu peculiar a la Hispanidad; que ese espíritu, valioso para la humanidad, es insustituíble para nosotros; que le tenemos medio abandonado, que lo necesitamos para el porvenir, que nos es posible recuperarlo íntegramente.[32]

Though essentially existing in the minds and hearts of individuals as an 'espíritu personal', it transcends them to become a collective 'espíritu objetivo', to which the art, literature, science, and all other cultural manifestations of a given nation testify. Unlike Hegel's world-spirit it has no independent autonomous existence, it is national and not universal. More especially, *it can fail*; either because the nation lacks the courage and vision to fulfil its imperatives, or because economic, geographical, or other conditions prevent such fulfilment. In such a case it would require reformation. Howbeit, 'la condición de toda grandeza histórica es la lealtad al propio espíritu'.[33] Spain, partly from poverty of resources, failed to fulfil her traditional ideals and for centuries ignored the need to renew it. But now, faced with the Bolshevik menace, 'El espíritu vivo siente como un milagro la vuelta del antiguo, como una resurrección'.[34]

Maeztu derived Spain's ideal directly from the heritage of Rome and from Catholicism, and indirectly from contrast with the liberal-humanist ideal which had triumphed over it because of 'la afirmación romántica de que el hombre es naturalmente bueno y está libre del pecado original' (61). For him, as for Ortega (see below, p. 200), the essence of nationality was a consensus of 'valores colectivos' projecting itself towards the future. But what separated him from the author of *España invertebrada* was his insistence on the timelessness and changelessness of these values, so far as Spain was concerned, since they were firmly anchored in Roman Catholicism, whose truths he now held to be absolute and exclusive. Thus, other nations, particularly non-Catholic ones, might have to modify their value-systems, but Spain had only one alternative: to strive for, or to betray, her collective, inherited values. Maeztu defined them as: belief in the essential equality of all men as human beings, that is as souls, endowed with free will, irrespective of class, wealth, or position; and secondly, belief in the universal capacity of men to achieve salvation. Belief, that is, in the moral unity of mankind and in its spiritual potentiality.

A great part of *Defensa de la Hispanidad* is given over to a broad interpretation of Spanish history in terms first of the rise of these beliefs, then of Spain's fidelity to them in her social system and imperial policy during the sixteenth and seventeenth centuries, and finally of her betrayal of them after 1750. The starting-point is put naturally at the conversion to Catholicism of King Recaredo in AD 586. The campaigns against the Moors and Jews (that is, against doctrines of fatalism and exclusivism) stiffened belief in the two underlying principles. They were reaffirmed categorically by the Catholic Kings in their instructions to the early *conquistadores* and by Diego Lainez at the Council of Trent in 1546. They were the guiding principles of the Spanish conquest of Latin America, ex-

emplified most clearly in the Jesuit missions of Paraguay, and survived there until the end of Spanish rule. The propagation of them
is the true mission of the Spanish spirit, which reveals itself through
them to be 'un espíritu generoso de servicio universal' (96).

Spain's spiritual mission implies a conception of the State radically
different from the liberal-democratic-secularist conception which
had grown up in Europe since the Enlightenment. Here Maeztu
gave full rein to his accumulated critiques of modern Western
societies and their political structures. His principal attack was
directed against what he called 'el naturalismo, la negación radical
de los valores del espíritu' (216), that is, communist materialism, and
'la confianza romántica del hombre en sí mismo' (72), that is,
liberal humanism. Both of these he associated directly with Anglo-
Saxon Protestant doctrines. He identified among their practical consequences the attempt to base societies on a falsely egalitarian legal
framework, the encouragement of an excessive degree of civil and
political liberty, a corresponding loss of absolute social sanctions, and
the reduction of collective aspirations to the sole aim of material
progress. This last, Maeztu considered, was insufficient to generate
the degree of self-sacrifice by one generation for the next which the
continuation of society demanded.

After 1750, Maeztu argued, because of the defeat of her old ideal
in the seventeenth century, and because of the folly and treachery of
her statesmen, Spain had gradually forsaken her tradition and been
won over to 'la superstición de lo extranjero' (45). He himself, he
lamented, had contributed tardily to the superstition in *Hacia otra
España*, a work which he now, not for the first time, repudiated.
Time had shown, he asserted in the key-section of the third essay,
'Los dioses se van', that the politico-social system which Spain had
been induced to copy was now revealing its total bankruptcy, not
only of ideals but of resources to pay for its multiplying functionaries
and growing welfare services. At the same time a rebirth of Catholic
belief was being accompanied by a restoration of 'authority' in
Fascist Italy and Nazi Germany. The time was therefore auspicious
for a Spanish reaction against the threat to what remained of her
spiritual heritage by the *antipatria* (implicitly, the new Republic).

Maeztu's ideal was a Spanish state explicitly wedded to the
primacy of religious ideals, and thus combining rather than separa-
ting religious and temporal authority. The *fuerza madre* on which
the state rested would thus become a spiritual absolute, as Spain
demanded, for 'El español cree en valores absolutos o deja de creer
totalmente' (71). It followed, for Maeztu, that the organization of
political life on such a basis could never be liberal or democratic as
he understood those terms. He advocated instead 'monarchy and
hierarchy' following the model established in the Middle Ages. For

the rest, he wrote: 'Partamos del principio de que un buen régimen ha de ser mixto. Ha de haber en él unidad y continuidad en el mando, aristocracia directora, y el pueblo ha de participar en el gobierno' (217). Not only, however, did he fail to specify how or to what extent popular participation in power was to be exercised, but he also failed to explain how the directing minority were to be converted from the tradition of seeing in state employment a source of private enrichment, to accepting 'un sentido del Estado como servicio'. He was content with the oracular affirmation that this would be so, and that once they achieved 'conciencia de haber recibido de Dios sus poderes, ese día se resolverán automáticamente los problemas' (220). Finally we must assume, from his vague reference to corporatism and to material progress as a necessary but subordinate adjunct to spiritual progress, that his plan automatically incorporated the main elements of his writings on the guild system and on the 'reverential sense of wealth'. *Defensa de la Hispanidad* closes the series of investigations into the 'Soul of Spain' which had begun with Ganivet's *Idearium español*.

Maeztu's work and thought possess a homogeneity which is absent from that of the other members of the Generation of 1898. His guiding ideas were few in number and comparatively easy to follow as they evolved. All centred in one way or another on the problems of modern state organization with particular reference to Spain. He brought to the study of those problems a closer familiarity and sympathy with Anglo-Saxon approaches to their solution, and a greater openness to European, especially German and French, intellectual influences, than we see elsewhere in 'regeneration' writings. But the concentration and compactness of his ideology had severe shortcomings. For a man who was all too ready to trap himself, like Ganivet, inside a narrow conception of historical determinism, Maeztu lacked a sense of historical orientation. As a young man he believed that the time for Spain's economic take-off had come in the years after 1898. In the 1920s he persuaded himself that it had begun to happen. Both views were hopelessly premature. In middle and later life he announced the collapse of liberal democracy in the West, as well as the utter failure both of British-type welfare reformism and Marxist communism. He went on to proclaim a return to Catholicism and to the authoritarian conception of the state and believed that this return inaugurated a new historical epoch. Within a few years of his death the error of these opinions was already amply apparent.

In retrospect we can see that Maeztu suffered from two great disadvantages compared to others in the Generation of 1898. While he recognized the collapse of absolute beliefs and the existential malaise of our time, he himself seems to have suffered little of the deep-seated spiritual tension which they generated in his companions. Since it is this last, in the end, which gives their work human significance, his by comparison seems limited. The other disadvantage was his lack of creative literary talent. Although he published some verse and short stories around the turn of the century, all his writings thereafter took the form of essays and articles. As the ideas and attitudes they dealt with became dated, the passion with which they were written ceased to stir the reader. The same is true of many similar essays by Unamuno, Baroja, and Azorín, and by Shaw, Chesterton, and Wells in Britain. But all of these latter writers had additional strings to their bow. Maeztu did not.

For this reason his role in the Generation of 1898 is doubly illustrative. It indicates, that is, more than just the fact that the living aspect of the Generation is its attitude to the human condition and not its response to the Spanish problem (as far as they can be separated). What Maeztu's role emphasizes most is the dangerous path on which the Generation as a body embarked when its members severed their original reformist allegiances and began elaborating approaches to the Spanish situation which were based on hypotheses about national character or mystiques of spiritual regeneration. Unamuno and Azorín in particular followed Maeztu part of the way towards the Right, where Ganivet's heart always was too. Baroja's political agnosticism and Machado's anti-jacobin liberalism did not immunize them against sporadic emotional nationalism with all its negative implications. Finally Ortega's conception of 'los mejores' leading 'las masas' is dangerously akin to Maeztu's more openly authoritarian hierarchical conception of society. In a distorted, but still disturbing, way Maeztu's *Hispanidad* all too often represents the *españolismo* of his fellow writers writ large.

NOTES

1. See Rafael Pérez de la Dehesa's extremely valuable *El grupo 'Germinal':* *una clave del 98* (Madrid, 1970), 55, 73–83. Maeztu's later polemics with Unamuno, which deserve further study, can be followed in *Los intelectuales y un epílogo para estudiantes*, 153–266.
2. 'Razones de una conversión' in *Autobiografía* (Madrid, 1962), 227.
3. *Defensa de la Hispanidad*, 4th ed. (Madrid, 1941), 217. Subsequent bracketed page-references are to this edition.
4. Uncollected.
5. *Hacia otra España* (Madrid, 1967), 81. Subsequent bracketed page-references are to this edition.
6. The five essays in question are: 'Nuestra educación', 'Gente de letras', 'Parálisis progresiva', 'Las quejas de Raventós', and 'Bilbao'.
7. See E. Inman Fox, 'Maeztu and Unamuno' in *Spanish Thought and Letters in the Twentieth Century*, 207–17, and Blanco Aguinaga, *Juventud del 98*, e.g., 100–1.

8. Included in *Los intelectuales y un epílogo para estudiantes* . . ., 47–72.
9. Both are included in *Autobiografía*.
10. Sergio Beser, 'Un artículo de Maeztu contra Azorín', *BH*, LXV (1963), 329–32.
11. *Autobiografía*, 133.
12. ibid., 27.
13. *Un ideal sindicalista* (Madrid, 1966), 88.
14. ibid., 107.
15. *Autobiografía*, 149.
16. Quoted V. Marrero, *Maeztu* (Madrid, 1955), 292.
17. See, for example, his article 'Las ideas dominadoras' in *Los intelectuales* . . ., 33–8.
18. *Los intelectuales* . . ., 123.
19. 'Las causas impopulares' in *Autobiografía*, 189–96. The quotation is from 192.
20. *El sentido reverencial del dinero* (Madrid, 1957), 17.
21. ibid. ('Concienciosidad'), 47.
22. 'De o en' in *Los intelectuales* . . ., 193–8.
23. See above, note 17.
24. In 'Una santidad que rectifica' in *Los intelectuales* . . ., 68–72. This was partly a misapprehension on Maeztu's part (see above, p. 10).
25. *Los intelectuales* . . ., 124.
26. *Autobiografía*, 267–8.
27. *Don Quijote, Don Juan y La Celestina*, 6th ed. (Madrid, 1948). Subsequent bracketed page-references are to this edition.
28. *Las letras y la vida en la España de entreguerras* (Madrid, 1958), 193.
29. *Ensayos* (Buenos Aires, 1948), 98.
30. ibid., 87.
31. *Los intelectuales* . . ., 25.
32. *Ensayos*, 162.
33. ibid., 169.
34. ibid., 170.

Chapter 5

BAROJA:
ANGUISH, ACTION, AND *ATARAXIA*

Like Unamuno and Maeztu Pío Baroja y Nessi was a Basque, born in San Sebastián on 28 December 1872. Though he was deeply attached to his mother, his novels consistently present parents and relatives in a disagreeable light, and he once declared that he had had an unhappy childhood. During his youth and adolescence the family moved successively to Pamplona, Madrid, and Valencia, where Pío completed a degree in medicine begun in the capital. He took his doctorate in 1893 with a thesis on 'El dolor, estudio psicofísico'. For a time he practised medicine near San Sebastián, but in 1895 seized the chance of managing his aunt's bakery in Madrid. Already he had published articles in the press on Russian and French novelists and in 1897 *Germinal* printed his short story 'Bondad oculta'.[1] He was soon contributing to other little reviews.[2] 1900 saw his first book of short stories, *Vidas sombrías*, published at his own expense, and his first novel, *La casa de Aizgorri*. Each sold less than a hundred copies. In October 1901 he and Azorín helped to found a magazine, *Juventud*, which carried articles by Unamuno, Costa, Giner, and other progressive intellectuals. When it collapsed in March 1902, Baroja moved to *El Globo*, a daily which had already serialized his next novel, *Aventuras, inventos y mixtificaciones de Silvestre Paradox* (1901). His first really outstanding novel, *Camino de perfección*, came out in 1902 and led to a banquet in his honour, attended, amongst other guests, by Galdós. Baroja's next novel, *El Mayorazgo de Labraz*, was sold for 2,000 pesetas at a time when a thousand pesetas a year was a typical starting salary and 3,000 was decorous.[3]

Thereafter his life was that of a bachelor son, living with his parents, saving his modest earnings from writing for occasional trips abroad and excursions inside Spain. A Swiss friend, Paul Schmitz (the Schultze of *Camino de perfección*), probably introduced Baroja to the work of Nietzsche. Schmitz's familiarity with northern Europe and Russia also influenced Baroja's tastes and curiosity. The two men's friendship played a major role in the conception of *El mundo es ansí*. In the 1909 elections and also in 1918 Baroja took part as a Radical Liberal, but was badly defeated both times. In between he had reached his creative peak with his best money-spinner, *Zalacaín*

95

el aventurero (1909), followed by the great central trio of novels: *César o nada* (1910), *El árbol de la ciencia* (1911), and *El mundo es ansí* (1912).

1912 was a key-year. In it Baroja concluded the first phase of his fictional work and began preparing the vast series of historical novels: *Memorias de un hombre de acción.* During the World War he was vaguely pro-German. Later he became friendly with Ortega and their debate in the press about the novel led to the latter's *La deshumanización del arte e ideas sobre la novela* (1925), the major doctrinal statement of its time in Spain. In 1923 Baroja visited Germany and Denmark. He was to work his impressions of them into his last important trilogy, *Agonías de nuestro tiempo* (1926–27). Also in 1926 *Zalacaín* was filmed for the first time, with Baroja in a minor role. He held aloof from both the Dictatorship and the Republic and in his resigned, pessimistic way awaited the civil conflict which he had prophesied in *La dama errante* (1908) and in *El árbol de la ciencia.*[4] In 1934 he was elected to the Spanish Academy; characteristically he had to buy his first dress suit for the ceremony. His mother's death in 1935 was a great blow. Worse followed when the Civil War broke out and Baroja was arrested by Nationalist troops. His release was followed by more than four years of dreary exile in France until the German invasion forced his return to Spain. The publication of his *Obras completas* (in censored form) between 1946 and 1952 marked the culmination of his literary career. He died on 30 October 1956. It seems a happy coincidence that among the mourners Hemingway seemed to represent writers outside Spain, while Cela's presence symbolized the link with a new generation of post-Civil War novelists.

I. HIS LITERARY PERSONALITY

When his first books were published, Baroja was twenty-eight. He was already an outsider. He rejected much of what passes for social integration, including marriage and a secure professional career. Under the influence of Haeckel and Spencer he had come to see human behaviour in often crude biological terms of survival of fittest, and society as a cruel struggle for selfish benefits. The rewards, he believed, went to those who accepted the morally degrading rules of *la lucha por la vida.* Baroja preferred to limit his aspirations to what he could achieve as a writer, and to cultivate his ideals of detachment, personal independence, and uncompromising ethical standards.

In common with others of the Generation of 1898 he suffered in late adolescence and early manhood a very severe crisis of ideas and beliefs. Despite the autobiographical material contained in *Juventud egolatría* (1917), 'La formación psicológica del escritor' (1934), and in his memoirs, *Desde la última vuelta del camino* (1944–49), its origins remain mysterious. The best account is in the early chapters of *El árbol de la ciencia*, whose hero, Andrés, Baroja described as 'una contrafigura mía'. Looking back in 1934 he claimed not to have had 'ni desde chico ideas trascendentales ultraterrenas' (*Obras completas*, Madrid, 1946–52, V, 880)[5] and he remained to the end staunchly agnostic. In *Las veleidades de la fortuna* (1927) and in *Rapsodías* (1936) he accepted that religious faith provided a powerful and perhaps irreplaceable basis for a harmonious interpretation of life. But he himself did not possess it. Catholicism repelled him because of the negative influence of clerical authority on Spanish social and political life. But, he admitted, 'Si el cura español es fanático y despótico, es porque el español lo es' (I, 1375).[6]

His scientific training provided him with the biological model for existence to which he stayed generally faithful; but it also revealed to him the limitations of scientific knowledge, and indeed of all rational understanding. Critics have been mistaken on this point. If in *El árbol de la ciencia* Andrés could assert: 'La ciencia es la única construcción fuerte de la humanidad' (II, 510), Baroja elsewhere insisted equally categorically: 'En esta progresión avanzará siempre la ciencia, siempre sin resolver los problemas capitales que más le interesan al hombre' (V, 1097).[7]

He turned, like everyone else in the Generation of 1898, to philosophy.[8] Kant, whom he interpreted in diametrically the opposite way from Maeztu, became a basic influence in his work. 'Kant', he wrote, 'vió que todas las maravillas descritas por los filósofos eran fantasías, espejismos; vió que las galerías magníficas no llevaban a ninguna parte ... Después de Kant el mundo es ciego' (II, 507–8). In Schopenhauer, the most important philosophical influence on the Generation of 1898 as a whole, Baroja found a totally congenial mind. Like the young Azorín, he learned from Schopenhauer that life was in its very nature suffering in various forms, that such suffering was proportionate to intellectual awareness, and that all action tended to intensify it. Schopenhauer's solution, which was to condition oneself to voluntary renunciation and resignation, and by self-limitation to seek release from suffering, and achieve *ataraxia* (resigned, negative serenity based on insight and detachment), became Baroja's ideal. Nietzsche, on the other hand, professed the aim of restoring to philosophy precisely what Ganivet had found missing from it in 1888: positive, life-directing ideals. The challenge Nietzsche presented to the individual was to shed demoralization, to reject Schopenhauer, and to plunge energetically into the biological struggle for its own sake. Existence was justified by the exhilaration of living intensely and dynamically, without moral restraints. The aim of each generation and individual was to collaborate actively and consciously with human evolution, hoping to transmit an improved set of acquired characteristics to future mankind. Baroja was momentarily dazzled by this prospect, which appealed to the strain of aggressiveness beneath his timidity. Hence his 1904 essay 'El culto del yo' with its utterly out-of-character slogan 'tenemos que inmoralizarnos'. But he soon qualified his enthusiasm. For the rest he repeatedly confirmed Ganivet's diagnosis of the ideological negativism of Spain's *fin de siglo* environment: 'De joven y sin cultura', he wrote, 'no iba a forjarme yo un concepto, una significación y un fin de la vida, cuando flotaba y flota en el ambiente la sospecha de si la vida no tendrá significación ni objeto' (V, 877).

II. APPRENTICESHIP AND EARLY WRITINGS

A deep sense of bitterness and repulsion at the squalor of life, the cruelty of people, and the harshness of society pervades *Vidas sombrías.* The characteristic themes of these short stories are the triumph of greed and fear over nobler impulses ('La sima', 'Un justo'), of disillusionment over love ('Playa de otoño', 'Lo desconocido', 'Águeda'), of misery and suffering over hope ('Marichu', 'Parabola', 'Hogar triste'), and the all-pervading reign of ignobility ('Conciencias cansadas'). Especially significant are 'El amo de la jaula', on God's deafness and indifference, and 'Nihil', which emphasizes the futility of revolutionary endeavour. What is interesting about *Vidas sombrías* is that not a single story has any direct bearing on the problem of Spain. Baroja here and for the rest of his life attacked social abuses, but he had no alternative to the system to advocate. Unlike Unamuno and Maeztu he never sympathized with socialism. He believed that its narrowly sectional interests were no less selfish than those of the bourgeoisie, and that its dogmatism would produce a regimented and restrictive society. Anarchism, as with Azorín, had more appeal. Its destructive policy *vis-à-vis* the state apparatus satisfied his deep-seated frustration, while its sentimental humanitarianism was in line with his basic sympathy with the oppressed. In *La casa de Aizgorri* (1901) the contrast between Yann, the anarchist, and the villainous socialist Díaz is heavily overdrawn. More anarchists appear in *La lucha por la vida* (1904–05); but while they and their hope of a better world are favourably depicted, Baroja's awareness of their movement's dreamy utopianism had already got the upper hand. In *La dama errante* (1908) his disgust with 'direct action' is visible in his treatment of the bombing incident near the beginning. His final position is revealed by the gently satirical treatment of both socialists and anarchists in *El mundo es ansí* (1912).

La casa de Aizgorri seems to owe something to Galdós's later manner in its dialogue-form and to Ibsen in its obtrusive symbolism. It combines the themes of family degeneration and the class-struggle. The former is shaken off by the heroine Águeda who, in contrast to her father and brother, possesses a hidden reserve of will-power, courage, and energy for love to bring out. The class-conflict is no less triumphantly foiled by Mariano, the young British-trained engineer who, with the help of Águeda, the local doctor, and a black-leg worker, successfully resists a violent strike. The book is dominated by two symbolic buildings: a distillery, which is finally destroyed along with its products, and a foundry, which stands for the re-invigorated, industrialized Spain of the future: Machado's 'España del cincel y de la maza'. It is the only such symbol in Baroja's work. He shared the Generation of 1898's desire for national improvement. 'Lo que queremos', he wrote in *Las horas solitarias* (1918), 'es que España mejore, que se robustezca, que llegue a ser una nación seria e inteligente que realice la justicia, que tenga una cultura vasta, original y múltiple' (V, 260). His own ideal was 'libertad con deberes morales e intelectuales' (V, 336): freedom with responsibility. But he was inclined to believe that little significant improvement could ever be brought about in society because of the resistance of human nature: 'Lo que hace la sociedad malvada es el egoísmo del hombre, y el egoísmo es un hecho natural, es una necesidad de la vida' (II, 515). Though he referred hopefully in *El mundo es ansí* to 'el nacimiento de la conciencia colectiva' (II, 822) (i.e., the welfare state idea), what he utterly failed to see is that the community is usually more easy to improve than the individual. It is this failure, shared unfortunately by others of the Generation of 1898, rather than the reactionary political attitudes discussed by Blanco Aguinaga,[9] which leaves Baroja open to criticism. Apart from toying with the impractical idea of dictatorship by an intellectual élite, he remained simply a destructive critic of Spain.

In his second novel, *Aventuras, inventos y mixtificaciones de Silvestre Paradox* (1901), he swung slightly towards Unamuno's *bufo-trágico* manner. The book depicts a gallery of shabby-genteel, jovial, and pathetic middle-aged eccentrics living on their wits in Madrid. Untidy and episodic, but highly entertaining, the story gives Baroja (who appears with his brother Ricardo in their bakery in chapters 10 and 20) ample scope for observation of the capital's *vie de bohème*, for biting satire and farcical caricature. The best comparison is Pérez de Ayala's *Troteras y danzaderas*, which explored the same world a decade later. Its carefree comedy throws into relief Baroja's bitter and pessimistic undertones. For all his drollery, the core of Paradox's personality is 'una amargura del pensamiento ... náusea de vivir, náusea de la gente y de las cosas' and 'el cansancio eterno de la eterna imbecilidad de vivir' (II, 57). However, in the last chapter, as Labarta (Baroja) declaims his poem in praise of death, reference is made to Nietzsche and to reaching with his help a compromise with el sentido trágico de la vida'.

III. THE FIRST MANNER

Camino de perfección (1902) has been interpreted by Villegas precisely in this sense.[10] Fernando Ossorio, Baroja's first really important fictional hero, is seen as an archetypal figure who with assistance from wise men (Schultze and Polentinos) overcomes temptation and weakness to achieve 'el triunfo aparente del superhombre'. Certainly Fernando develops the pattern of overcoming negative hereditary and environmental factors by energy and will-power, already sketched out by Baroja in Águeda de Aizgorri. But even with the qualifications Villegas introduces, Fernando's 'triumph' is more ambiguous than this critic suggests. His character achieves no clear profile in the early chapters. Baroja, 'entusiasmado con las ideas de Zola' he tells us in chapter 1, makes play with hereditary factors and crudely conflicting childhood influences to justify Fernando's incipient hysteria and hallucinatory symptoms. Only gradually do we come to recognize the spiritual vacuum beneath his *abulia* and his aggressive rejection of life and his fellow men. Not until chapter 20 is it clear that Fernando, like Antonio in the companion novel by Azorín, *La voluntad*, and the other will-less fictional heroes of the Generation of 1898, illustrates Ganivet's original assertion that *abulia* is inseparable from the loss of 'ideas directivas'.

The particular life-directing principle to which Fernando is instinctively drawn is traditional religion, which Baroja always regarded as the most effective *mentira vital*. His journey to Toledo, 'la ciudad mística soñada' (VI, 63), is thus a kind of pilgrimage. But it is unsuccessful. The central section of the novel, which now opens, is crucial not only for Fernando but also for a wide area of Baroja's later work. Religion, art, and the senses (a combination, one notices, which is typically *modernista*) having failed Fernando, Baroja prepares to explore three other avenues towards reconciliation with life. The first, postulated but held in reserve for the conclusion, is love ('la única palabra posible era amar') (67). The second is the acquisition of a conscious ethical ideal. It is achieved in chapter 31, after Fernando has resisted the temptation to seduce Adela: 'Empezaba a sentir un verdadero placer por no haberse dejado llevar por sus instintos. No; no era sólo el animal que cumple una ley orgánica:

era un espíritu, era una conciencia' (82). The third, implicit already
in Schultze's proposed therapy: exercise and Nietzschean vitalism, is
acceptance of life for its own sake, ignoring its absence of transcendental meaning: 'Vivir y vivir ... ésa es la cuestión' (111). It is not
made wholly clear by what process Fernando in Marisparza and
Alicante throws off his spiritual oppression, though a turning-point
seems to be indicated by his reflections in front of the bishop's
mummy in chapter 13. It is the consequences that are important.
The first is Fernando's abandonment of art, when he blithely sub-
stitutes a coloured photograph for a portrait. The second is his re-
acquisition of energy, like Águeda, which allows him to brush aside
his rival for the hand of Dolores. A third is his marriage to her,
leading to the birth of his child and the symbol in chapter 59 of life
triumphing over the anti-vital spirit of traditional religion. In the
last sentence of the novel, however, Baroja leaves religion preparing
its counter-attack.

Camino de perfección occupies a key-position in Baroja's early
evolution.[11] He never again presented marriage as directly connected
with the recovery of existential confidence. Henceforth marriage
involved either compromise with society's dictates, as in the cases of
Hasting and María Aracil, or was interrupted by death, as in
El árbol de la ciencia and *César o nada*, or else was a source of
unhappiness, as in *El mundo es ansí*. Baroja was in any case ill-
equipped to handle love-situations in any depth or detail, from lack
of private experience, and these are usually severely foreshortened
or unconvincingly presented. A particularly extreme example is
El mundo es ansí in which, though Sacha marries twice, there are
no love-scenes, no proposals, and the honeymoons are both spent in
company with other people!

Ethical behaviour and vitalism, on the other hand, emerge from
Camino de perfección as powerful forces in Baroja's ideology. They
were at once to find themselves in conflict, as for the rest of the
decade Baroja continued to experiment with characters whose chief
characteristic is the strength of will and freedom from religious,
moral, and social restraints Fernando dreamed of for his son at the
end of *Camino de perfección*. Azorín, too, was writing at this time in
La voluntad:

El primer deber del hombre, el más imperioso consistiría en llegar a todos
los placers por todos los medios, es decir en ser fuerte. Nietzsche cree que,
aun sin la conciencia, es ésta la necesidad única. Yo también lo siento de
este modo; sólo que la energía es algo que no se puede lograr a voluntad.
(*Obras completas*, I, 935)

Ramiro de Labraz in *El Mayorazgo de Labraz* (1903) is the first to
proclaim his independence from any 'código religioso o moral'. But
his rhetorical self-justification is merely the prelude to a particularly

contemptible and repulsive crime. Quintín Roelas in *La feria de los discretos* (1905), though less villainous is hardly less unscrupulous, and what is worse hardly less pretentious. Not until *César o nada* did Baroja solve the problems connected with presenting an active and successful vitalist as the hero of a full-scale novel set in the present.

Logically he should have seen in the social struggle a perfect field of operations for the man of action. But when he develops the idea in *César o nada*, we notice that Spanish society is no longer presented as a brutal free-for-all to be enjoyed for its own sake by forceful individuals like Hasting in the first trilogy; it is now presented in quite different terms as a conspiracy by the mediocre to repress men of outstanding talents and character. At the same time the qualities of the man of action are suddenly redefined (in very different terms from those of Nietzsche and of 'El culto del yo') as those of courage, energy, and goodness. The argument has shifted from the justification of immorality as the expression of 'energy' to the assertion of a higher morality than that which society normally recognizes. This explains how César differs from Ramiro and Quintín. Though like them he is prepared to infringe moral conventions, his aim is not mere selfish gain. Baroja's claim is that disinterested social reformers can sometimes be exempted from certain of the rules. César is Baroja's only attractive immoralist because his immoralism, such as it is, is well-intentioned. He is in fact only a devil's advocate who finally turns out to be on the side of the angels. In the last part of the novel César gradually gives way before his emotions and the emphasis shifts from the struggle with society to the struggle with self. This enhances his stature greatly by comparison with that of Quintín. Instead of remaining like him a character in one piece, wise in his own conceits and absolved from normal doubts and conflicts (including emotional ones), César evolves consistently and convincingly.

He is the nearest approach Baroja ever made to depicting a practical vitalist with a social aim. Like Ganivet's Pío Cid, César sets about reforming Spain single-handed and according to his own private formula. When he comes too near to success, he is the victim of a murderous attack and the ideal of action in a modern context collapses. The conflicts which his death concludes, but does not solve, have their origin much further back in Baroja's career. The first to formulate the action-ideal clearly had been Roberto Hasting in the first trilogy *La lucha por la vida* (*La busca*, 1904; *Mala hierba*, 1904; and *Aurora roja*, 1905). His remarks in the first-mentioned novel are of cardinal importance:

> ¡Creeme! En el fondo no hay más que un remedio y un remedio individual: la acción ... Ya que nuestra ley es la lucha, aceptémosla, pero no con

tristeza, con alegría. La acción es todo, la vida, el placer. Convertir la vida estática en vida dinámica; éste es el problema. La lucha siempre, hasta el último momento, ¿por qué? Por cualquier cosa. (I, 635)

Two points emerge clearly from this outburst. One is its lack of collective social implications. The other is the lack of any necessary aim or finality at all. Worse still, at the very moment Hasting preaches his doctrine to Manuel, he is himself acting contrary to it by saddling himself with Ester, one of the weaklings he advocates brushing aside. Before long, in *Mala hierba*, we find him associating *voluntad* and *energía* not with success in the struggle for life or the mere exhilaration of action, but with 'sentimientos altos' and 'la idea de la justicia' (I, 384). Alongside his vitalistic ebullience ethical convictions suddenly emerge: 'Yo tengo mi conciencia. Quizá sea rectilínea como mis aspiraciones' (444). Precisely the same is true of César's friend Carlos Yarza, who had originally appeared in *Los últimos románticos* (1906) and its sequel *Las tragedias grotescas* (1907). Despite his slogan 'hay que ser lobo', he too protects a weakling in the struggle for life, Paulina Acuña, and ends by fighting for the dream of liberty alongside the Paris *communards*.

María Aracil, the heroine of *La dama errante* (1908) and *La ciudad de la niebla* (1909), completes the pattern. Once she leaves her father she is committed by her sex to the struggle for life on highly disadvantageous terms. She lacks none of the energy required to achieve her independence as a single woman. But she is forced to recognize that ethical compromise is the condition of her emancipation. Iturrioz, Baroja's mouthpiece here, as in *El árbol de la ciencia*, puts the issue to her bluntly: ' ¿Tu quieres ser libre? Tienes que ser inmoral' (II, 443). Instead María accepts submission and settles for a husband and family in Madrid.

By the end of the first decade of his career as a novelist Baroja had come to realize that the ideal of vitalism, acceptance of life on the basis of self-realization through struggle, effort, and conscious volition, was unacceptable for three reasons. First, it was purposeless. Second, it required an effort of will which few could make consistently. Finally it conflicted with the ethical imperative. As early as *La feria de los discretos*, one of the minor characters, Escobedo, declares: 'Nos hablan de la eficacia del esfuerzo, nos dicen que hay que luchar con voluntad . . . y luego vemos que no hay lucha, ni triunfos ni nada; que la fatalidad baraja nuestro destinos y que la ausencia de la felicidad está en nuestra misma naturaleza' (I, 743). In 1917 Baroja accepted the failure of the action ideal in his brief autobiography *Juventud, egolastría*. 'Yo también he preconizado un remedio para el mal de vivir, la acción', he wrote. 'Es un remedio viejo como el mundo, tan útil a veces como cualquier otro y tan inútil como todos los demás. Es decir que no es un remedio' (V, 173). It was the epilogue to an entire phase of his work.

Of the works between *Camino de perfección* and *César o nada*, the first trilogy, *La lucha por la vida*, is clearly the most important. Its hero, Manuel Alcázar, typified the immigrant workers who were arriving in Madrid from the countryside in thousands at the end of the last century. Unskilled, the son of a homeless domestic servant, in a city without industries to absorb the surplus of labour, he alternates between casual employment and petty crime among the capital's social rejects. Soledad Puértolas[12] has amply documented the accuracy of Baroja's descriptions of an area of reality which Galdós had only glanced at in passing: the world of the *golfos*, criminals, prostitutes, beggars, and alcoholics of the slums. Manuel shares to a very important degree the instinctive moral sense which distinguishes even the 'struggle-for-lifeurs' (as Baroja calls them), including his friend Hasting. But unlike the latter he lacks analytical intelligence and strength of will. His passiveness allows Baroja to slot him successively into different levels of slum and criminal life in order to describe them. Grouped around him are a number of characters who represent the choices open to him, appealing to one or the other of his two basic tendencies: his 'respeto a todo lo establecido' and his 'instinto antisocial de vagabundo'. Opposite each other in this respect stand Hasting with his creed of self-discipline, work, and tenacity, and Vidal, who attracts Manuel downwards into idleness and crime. A comparison of their respective fates underlines the crudity of the contrast. But it is the feminine influences which really predominate with Manuel:[13] his mother, who represents humility and submission, Doña Violante, with her thriftless parasitism, but above all Justa and Salvadora. The former's attempt to find an easy way out of poverty ends in the gutter, while Salvadora, by force of character, hard work, and commonsense, achieves modest respectability. Her intuition and curiosity prevent the anarchist's Passalacqua's hare-brained bomb-plot from ruining Manuel and his brother. Her influence gradually attracts Manuel into bourgeois social conformity.

Aurora roja is, sociologically speaking, the most significant novel of the Generation of 1898. It examines with affectionate scepticism the formation by Manuel's brother, Juan, of a well-intentioned, but ideologically confused and ineffectual, anarchist group. To argue, with Blanco Aguinaga and Puértolas, that despite the subsequent failure of the Left in Spain Baroja's scepticism was unjustified, seems illogical. The opposite is rather the case. The really valid criticisms of Baroja in this trilogy relate rather to the petty-bourgeois angle from which he sometimes appears to be observing the social conditions he describes, and the untypical political alternative to the regime which then prevailed which he chooses to discuss in *Aurora roja*. By giving his attention to anarchism, which was in Spain basically a rural movement, and which was weak in Madrid, rather than to socialism, which was quite strong and presented the real alternative, Baroja falsified his picture of the nascent Spanish class-struggle. It was an opportunity lost. That Baroja should have lost it underlines yet again the unwillingness of the Generation of 1898, despite its ideal of regeneration, to look the facts in the face.

Los últimos románticos and its sequel *Las tragedias grotescas* were potboilers. But they illustrate, along with *La dama errante* and *La ciudad de la niebla* which followed, an interesting aspect of Baroja's outlook and technique: his presentation of the other sex. About this he had no illusions. 'Yo no he pretendido nunca', he wrote in his memoirs, 'hacer figuras de mujeres miradas como desde dentro de ellas, estilo Bourget, Houssaye, Prévost; esto me parece una mixtificación; las he dibujado como desde fuera, desde esa orilla lejana que es un sexo para otro' (VII, 1053). In Clementina Bengoa and Rita Gálvez of *Los últimos románticos* and its sequel, Baroja painted a savage picture of genteel feminine depravity, which reappears only slightly attenuated in Mrs Roche, when María Aracil meets her in *La ciudad de la niebla*, which is of course London. María was Baroja's first full-scale fictional heroine. She occupies a minor, but unique, place in the modern Spanish novel because she is the first example of sympathetic treatment by a major novelist in Spain of the modern woman on her way to emancipation. Unhappily, like Sacha in *El mundo es ansí* and Laura in the novel of that name, she is not a fully convincing representative of her sex. Rather than revealing an individual and recognizably feminine pattern of outlook and priorities, Baroja's heroines, from Águeda de Aizgorri onwards, seem to have been created chiefly to contrast with what Baroja conceived to be the predominant qualities of middle-class Spanish women in whose make-up he affected to discern 'Una mezcla de fregona, de cortesana, de cómica, y de agente de negocios' (II, 372). His popularity with the feminine reading public was, we may note, undiminished by such outbursts.

The most important consequences for his novels of his anti-feminine prejudice was the role frequently allotted to women in relation to the hero's problems. A noteworthy early figure is Asunción, whom Carlos Yarza thought of marrying in *Las tragedias grotescas*. She is characteristically incapable of understanding Carlos's principles and way of life: 'Le parecía que Carlos tenía la ocurrencia tonta de querer vivir mal. Si Carlos hubiese querido ser como todo el mundo, ella sería su mujer y le adoraría' (I, 996). Fortunately Carlos avoids too great an involvement with her. But in later novels, where the hero's need for understanding and support is greater, the leading female figures are sometimes made to play a slightly contemptible part. Ana in *La sensualidad pervertida* (1920), Pepita in *Los amores tardíos* (1927), and Concha in *Las noches del Buen Retiro* (1934) each engages the hero's hopes and allows herself to become deeply implicated in his search for an acceptable life-formula. But once they are called upon to make a decision on his behalf which involves effort and sacrifice, they conspicuously fail to respond. At the critical moment they prove unequal to the task of comforting the hero in his spiritual isolation and sharing his painfully achieved standards.

Sacha Savarof, in *El mundo es ansí*, Baroja's full-length portrait of a woman, belongs to the inner circle of Baroja's central characters which also includes Ossorio, Hurtado, Murguía, and Larrañaga. They are all characterized by the fragility of their ideals and illusions, their search for emotional and intellectual security, their conscious ethical standards, and by a compulsion to submit their outlook and actions to the test of rational analysis. All of them struggle with the 'lepra sentimental', the human need for an emotional and sexual outlet, which we have already seen complicating the efforts even of men of action like Hasting and Yarza to come to terms with life. For Sacha, as a woman, love is the instinctive 'mentira vital', marriage the natural choice. The obstacle to happiness is her analytic mind, which denies her the experience of real passion but does not protect her against the irrational tug of her feelings. Instead of preventing her from acting, it prevents her from holding on to comforting illusions after she has acted. The key-word for her character is *lucidez*, which Baroja repeats in the last sentences of the novel's middle chapters (Part II, 5 and 6). These chapters present a deliberately ironic contrast between Sacha's conscious outlook and the instinctive tendencies which lead to her two unhappy marriages. In each case lucidity comes into play too late. Sacha is left at the end of the book frustrated and lonely, supported only by a sense of moral and intellectual superiority.

Laura Monroy in *Laura, o la soledad sin remedio* (1939) completes the trio of Baroja's foremost heroines. Like María she is forced to fend for herself abroad, during the Civil War. Like Sacha she studies medicine and frequents exiled Russian circles before seeking in marriage to an expatriate Russian a solution to her personal and economic problems. But she is not, like María, striking a blow for emancipation, nor does she, as was the case with Sacha, offer Baroja a splendid opportunity to survey the Spanish scene through the eyes of a foreigner. Laura shares the cool lucidity, the lack of romantic illusions, and the contempt for coquetry of the two earlier heroines, but she lacks their idealism and energy. Baroja seemed to be trying to study a woman's feelings of loneliness and inadequacy without either motivating them sufficiently or providing Laura with enough resources to overcome them. While realizing instinctively that passion would release her from solitude and indecision, Laura consciously imposes on herself an ideal of emotional restraint, only to find that her achievement of it with Golowin fails to satisfy her. In this she is not untypical of Baroja's later central characters, all of whom tend to find that emotional fulfilment eludes them.

In 1911 Baroja published *El árbol de la ciencia*, his masterpiece. It begins with an account of the youth and early manhood of the hero, Andrés Hurtado, with special emphasis on his ideological and spiritual evolution. So far it is not unlike *Camino de perfección*. What distinguishes it from the earlier novel is the much clearer analysis of Hurtado's developing outlook and the attempt to relate it to his human and social environment. The technique of symbolic references to Nature which, as García Sarriá has shown, Baroja used with great effect in 1902, gives way to a more direct approach. The novel opens with Andrés's experiences as a medical student. They are used to ram home the message that the main powerhouse of Spanish thought, Madrid University, had collapsed into intellectual indigence. Andrés's home-life emphasizes, through the portraits of his father and elder brothers, the moral and ideological bankruptcy of the Spanish middle class just as the disaster of 1898 was to offer it the opportunity to assume its full social and political responsibilities. Unable to derive a satisfactory pattern of mental and spiritual allegiances either from his family or from Spain's intellectual establishment Andrés becomes progressively alienated. Logically his thoughts turn to revolutionary radicalism.

By now *El árbol de la ciencia* has all the makings of a novel of political and social protest. In part II especially the story marks time while Baroja devotes a block of eight chapters to savaging every class in Spain from the royal family and the aristocracy at one end of the scale to Doña Leonarda's circle of parasites and near-prostitutes at the other. It includes a sharp attack on the slave mentality of the self-respecting working class, represented by Venancia. The scene is thus set for Andrés to assume the role of a committed political activist. What actually happens is quite different. The cynical remarks of his friend Julio Aracil encourage Andrés to slip into a convenient attitude of 'anarquismo espiritual, basado en la simpatía y en la piedad, sin solución práctica ninguna' (II, 471). When to his disillusionment with life in Madrid is added his disgust with life in a *pueblo*, Alcolea, his revolutionary impulse revives. He indulges in childish fantasies of burning the town and hanging its political bosses. In practice, when consulted by the local young republicans, his advice to them is to drop all thought of intervention in society and to emigrate! The scene symbolizes the refusal of the

Generation of 1898 to face the logical consequences of its critique of Spain.

Instead of doing so, Baroja, like the others, preferred to reformulate the problem in purely individual terms. What is alleged to prevent Andrés from taking positive action is not so much his lack of faith in collective endeavour as his own private tendency, reinforced by his personal situation and by his reading of Schopenhauer, to regard life as intrinsically evil, blind, and futile: 'una cosa fea, turbia, dolorosa e indominable' (460) ... 'una corriente tumultuosa e inconsciente, donde todos los actores representaban una comedia que no comprendían' (471). The social problem is thus once more subordinated to the spiritual problem. What Andrés is looking for is not just a solution to his country's difficulties, but an answer to his own inner dilemma; not just a programme, but 'una verdad espiritual y práctica al mismo tiempo' (465). The death of his younger brother, Luisito, awakens him from a brief interval of psychological relaxation to an even deeper awareness of life's malignity. Luisito is not the only child who dies in Baroja's novels: the arbitrary destruction of an innocent existence calls into question all comfortably positive interpretations of human destiny.

Crushed, Andrés finds himself completely bereft of vital directions: 'Uno tiene la angustia, la desperación de no saber qué hacer con la vida, de no tener un plan, de encontrarse perdido, sin brújula, sin luz adonde dirigirse. ¿Qué se hace con la vida? ¿Qué dirección se le da?' (507). Part IV of the novel contains a long discussion between Andrés and his main interlocutor, Iturrioz, which is the core of the book. Both agree that the basic need is to accept the realization that life has no meaningful finality and cannot be explained by reference to any standard of absolute truth. What separates them is the method they adopt to adjust themselves to this recognition and the extent to which they are successful in doing so. Andrés, younger and more extreme, takes the view that intellectual analysis must be carried through regardless of the consequences. He retains some residual confidence in the result, based on scientific progress and social amelioration. Iturrioz more prudently insists on the need for 'mentiras vitales': life-enhancing illusions which provide the individual with some basis for positive action. His doctrine is that eating of the Tree of Knowledge leads directly to misery and aboulia: 'La verdad en bloque es mala para la vida ... se necesita una fe, una ilusión, algo que, aunque sea una mentira salida de nosotros mismos, parezca una verdad llegada de fuera' (510, 517).

Having spent periods in Madrid and Valencia, Andrés moves to Alcolea. The pattern (capital city, provincial city, small market town) is aimed at producing a cross-section of Spain, metropolitan, urban, and rural. In addition Alcolea is very effectively presented as a microcosm of the nation as a whole. It is politically corrupt and economically stagnant. Its idle, parasitic aristocracy, represented by Don Blas Carreño, lives in the past. Middle-class opinion is led by Dr Sánchez who, like Hurtado's friend Aracil in Madrid, is ready to stoop to any abjection where money or social position is at stake. The workers and peasants (Pepinito, Garrota) vegetate in ignorance and passive resignation, manipulated socially and politically by their exploiters. Social behaviour is regulated by outward observance of rigid sexual conventions and characterized by a total absence of community spirit.

Disgusted, Andrés returns to Madrid and a further confrontation with social iniquity as a slum-doctor. In contrast to Blasco Ibañez and Concha Espina's naïve interpretations of the class-struggle, Baroja shows the proletariat actively collaborating with the processes which perpetuated bourgeois domination. 'La verdad es', he comments sadly, 'que si el pueblo lo comprendiese, se mataría por intentar una revolución social' (552). But disillusioned by his experiences, Andrés is in no mood to start a crusade for popular political consciousness. He remains absorbed in his own attempt to close up what Baroja calls his private window on to the abyss: to overcome his insight. Marriage and private employment as a translator produce a temporary sense of release. But the death of his wife in childbirth, like that of Luisito earlier, forces the window open again. Like Azorín's sick man in *Diario de un enfermo* in similar circumstances, Andrés commits suicide. The ending of *El árbol de la ciencia*, followed by that of *El mundo es ansí* in which Sacha is left simply to endure the cruelty of a life she cannot even end by imitating Andrés, reveals that by 1912 Baroja had reached an impasse. He was not to write another novel set in the contemporary period until eight years later.

IV. BAROJA'S THEORY OF THE NOVEL

By this time his theory and practice of the novel were fully developed.[14] Like Wells in Britain, he regarded the natural as an aspect of the beautiful. The real enemy of artistic creation was, for him, not technique as such, but *conscious* technique, which kills spontaneity. Spontaneity and observation are the two essential words in respect of his theory of fiction. He believed that the ability to write creatively is something totally inexplicable, a mysterious gift, which knowledge of literary doctrines and rules cannot replace, and which constantly eludes their constraints. 'La verdad es', he bluntly insisted, 'que en el arte de hacer novelas, como en casi todas las demás artes, se aprende muy poco. La cuestión es tener vida, fibra, energía o romanticismo o algo que hay que tener porque no se adquiere... Lo que salva al novelista es lo que pone y no se puede aprender' (V, 253). For such a gratuitous natural gift Baroja demanded complete freedom of action. Just as he loathed every rule of organized society as a restriction on his individual liberty, so he dismissed every fictional convention as a restriction on his personal creative talent. The nearest Baroja ever came to a definition of creativeness itself was in his chapter on intuition and method in *La caverna del humorismo*. Like Wells he distrusted the attempt to analyse what one was doing, comparing the writer to someone learning to use a sewing-machine: 'mientras piensa en lo que hace le sale mal'. Only what was instinctively right was effective: 'toda obra literaria es un resultado de la intuición y no del método... Ni en la literatura, ni en el arte, ni en la ciencia, puede haber ni reglas, ni métodos para una cosa tan íntima y tan subjetiva como la creación' (V, 446).

What part does reality play? Here Baroja was more explicit. Oddly, for a writer who set absolute store by intuition, he was totally opposed to the notion of pure creative imagination, that power of magical fantasy which some writers (including Ortega) have regarded as the literary artist's essential faculty. In his most important statement about his approach to the novel, the prologue to *La nave de los locos* (1925), he synthesized his objections to Ortega's ideas, which had themselves been formulated partly in reply to his manifesto at the beginning of *Páginas escogidas* (1917).[15] In contrast to Ortega's view of the novel as an aesthetic artefact, Baroja demanded significant content; in contrast to Ortega's stress on 'lo irreal y fantástico', Baroja stood out for accurate observation of life. Personally he emphasized his dependence on the rich and varied impressions deposited in the depths of his mind, like a fertile sediment, by the experiences of his adolescence and early manhood. 'El novelista vive de ese fondo', he stated categorically, 'es lo que da carácter al novelista, lo que le hace ser lo que es' (IV, 325). The critical period in his own case had been the years between about 1884 and 1898, in the course of which his outlook and personality had gradually crystallized. Thereafter, he explained in *Las horas solitarias* (1918), his novels tended to be inspired by places, which suggested to him scenarios for events and people. He let his impressions settle, and then made notes. Gradually, by accretion, he acquired 'un conjunto de impresiones reunidas y de tipos ideados' and 'algo aproximado a un plan' would begin to emerge. At this point he would begin writing 'a la buena de Dios', letting the novel acquire its own shape as he went along. The process can be defined as a reapplication to reality of a personal perspective acquired from contact with it during his formative period. From this inner framework of experience Baroja took the theme and the main features of the central character's personality and outlook. The rest, he argued, was *reportaje*: 'cosas tipos vistos'.

Everything thus remained fast anchored to experience and observation. Pure invention, without 'el trampolín de la realidad', could hardly rise above the level of fairy-tales: 'El escritor puede imaginar, naturalmente, tipos e intrigas que no ha visto; pero necesita siempre el trampolín de la realidad para dar saltos maravillosos en el aire' (IV, 320). So far, Baroja was fully within the realist tradition. Where he differed from it was in his conscious rejection of the illusion of authorial objectivity. 'No sé si puedo llamarme realista', he once declared, 'no sé lo que es la realidad' (V, 414). Like Azorín he advocated looseness of construction and condemned the Flaubertian ideal of the well-made novel. Though neither writer seems to have been fully aware of it, their dislike of neatly fashioned plots and sharp outlines of character followed logically from their views about life. Any kind of plot is a 'sense-making paradigm', a way of organizing reality which we know to be, in fact, simply a flux. It confers a purposiveness, a significant end, to a sequence of events, removing them from the mere successiveness which characterizes most of our experience. The same is true of fictional characters, who have tended in this century to evolve away from being 'slaves of fake omniscience' on the part of authors and to achieve a certain indeterminacy. In other words, all artistic selection implies something about the author. Form is in one important sense a refuge from the aimless surge of happenings we live in. Since every serious literary novel is in some degree 'a novel-shaped account of the world', it follows that the reaction against tidy plots and clear definition of character, visible in all the novelists of the Generation of 1898 (but most clearly enunciated theoretically by Baroja), is fully in line with their general vision of life as mere contingency without purpose or pattern. This, then, is what underlines Baroja's demand for open-ended, free-flowing narratives.

The typical Barojan novel tends to lie somewhere close to the *Bildungsroman*, in which the central character serves his apprenticeship to life and experience, and the straight novel of ideas. Baroja was not in a true sense a psychological novelist, because what he traces is nearly always the hero's or heroine's *conscious*, ideological, evolution, without attempting to probe into the emotions, the instincts, or the sub-rational motivations. He affected not to believe in the possibility of extending detailed psychological analysis to the point of filling an entire novel with it, while at the same time avoiding rhetoric (IV, 321). The evidence, in this case, is against him. Structurally Baroja's novels are usually simple, though it is beginning to be recognized that this simplicity is at times more apparent than real.[16] There is generally only a single chain of events without sub-plot or internal complexity. The early novels, *La casa de Aizgorri* and *El Mayorazgo de Labraz*, are recognizable as such by their employment of a more conventional technique of division into parallel chains of episodes evolving simultaneously. Baroja seems to have contemplated using this method in *La lucha por la vida*, using Hasting as an autonomous character with his own story. But he did not persevere, and in *Aurora roja* relegated even Manuel to a secondary position so as not to split the story between him and the new hero, his brother Juan.

Around the central character, who dominates the work and whose evolution gives the book its general shape, are normally grouped a small number of friends, relatives, or casual acquaintances. Their function is to act either as foils for the main figure, bringing out aspects of his character by contrast or re-emphasis, or to serve as interlocutors, clarifying his or her attitudes in conversations, and sometimes modifying them considerably. Obvious examples are Iturrioz and Aracil in *La ciudad de la niebla* and *El árbol de la ciencia*. The contemptible moral elasticity of Aracil is used to emphasize the integrity and ethical superiority of María and Andrés. In regard to the latter Baroja quietly adds a point of irony by making him beholden to Aracil for employment. Iturrioz plays the same role in both novels: that of a sympathetic conversational partner whose views clarify those of the protagonist. Neither Aracil nor Iturrioz has any role to play independently of the central character and in *El árbol de la ciencia* never appears except in Andrés's company. The hero's field of vision is in fact the stage of most Barojan novels; to leave that stage is usually to disappear completely. Other examples of foils are easy to find. Hasting's activeness and energy underline Manuel's *abulia*. Sacha Savarof's lucidity is deliberately contrasted with the unanalytic and passionate character of her friend Vera. Laura Monroy is no less consistently contrasted with her energetic cousin Mercedes. Larrañaga and his brother-in-law in the earlier part of *Agonías de nuestro tiempo* are a similar case in point. Azorín, too, used this simple but effective technique of paired characters. Other typical interlocutors are Polentinos and the *Escolapio* priest in *Camino de perfección*; César's sister, Alzugaray, and Kennedy in *César o nada*; Pepita, Soledad, and Olsen in *El gran torbellino del mundo*; and Leguía, who doubles the roles of interlocutor and narrator in some of the Aviraneta novels.

Since the central character is always on stage there is an almost total predominance of scene over summary. The reader enjoys the illusion of being shown events as they happen, with a minimum of flash-backs and reported incidents. A possible disadvantage is the strong tendency away from drama and suspense. Except in the case of adventurers like Zalacaín or Aviraneta, there is a narrow limit to the number of novelesque incidents that can be made to happen to individuals without straining the reader's credulity. Baroja's claim to have avoided melodramatic happenings was thus perhaps making a virtue of necessity. In any case it is not fully justified. But in his best novels of contemporary life Baroja played down excitement, just as he played down sex, deliberately refusing to fall in with the theatricality of plot and near-pornography which dominated so much fiction in Spain before the Civil War.

The resulting slow tempo and absence of conflict in Baroja's novels set in the present are disguised in various ways. First, by very heavy concentrations of dialogue. Second, by vivid first-hand descriptions of places and ways of life as the central character moves about. This 'travelogue-technique' designed to lend an appearance of movement to an otherwise sluggish narrative by rapidly shifting the background, begins with Fernando's walking-tour in *Camino de perfección*. We see it expanded in the flight of Aracil and María to Portugal in *La dama errante* and the peregrinations of Sacha Savarof and Laura Monroy around Europe. César Moncada moves from Italy to Spain. Larrañaga in *Agonías de nuestro tiempo* from Holland to Scandinavia. In *Los visionarios* (1932) and *El cantor vagabundo* (1950) the protagonists are continually on the move around Spain. Novels like *El cura de Monleón* (1936), in which the background is static and limited, are exceptional. A third feature which helps to disguise his novels' leisurely rhythm and loose narrative texture is Baroja's taste for saturating his stories with minor characters who stream across the stage animating the atmosphere with their comments, opinions, and at times dramas, but always enlivening it with their mere presence. 'Todo lo que sea poner muchas figuras es, naturalmente, abrir el horizonte' (IV, 318), he asserted.

These bit-parts and extras form an outer circle of humanity around the central character and his immediate companions. Often drawn from life, they may exist simply for their own intrinsic human interest. More commonly they personify attitudes or social groups Baroja wished to attack either directly or by satirical caricature. The former are presented flatly as abject, contemptible, or merely disagreeable. Foremost are the parents and family connections of his heroes and heroines. The warped and petty values of the Ossorios, Sacha Savarof's in-laws, Murguía's Aunt Luisa (in *La sensualidad pervertida*, 1920), and numerous others represent, for Baroja, the normal and natural values of society. They are regularly seconded by teachers and priests, whom Baroja saw in this connection as agents of authoritarian social restraint. Less commonly Baroja relaxes sufficiently to turn some of his secondary characters from knaves and fools into mere grotesques like Don Calixto and the notables of Castro Duro in *César o nada*. The result is the same. The folly, vices, egoism, and cruelty of the mass of mankind form a background which throws into relief the rather unfair monopoly of decency with which Baroja invests his central characters.

A final, and signally important, feature of Baroja's theory and practice of fiction is his contribution to the renovation of style. One of the clearest formulations of his attitude to style is found in Part III, chapter 14, of *El mundo es ansí*:

> Uno va buscando la verdad, va sintiendo el odio por la palabrería, por la hipérbole, por todo lo que lleva obscuridad a las ideas. Uno quisiera estrujar el idioma, recortarlo, reducirlo a su quintaesencia, a una cosa algebráica; quisiera uno suprimir todo lo supérfluo, toda la carnaza, toda la hojarasca.
> — ¿Para qué?
> — Para ver claro, sin obscuridades, sin brumas.
> — Pero lo brumoso tiene también sus encantos.
> — A mí no me gusta más que lo claro, lo frío, lo agudo, lo que está desprovisto de perífrasis ... (II, 829)

Baroja's style illustrates the ideal of brevity, limpidity, and precision which all the Generation of 1898 pursued in their prose. Reacting consciously against the prolix, rhetorical, cliché-ridden *estilo castelarino* which had set the tone in the previous generation, Baroja also aimed to avoid the deliberately brilliant 'artistic' style of Valle-Inclán in the *Sonatas* or the polished elegance of Pérez de Ayala and Miró, whose prose he regarded as *atildado* and artificial. His aim was clarity and exactitude: style as a vehicle for thought. There is never in his work after *Camino de perfección* any attempt to interpose his style between the reader and the content, even for aesthetic effect. Critics until Ciplijauskaite[17] have in general failed to recognize the effort that Baroja put into his prose. He himself protested that what he called his *contra-estilo* 'no es como creen algunos, resultado de la indiferencia por la expresión, sino resultado de preocupaciones más o menos justas por ella' (V, 844). Except for occasional lyrical interludes, Baroja's prose settled down into straight functionality. Its force lies in its unadorned natural simplicity of phrasing, based on the spoken, not the earlier written, language. The crisp brevity of sentences and paragraphs, in which he saw his main departure as a stylist from Galdós, the rare similies, the visuality, the gentle touches of humour, the avoidance of poetic effects, alliteration, obtrusive rhythms, and the like, add up to what he christened in *Juventud egolatría* 'retórica en tono menor': a style of deliberate, salutary unpretentiousness.

Baroja's ideas and methods are open to criticism on various grounds. His view of the novel as 'un saco en que cabe todo'[18] is correct as far as it goes; but this does not mean that his reliance on a spontaneous, instinctive manner of putting his novels together always works. Some of his best novels, *El gran torbellino del mundo*, for example, are clumsily constructed. The worst novels sprawl and fall apart, dispersing the reader's interest. *Los últimos románticos, Las noches del Buen Retiro,* and *El hotel del Cisne* all lack an indispensable minimum of shape and architecture. Baroja's love of a crowded stage, too, can play him false. *El amor, el dandismo y la intriga,* for example, seems to be a mere pretext for sketching a whole gallery of 'tipos vistos'. The predominance of the central character indicates the only constructional principle of any importance – chronological biography – that Baroja consistently accepted. 'Supongo que mi vida debe tener su unidad', Murguía remarks at the beginning of *La sensualidad pervertida,* 'y la unidad de mi vida hará la unidad de esta historia' (II, 848). But this principle can carry with it the excessive subordination of other characters. The poor love-interest in so many of Baroja's novels is partly due to his reluctance, after *La casa de Aizgorri,* to start his stories off with both a hero and a heroine. Instead partners are introduced or brought to the fore only when the central character's development has reached an appropriate stage, and tend to occupy only a fraction of the narrative.

Baroja never seems to have asked himself the question which so preoccupied Azorín in the middle of his career as a novelist: where he should situate himself, as author, in relation to his material. Baroja was always close up to, and deeply involved with, what goes on in his novels. So much so, Ortega remarked, that he seemed to write them 'para satisfacer una necesidad psicológica suya personalísima'. This motivates the most serious single criticism of Baroja as a novelist: his habit of openly manipulating the narrative, selecting the incidents, and adjusting the motivation of certain characters to make them fit his preconceptions. As a result a number of familiar aspects of reality are all but excluded from his work, and a view of life emerges which in the extreme case conflicts with everyday human experience. To take a single instance: both Sacha Savarof and Laura Monroy are basically unhappy, but each has a child. Having included this last fact, Baroja deliberately refuses to take it into account. For to admit the possibility that these two women might find in motherhood the fulfilment they could not find in marriage would have conflicted with his determination to present life as unremittingly hostile. We are entitled to question the way in which Baroja too often adapts his world to his attitude. Whenever a central character seems dangerously close to success or serenity, ignobility, cowardice, violence, or death intervenes. Zalacaín is killed; César's survival (in the revised editions of *César o nada*) is in doubt. Andrés Hurtado loses Lulú, Murguía loses Adelita, Larrañaga loses Nelly. The aboulic Arcelu finds enough energy to leave the country just as Sacha discovers her need of his love. There is no need to extend the list.

Finally we must mention commentary. Given the large amount of dialogue, the sometimes slanted portraits of secondary figures, and the ostentatious selection of incidents referred to earlier, there is a constant danger that commentary will acquire disproportionate importance. The fact that Baroja is far from loath to intervene himself at intervals to give the reader a piece of his mind aggravates the situation. The whole of Part I of *El gran torbellino del mundo* (1926), for example, is one vast dialogue in which Baroja took stock of his intellectual attitudes. Such a block of thinly disguised authorial reflections is apt to tire the patience of readers who do not share Baroja's interests or prejudices. To the critic, the weight of commentary, direct and indirect, with which Baroja ballasts his novels, indicates a certain reluctance to let them speak for themselves.

V. THE NOVELS OF ACTION AND ADVENTURE

The publication of *La feria de los discretos* brought from his fellow novelist Ricardo León the comment that Baroja had the makings of a first-class writer of adventure stories. In fact, as the ideal of action in a modern setting came to seem increasingly hollow, the temptation to transfer it to the context of the nineteenth century became irresistible. There its possibilities could be exploited on land and sea, or against the background of Civil War, without any pretence of making it relevant to present-day problems. So in 1907 Baroja began *Zalacaín el aventurero* (1909). It was followed in 1911 by *Las inquietudes de Shanti Andía*. In them the man of action ceases to be a man of insight at the same time. Zalacaín and Shanti enjoy an uncomplicated attitude to life. They have no problem except that of finding outlets for their surplus of energy. Putting aside his deeper vision, Baroja wrote these novels with a gusto which contrasts with the reflectiveness of his most characteristic work. Some features of the usual fictional formula are retained, notably the predominant central character and the rapidly shifting background. But now the figure in the centre, instead of talking, acts. Dialogue and commentary are far less prominent Conflict and suspense return; even love-interest is allowed a less subordinate role. *Zalacaín* is, in fact, a highly successful compromise between the technique Baroja had been elaborating hitherto and that of the standard novel of adventure. Book I is a masterly example of skilful organization. The telling contrasts between Zalacaín and his parents, between his upbringing and conventional education, and between his values and those of the wealthy and traditionalist Ohandos, are underlined by the influence of Tellagorri, Zalacaín's kindly but subversive mentor. The whole opening is a broadside against social conventions. As Tellagorri represents, in certain respects, Baroja's ideal, so the Ohandos, rich, despotic, and priest-ridden, join the Ossorios, the Arellanos, the del Hierros, and all the other Barojan figures who stand for what he detested. Catalina Ohanda, the heroine, is of course excepted. But like so many women in Baroja's novels she still clings to conformity. Her complaint is that of Asunción in *Las tragedias grotescas*: '¿Por qué no eres como los demás chicos?' (I, 177). In chapter 5 Baroja even provides a hint of interior duplication in the story before the family quarrel between the Zalacaíns and Ohandos develops into an open feud.

From Book II on, we see the man of action, with the Carlist War providing the perfect context. Following his usual method, Baroja provides Zalacaín with a foil, Batista, whose reflective caution highlights the former's spontaneous commitment to immediate action. The story advances at a uniformly brisk pace through three dramatic episodes until in Book III it can be wound up to a heroic climax, the apotheosis of Zalacaín who fulfils himself in a burst of sustained activity before Baroja reintroduces the treacherous Ohandos and allows the drop to fall. Zalacaín represents the chronic stage of Hasting's ideal: complete inability to live without the stimulus of action. 'Ahora no tengo obstáculo, y ya no sé qué hacer', he explains to Briones (I, 249), 'necesito la acción, la acción continua'. And so, like César Moncada, he is eliminated.

It could not be otherwise. Action for its own sake can only lead to sudden death or to the exhaustion and cynicism of the elderly Aviraneta or Shanti Andía. In this case Baroja, in a rare concession to the audience, takes on an ending which is unique in his work for its saccharin romanticism. *Zalacaín* has remained his most popular novel. By comparison with it *La inquietudes de Shanti Andía* is diffuse and episodic. Shanti presents himself both as belonging to the same human category as Zalacaín: 'habiá en mí una exuberancia de vida, un deseo de acción . . . yo necesitaba hacer algo, gastar la energía, vivir' (II, 1044) and at the same time as 'indolente, indiferente y apático' (998). Beneath this ambiguity we recognize a fictional device. Baroja needed a character who would be active enough at first to attract the reader's interest, but who as a middle-aged narrator of his adventures would be reflective enough to make an adequate mouthpiece for comments and opinions belonging to the author. Much of the action, which includes slaving and piracy, an escape from a British prison-hulk clearly suggested by the opening of *Great Expectations*, mysterious aliases, and buried treasure, is recounted by others. The method of interlaced narrations loosely connected with the central figure, in this case Shanti, is, however, important. It portends in miniature the technique of the *Memorias de un hombre de acción*.

In the autumn of 1911 Baroja began researching into the life and times of one of his mother's distant relatives, Eugenio de Aviraneta.[19] A Liberal conspirator, spy, and agitator between the end of the Napoleonic period and the middle 1860s, Aviraneta had been connected with many of the plots and manoeuvres which accompanied the long-drawn-out struggle between progressives and traditionalists in nineteenth-century Spain. Much of the material Baroja accumulated was destroyed when his house in Madrid was bombed during the Civil War, but by then it had provided inspiration for no fewer than twenty-two novels, a third of Baroja's entire production, and a biography of Aviraneta. The standard comparison for the *Memorias* is of course with Galdós's *Episodios nacionales*, but the differences are crucial. Galdós broadly accepted the existing pattern of society and ultimately took for granted the Liberal interpretation of history according to which progress towards greater liberty and civilization was part of a pattern of historical determinism. Despite his growing pessimism and disillusionment, Galdós never really criticized the bourgeois social system as such. He attacked only what he saw as its shortcomings. His aim was to explore Spain's recent past in order to lay bare the origins of the ideological, social, and political forces operating in his own day. Moreover, Galdós wrote with a very strong sense of audience appeal, picking out exciting events and making the fullest use of drama, pathos, and patriotic idealization. From the opposite, Carlist, standpoint, and with a more deliberately rhetorical approach, Valle-Inclán did much the same in *La guerra carlista* (1908–09).

Baroja had no such intentions. Sceptical alike of bourgeois social ideals and the onward march of man in any direction, he wrote from a standpoint outside the system, hostile to it and to programmes promising improvements to it. In so far as the *Memorias de un hombre de acción* project any view of history, it is a static one. The same violence and fanaticism, the same stupidity and venality, the same hypocrisy and self-seeking characterized life under the first Queen María Cristina as they did under her great-grandson Alfonso XIII. History for Baroja was 'siempre una fantasía sin base científica' (IV, 13). Its operations were mysterious, its personalities contradictory, and its facts obscure. The activities of each political, social, or military group were chiefly characterized by errors, follies, and vices. There are thus plenty of knaves and fools in Baroja's picture of nineteenth-century Spain, but no heroes.

Aviraneta's complex and at times contradictory character includes many of Zalacaín's basic traits: irrepressible energy and will-power, courage, resourcefulness, and the determination to use these qualities in a dangerous and unorthodox direction. 'Para Aviraneta', we read in *Los caminos del mundo*, la única vida estribaba en hallarse metido en un infierno de dificultades, en un torbellino ciego, al cual pretendía dominar. Esta tensión de la voluntad era en él lo principal; las ideas, en el fondo, creo que le preocupaban menos de lo que él se figuraba. Tenía la furia de hacer por hacer. (III, 295–6)

Baroja resisted the temptation to present Aviraneta as nobly employed in the furtherance of a great cause: that of the Spanish Liberals. He is not portrayed heroically, and he is in the end a failure. A man of fundamental probity, he is intelligent but lacking in real insight: an 'hombre dinámico ante todo, que no había llegado a un estado completo de conciencia' (III, 422). The consequences are twofold. His purely emotional commitment to liberalism renders him over-confident and unrealistic, as we see from his actions in Aranda. Secondly, his actions tend to be the fruit of mere impulse, with only short-term aims and little regard for the human consequences. His only elaborate plan, that of disrupting the Carlist war-effort using the forged documents of 'El Simancas', produces fearful suffering and bloodshed without significantly altering the course of events. Aviraneta's evolution with age is accompanied by his realization of the lack of intelligence of the Spanish Liberals and the unreadiness of the people for radical change. At the end of his career, in poverty and faced with the meagre results of a lifetime's effort, he can still comfort himself with the thought 'Lo único que me queda para vivir es la idea de haber obrado siempre con arreglo a mi conciencia' (IV, 1032).

Almost all the novels of the *Memorias* are cast in the form of memoirs by secondary figures, a simple way of avoiding pseudo-omniscient narration, varying the narrative standpoint and creating the illusion of a first-hand description of events. The fact that Aviraneta frequently appears as a disillusioned mature man contributes a note of irony to the picture of Liberal activities and hopes. The structure of the series has been analysed in some detail by J. Pérez Montaner.[20] He draws attention to the death of *El Empecinado* at the end of *Los contrastes de la vida* as marking the end of a phase in the cycle, to the novels dealing with the regency of María Cristina after the death of Ferdinand VII as the central nucleus, and to Baroja's attempt to impose a measure of circularity on the series in the last two novels. J. Sánchez Reboredo[21] in a complementary article advances a major criticism: Baroja's obsessive adherence to accuracy in minor details combined with a doctrinaire refusal to incorporate into the novels a measure of historical interpretation. Just as Baroja's ingrained distrust of his own repressed idealism prevented him from adjusting the balance between Aviraneta's disinterestedness, courage, and sacrifice and his cynical, at times irresponsible, extremism and opportunism, so too Baroja's intellectual scepticism discouraged him from attempting to analyse the underlying political, social, and

economic forces at work. All the same, his picture of Spanish political
and social life in the last century remains impressively original.

VI. THE SEARCH FOR *Ataraxia*

The last chapter of *Las horas solitarias* (1918): 'Lamentación pedan-
tesca acerca de la ataraxia', complements Baroja's earlier explicit
rejection of the action-ideal and defines his later aspiration. There
was no break in the continuity of his thought. *La sensualidad pervertida* (1920) takes up possibilities already hinted at in *El árbol de la
ciencia* and *El mundo es ansí*. Like Arcelu in the latter novel,
Murguía is a strangely appealing figure, as obvious a self-portrait
of Baroja in middle life as Hurtado was a reflection of his youth.
Repressed, different, distrustful of personal and social involvement,
he has none of Hurtado's 'indignación ética' or of Sacha Savarof's
emotional impulsiveness. He retains only their lucidity and vulner-
ability, qualities which, combined with 'un fondo de probidad
intelectual un tanto absurdo, resto de ingenuidad infantil' (II, 909),
orientate him towards a solitary, contemplative pattern of life on
the edge of society. By remaining unmarried and minimizing his
needs, he is able to preserve what he most values: almost complete
independence. By the middle of the novel he has reached a fragile
accommodation to life, modelled on Baroja's own formula: self-
employment and seclusion together with asceticism. *Ataraxia*, serenity
achieved by self-limitation and detachment, seems within reach. But
here and in the next trilogy, *Agonías de nuestro tiempo*, Baroja introduces a subtly personal element of perturbation: sexual and emotional
frustration. As Baroja sets out in his later work to explore the
Schopenhauerian ideal of abstention, the problems of love and sexuality become central issues. Baroja's own position had been frankly
stated in *El mundo es ansí*, chapters 9 and 13, and in *Juventud,
egolatría*: 'La tragicomedia sexual'. Love, like religion, was a major
mentira vital: a life-enhancing illusion. Murguía, like Baroja, is unable to share it, partly because of his analytical mentality and partly
from a distrustful reluctance to compromise what he regards as his
precious 'autonomía espiritual'. But the need for some kind of
emotional and sexual outlet, however unromanticized, remains, and
with it the longing for a lasting relationship which does not involve
submission to social pressures. The centre of the novel shows Murguía
struggling with these impossible conditions through a series of abortive relationships, and meanwhile contemplating the squalor and
moral degradation attendant on most of the sexual affairs – matri-
monial, adulterous, and homosexual – that come within his field of
vision. In early middle age Murguía unexpectedly recovers the

capacity for emotional illusion only to be confirmed in his prejudices by Ana de Lomonosoff's unmotivated rejection of his timid overtures. Again the novel ends with a deliberate manipulation of events. Murguía is left ageing, resigned, and rather pathetic. Except in one respect. True to his method, Baroja introduces as a foil for him his cousin Joshé Mari, whose familiar blend of social success and elastic morality is combined with a taste for extra-matrimonial adventures. The confrontation between the two comes characteristically:

– Tu has tomado en la vida, le dije, la posición mejor y más cómoda ... Ahora, que te falta experimentar una sensación que ya no experimentarás nunca.
– ¿Cuál?
– La sensación de lo ético ... Eso no sabes tú lo que es; ya no lo sabrás en la vida. (II, 928)

However much Baroja at times seemed to envy the uncomplicated, socially-integrated lives of the Enrique Aracils and the Joshé Maris he portrayed, the moral superiority of his figures of insight is never in doubt.

In the trilogy *Agonías de nuestro tiempo* (*El gran torbellino del mundo*, 1926; *Las veleidades de la fortuna*, 1927; and *Los amores tardíos*, 1927) Baroja continued to explore the abstention-ideal. For its hero Larrañaga, the way of life which Andrés Hurtado experimented with in Alcolea, and which is only gradually adopted by Murguía, is already a reality. The question is whether it can last. Middle-aged when the novel begins and living abroad, Larrañaga has certain initial advantages over Murguía, but otherwise the likeness is strong. There is the same 'instinto de sensualidad comprimido' (I, 1350) struggling against the restraints of reflection, self-distrust, and ethical scrupulousness. Larrañaga's character unfolds at first by way of the grand review of intellectual attitudes mentioned already as the chief feature of the trilogy's opening. But behind this impressive frontage of conscious opinions a latent sensibility awaits the turn of events which will release it. This occurs with the chance meeting with Nelly. Her passive but appealing character and the pathos of her situation are perfectly adapted to meet Larrañaga's requirements. While providing him with an emotional outlet, she presents no threat to his painfully acquired independence and equilibrium. Nelly *represents* more than she actually *is*: the possibility of striking a balance between abstention and emotion. The platonic nature of her relationship with Larrañaga, which he shows a significant reluctance to alter, and her total dependence on him emphasize (but how artificially!) the one-sided restrictions Baroja imposes on her role. She can give and receive emotional support, but has no scope for creating difficulties. Having dangled this solution in front of Larrañaga for a few months, Baroja snatches it away with Nelly's death.

The rest of the trilogy analyses the reaction of Larrañaga, now crushed and irresolute, to a new situation. This is created by his sensual, demanding, active, and decisive cousin Pepita, who happens to be at loggerheads with her husband, another of Baroja's now rather stereotyped socially successful blackguards. The ironic contrast between Larrañaga's heightened consciousness of the risks involved, the legacy of his experience with Nelly, and the demands of his newly-awakened emotions, produces an indecision which, caught between insight and desire, he struggles ineffectually to resolve. Pepita, unlike Ana de Lomonosoff, has no scruples about adultery, but this contrast does not affect the similarity of the two women's behaviour. In the end Pepita, too, returns to her husband, to social conventionality, to what Baroja sadly recognized as normality.

Abstention is a theme which lends itself to few variations. Baroja seems to have accepted the dead-end reached in *Los amores tardíos*. In *El Hotel del Cisne* (1946) and *Los enigmáticos* (1948) the age of the central characters is the decisive factor. It does not of itself bring serenity, but it brings immunity from sexual entanglements and, for the first time, genuine resignation. Meanwhile the emotional situations of Murguía and Larrañaga had been reworked in *Susana* (1938) and those of Sacha Savarof and Laura Monroy in *La sirena de Jáuregui* which forms part of *El puente de las ánimas* (1945). The death of the heroine in each case confirms Baroja's awareness of having reached an impasse. Despite a number of innovatory features, in particular the exploration of Pagani's dreams in *El Hotel del Cisne*,[22] these novels lack tension and tend to seem humdrum and repetitive. It is interesting to notice that the abandonment of serious narrative elements altogether, and their replacement by satirical travelogue-reportage in *Los visionarios* (1932), resulted in a conspicuous improvement.

Galvanized by the proclamation of the Republic in April 1931, Baroja made successive trips to Jaca to study the abortive military *coup* there, and to Andalusia to observe conditions, before pouring out at his usual fantastic speed the trilogy *La selva oscura* (*La familia de Errotacho*, 1932; *El cabo de los tormentos*, 1932; and *Los visionarios* (1932). Intended to 'dar una impresión de conjunto de las conmociones españolas de estos últimos años' (VI, 258), it exhibits the characteristics of piecemeal writing already visible in parts of the *Memorias de un hombre de acción*. The first two volumes consist of seven short novels, one of which (*El contagio*) was suppressed by the censor when the so-called *Obras completas* were prepared. They deal with the political and social disturbances surrounding the end of the dictatorship of Primo de Rivera. *Los visionarios* itself has a greater degree of unity, though the view of Varela Jacome that it has 'una estudiada estructura' seems an overstatement.[23] On a larger scale than in the journey of Aracil and María in *La dama errante*, Baroja uses a similar technique to combine political and social discussion with journalistic documentation. His depiction of class-conflict already moving towards a climax is the more objective for being critical of both the Left and the Right. Sociologically considered, Baroja's nihilistic scepticism in *Los visionarios* can be seen as the last significant expression by a member of the Generation of 1898 of the frustration felt by Spain's petty-bourgeois intelligentsia caught between the forces of left-wing maximalism with mass working-class support and the entrenched resistance of the traditional élitist power-groups.[24]

After the end of the Aviraneta series and *La selva oscura* in the early 1930s Baroja wrote only three more novels worthy of mention. *Laura* (1939) we have already discussed. The other two were *El cura de Monleón* (1936) and *El cantor vagabundo* (1950). In the former, Baroja selects a figure from the one social category for whom the life-style adopted by Murguía and Larrañaga might be expected to prove viable: a priest. Sustained by faith, sworn to celibacy, and excluded by his office from many forms of social involvement, Javier Olarán seems well equipped to practise the formula of abstention within the wider context of religious asceticism. As long as he is able to remain cocooned inside the protection of his faith – always, for Baroja, the strongest of the *mentiras vitales* – self-limitation works. But little by little as Javier is forced closer to reality by daily contact in the confessional with unembellished human nature, and by political disturbances in his parish, the analytical mind which is the hallmark of Baroja's most authentic central characters comes belatedly into play. As Javier, in a long and excessively undigested section of the novel, examines the basis of his faith, it fades and finally vanishes. When he returns to the world in a double sense, leaving both his priestly office and his life of seclusion in Alava, Javier's difficulties are only just beginning. For the first time, he must face life without the support of a vital illusion. The picture is still the same as before.

Luis Caravajal in *El cantor vagabundo* completes the list of Baroja's significant later heroes in a rather unexpected way. Born, like Baroja, in the early 1870s, he is the last of his creator's many transparently disguised spiritual self-portraits. His philosophy comes down in the end to Baroja's: 'abstenerse en la lucha, vender romances como vendo yo' (VIII, 482). The novel opens dramatically with his arrest by the Republican militia during the Civil War, but soon re-lapses into a biographical flashback including familiar travelogue sequences centring on Paris, London, and North Africa. What is interesting is that there is no process of developing insight associated with Caravajal's experiences. His conversation with Brissac in Part VIII, chapter 13, corresponds to that of Andrés Hurtado and Iturrioz in *El árbol de la ciencia*. It contains the nub of the whole novel:

> – Y ¿Vd cree que es mejor vivir así, sin ilusiones y sin esperanzas?
> – A mí me parece el principio de la sabiduría. La limitación creo que es lo más higiénico que puede hacer el hombre. (VIII, 545)

but it has no immediate effect. Only at the end, when Silvia, conveniently desexualized and undemanding, but affectionate and intelligent (a bachelor's fantasy, like Nelly), offers the possibility of a stable relationship with no threat to Caravajal's non-involvement, does Baroja show his hand. Caravajal's unhappiness, like that of Laura Monroy, is ascribed not to any deeper understanding of life as it really is, but to an arbitrary incompatibility with the world: 'una neurosis de angustia' (409). Caravajal describes it as 'una tristeza física, orgánica que no es razonable. No procede de mis ideas . . . Viene como si fuera una enfermedad de inquietud' (589). Baroja's readiness at the end of his creative life to accept the possibility that the agnosticism and rejection of illusion on which so much of his life and work had been based might be no more than a symptom of neurosis, is a final tribute to his intellectual honesty.

VII. CONCLUSION

To suggest, as Ricardo Gullón has done, that Baroja's work was neglected between his death in 1956 and his centenary in 1972 is patently misguided, though it must be admitted that in general the quality of Baroja's criticism does not compare with that devoted to Unamuno, Machado, or even Azorín. Confirmation of this can be all too readily found in the sorry collection of *homenajes* published in connection with the centenary itself. Like Hardy in England, Baroja tends in the long run to alienate the sympathies of readers and critics by his dogged refusal, outside his adventure stories, to admit life's more pleasurable possibilities into his novels, his negative vision of society, and his jaundiced view of human nature in all but a tiny minority of intellectually and ethically conscious individuals. Perhaps the main mitigating factor is his humour, when it appears.[25] This, together with his utter sincerity and the determined subversiveness he showed towards all established values and institutions, guaranteed him an audience in an environment dominated by hypocrisy and enforced conformism.

In retrospect Baroja emerges, alongside Unamuno and Machado, as one of the 'big three' of the Generation of 1898. In breadth and quality his work, which like that of Galdós is quite insufficiently known outside the Spanish-speaking countries, compares with that of Arnold Bennett or Roger Martin du Gard in France. He is outstanding as Spain's great modern novelist of intellectual protest. His influence on the younger generation in the 1920s has been remarked on by Valbuena Prat.[26] Sender testified to it in the next decade.[27] Goytisolo in 1959 referred to Baroja as 'el último novelista español que mantuvo contacto con el público'.[28] His impact on later novelists writing in Spanish was such that Cela felt able to declare that 'de Baroja sale toda la novela española a él posterior'.[29] In Latin America novelists of the stature of Mallea and Carpentier have acknowledged his influence, Neruda read him avidly, and critics including Eugenio Matus, Juan Uribe Echeverría, and Carlos Nallim have contributed book-length studies of his work. Few will contest the view of another outstanding Latin American critic, Guillermo de Torre, that in Baroja we find 'el más poderoso temperamento novelesco con que después de Galdós cuenta las letras hispánicas'.[30]

NOTES

1. It was not the first to be written. 'Medium' (1892?) and 'Grito en el mar' (1896) probably antedate it.
2. Luis Urrutia Salaverri has gathered Baroja's early uncollected writings between 1890 and 1904 into *Pío Baroja. Escritos inéditos: Hojas sueltas* (2 vols, Madrid, 1973). See also *Baroja, escritos de juventud*, ed. M. Longanares (Madrid, 1972).
3. See the extremely illuminating article by Rafael Pérez de la Dehesa, 'Editoriales e ingresos literarios a principios de siglo', *RO*, 24, no. 71 (1969), 217–28.
4. Cf. the comment of the village priest: 'Eso traerá, a la larga, una revolución en España' (*La dama errante, OC* II, 303) and the quotation from *El árbol de la ciencia*, above, p. 109.
5. All subsequent bracketed references are to this edition.
6. On this point see I. Elizalde, 'Los curas en la obra de Pío Baroja', *Letras de Deusto*, II (1972), 51–114 and Francisco Pérez Gutiérrez, 'Los curas en Baroja' in *Barojiana* (Madrid, 1972), 67–111.
7. F. López Estrada, *Perspectiva sobre Pío Baroja* (Seville, 1972), 100–3 collects (once more) quotations in support of Baroja's early confidence in science, but emphasizes his disillusionment with it in old age (e.g., *OC* VII, 972; VIII, 543). He overlooks the fact that this disillusionment was already present in the article 'Los productos de la cultura' here quoted.
8. For a fuller account see Carmen Iglesias, *El pensamiento de Pío Baroja* (Mexico, 1963), ch. 1: 'La filosofía'.
9. Blanco Aguinaga, *Juventud del 98*, ch. 6, esp, 271–90. See also Franco Díaz de Cerio, 'Baroja y la política', in *Letras de Deusto*, II (1972), 11–49 for another hostile account of Baroja's political ideas.
10. Juan Villegas, *La estructura mítica del heroe* (Barcelona, 1973), 139–175.
11. Hence the five articles on it in *CHA*, 265–7 (1972). See also the excellent essay by Francisco García Sarriá, 'Estructura y motivos de *Camino de perfección*', *Romanische Forschungen*, LXXXIII (1971), 246–66.
12. Soledad Puértolas, *El Madrid de La lucha por la vida* (Madrid, 1971). See also E. Alarcos Llorach, *Anatomia de La lucha por la vida* (Oviedo, 1973).

13. See the very useful article by Javier Martínez Palacio, 'Las mujeres de *La lucha por la vida*', *El Urogallo*, XV (1972), 106–10.

14. The main sources for Baroja's views in this connection are: the prologues to *La dama errante, Páginas escogidas, Los amores tardíos, El laberinto de las sirenas,* and (especially) *La nave de los locos;* the discussions of literary theory and practice in *La caverna del humorismo* and *Las horas solitarias;* and the articles 'Sobre la técnica de la novela' (in *El tablado de Arlequín*, 2nd ed., 1924, but not in *OC*) and 'Sobre la novela realista', another version of the prologue to *La nave de los locos.* Luis Granjel, *Retrato de Pío Baroja* (Barcelona, 1954), 132–44 is excellent. C. O. Nallim, *El problema de la novela en Pío Baroja* (Mexico, 1964) despite its title is largely irrelevant. On individual works see Corpus Barga, 'Una novela de Baroja', *RO*, 3 (1925), 106–125 and my article, 'Two novels of Baroja. An Illustration of his Technique', *BHS*, XL (1963), 151–9.

15. See Carmen Iglesias, 'Controversia entre Baroja y Ortega acerca de la novela', *Hispanófila*, II (1959), 41–50, which goes over the same ground as my article 'A Reply to *deshumanización*: Baroja on the Art of the Novel', *HR*, XXV (1957), 105–11.

16. See, for example, the analysis of *Camino de perfección* by García Sarriá mentioned above, note 11, and that of *El mundo es ansí* by Eamonn Rogers, 'Realidad y realismo en Baroja', *CHA*, 265–7 (1972), 575–90, together with my introduction to the same in my edition of it (Oxford, 1970), esp. 18–22.

17. Birute Ciplijauskaite, *Baroja, un estilo* (Madrid, 1972).

18. *Páginas escogidas* (London, 1917), 10.

19. On Baroja's use of materials see C. A. Longhurst, 'Pío Baroja and Aviraneta', *BHS*, XLVIII (1971), 328–45 and more generally L. M. Ugalde, 'El supuesto antihistoricismo de Pío Baroja', *Hispanófila*, XXXVI (1967), 11–20 and F. Flores Arroyuelo, *Pío Baroja y la historia* (2nd ed., Madrid, 1973).

20. 'Sobre la estructura de *Las memorias de un hombre de acción*', *CHA*, 265–7 (1972), 610–20.

21. 'Notas sobre la estructura de *Las memorias de un hombre de acción*', *Revista de Letras* (Puerto Rico), XV (1972), 379–95.

22. See the rather quaint essays by Juan P. Quiñonero, 'Baroja, surrealismo, terror y trasgresión', *CHA*, 265–7 (1972), 328–62 and L. García Abrines, 'Baroja y el automatismo subconsciente', *RHM*, XXXV (1969), 103–5.

23. B. Varela Jacome, 'Estructuras de la trilogía *La selva oscura*', *Revista de Letras* (Puerto Rico), XV (1972), 358–78 and E. González López, *El arte narrativo de Pío Baroja en las trilogías* (New York, 1971), chapters 39, 40.

24. For the predictable reaction of the new Left in Spanish criticism see A. Elorza's excellent essay 'El realismo crítico de Pío Baroja' in *RO*, 21, No. 62 (1968), 151–73.

25. See the prize-winning essay by Luis López-Delpecho, 'Perfiles y claves del humor barojiano', ibid., 129–50.

26. A. Valbuena Prat, *Literatura española en sus relaciones con la universal* (Madrid, 1965), 496.

27. Sender, op. cit., 126.

28. J. Goytisolo, 'Para una literatura nacional popular', *In*, 146 (1959), 6, 11.

29. Camilo J. Cela, *Don Pío Baroja* (Mexico, 1958), 75.

30. Guillermo de Torre, *Del 98 al barroco* (Madrid, 1969), 117.

Chapter 6

MACHADO: THE ROAD TO EMPTINESS

The other major Spanish poet who, along with Unamuno, successfully resisted the main impact of *modernismo*, was Antonio Machado.
Born in Seville on 26 July 1875, at the age of eight he moved with
his family, including his older brother Manuel Machado, also a well-
known minor poet, to Madrid. There he studied until 1888 at the
Institución Libre de Enseñanza, absorbing the cult of intellectual
liberty, the deep attachment to ethical values, and the strong sense of
responsibility to the national community as a whole which was
its characteristic imprint. Before long the family was in financial
difficulties. Nevertheless, until he was thirty-two Machado was able
to avoid choosing a career and to live the life of a hopeful young
writer among the cafés and literary *tertulias* of the capital. He did
some bit-part acting and managed two trips to Paris, in 1899 and
1902, meeting Oscar Wilde and Moréas and making friends with
Darío there. He also made extensive tours of the Spanish countryside,
which Giner tirelessly taught his disciples to appreciate. 1901 saw
Machado's first published poems, 'Desde la boca de un dragón' and
'Siempre que sale el alma', later discarded, and in 1902 (though the
book is dated 1903) he published privately his first verse-collection
Soledades. It contained 42 poems which he had written since 1899.
Unsold copies were remaindered under a different cover in 1904.
A modern edition (Madrid, Taurus, 1969, edited by Rafael Ferreres)
reproduces the original. This is of some importance, for when
Soledades was republished in 1907 by Machado as *Soledades,
Galerías y otros poemas* (hereafter *SGOP*), 13 of the original poems
had been dropped, changes were made in the remaining 29, and 65
new ones were added. What we now normally read is not, therefore,
what was first printed.

In the same year, 1907, Machado went to teach French in the
little Castilian town of Soria. There in 1909 he married Leonor,
the daughter of his landlady, and in 1910 with the help of a scholar-
ship took her to Paris, where he attended a course of lectures by
Bergson which confirmed some of his own cherished intuitions about
Time. Unhappily in mid-1911 Leonor became gravely ill and had to
be taken home to Soria, where she died at the age of eighteen on

1 August 1912. The year was the turning-point in Machado's life, for it also brought, in June or July, the publication of his most famous collection of poems, *Campos de Castilla*.

Immediately after Leonor's death Machado had himself transferred to the southern town of Baeza where he continued teaching, writing, and travelling around Andalusia, until 1919, when he moved back to Segovia in Castile. In 1917 he had published a selection of *Poesías escogidas* and the first edition of his *Poesías completas*. These were followed in 1922 by the second edition of *SGOP* and in 1924 by *Nuevas canciones*. In 1927 he was elected to the Royal Academy of Letters, but never formally took his seat. Ortega's *Revista de Occidente* published poems by Machado, including in 1929 *Canciones*, now known as *Canciones a Guiomar*. During the previous year, it is now accepted, Machado had met and fallen in love with the minor poetess Pilar de Valderrama, the Guiomar in question. Their relationship seems to have lasted until 1926. By this time Machado had obtained his final transfer to Madrid (1932). As early as 1926 he had adhered to the *Alianza Republicana* and during the Civil War the Republican government found in him an unconditional adherent.[1] In January 1939 he was forced to flee to France, where he died on 22 February in Collioure.

All those who have examined the items suppressed from *Soledades* after 1903 are unanimous that Machado's principal aim was only to remove weaker poems, but also to eliminate *modernista* survivals.[2] Of the individual poems which were dropped, the most obviously *modernista* example was 'El mar triste' which contained clear reminiscences of 'Sinfonía en gris mayor', the first of Darío's poems to be published in a Spanish literary magazine. While the colour references and 'exquisite' vocabulary of these lines from 'La fuente':

> el sol la surca de alamares de oro,
> la tarde la cairela de escarlata
> y de arabescos fúlgidos de plata

are practically *modernista* call-signs, the insistent use of words of vaguely religious association: *salmo, salmodia, salterio, mirra, inciensos, campana, plegaria*, is related by Ribbans rather to 'el simbolismo francés de signo menor', and the recurrent references to April to a deliberate reaction against Verlaine's autumnal inspiration.

These discarded poems, then, sufficiently declare the early influences operating on Machado. He himself did not seek to minimize their impact, which remained important to his poetry up to and including the revised version of the *Soledades*. It is plain from the 1919 prologue to the second edition of *SGOP* that Machado's acquaintance with *modernismo* and with the French Parnassian and Symbolist poetry to which *modernismo* was so closely related, served essentially to open his eyes to the limitations of the older generation of Spanish poets. Only Bécquer, whom Machado in 1904 called 'el primer innovador del ritmo interno de la poesía española',[3] and Rosalía Castro survived. What emerges from the prologue to the 1917 edition of *Soledades* and from numerous other remarks by Machado, is his choice of a different direction from that adopted by Darío and the *modernistas*: 'Pensaba yo', he wrote,

> que el elemento poético no era la palabra por su valor fónico, ni el color, ni la línea, ni un complejo de sensaciones, sino una honda palpitación del espíritu; lo que pone el alma.

This explicit rejection of two fundamental elements of *modernismo*: the renovation of diction along lines determined by emphasis on sensation, rather than emotion, and the implicit charge – more justified in Spain than in Latin America – that *modernista* poetry lacked a spiritual dimension, being too bound up with the senses, reveal Machado's eventual divergence from the movement. Admittedly the *Soledades* themselves do clearly illustrate the difficulty of always drawing a hard and fast distinction between *modernismo* and *noventayochismo*, particularly as regards poetry. While the two movements can now be seen separately, following Salinas and Díaz-Plaja, their intellectual and spiritual origins were very similar. Though their response to it was different, they shared a common existential malaise. This is why Azorín in 1913 could still regard Darío as a member of the Generation of 1898, and why Juan Ramón Jiménez persistently regarded *noventayochismo* as a branch of *modernismo*. But these views are now outdated.

In a letter to Unamuno of 1903 he asserted: 'el artista debe amar la vida y odiar el arte, lo contrario de lo que he pensado hasta aquí' and a year later defined poetry as 'un yunque de constante actividad espiritual'.[4] Though Machado never clearly explained what he meant by this definition, we can approach an understanding of it both from the criticisms he directed at other poetic movements and from his own direct statements. His hostility to *modernismo* had emerged as early as 1904 in a review of Juan Ramón Jiménez's *Arias tristes* (*El País*, 14 March 1904).[5] It illustrates his rejection of poetry which sought in formal beauty a refuge from lived reality, which prized sensations above emotions, and which had deliberately embraced narcissistic subjectivity. He called instead for a deeper self-inspection and closer contact with active life.

The same outlook is visible in his later writings on poetry, especially his article on Gerardo Diego published in *La Voz de Soria* on 29 September 1922, 'Reflexiones sobre la lírica' (1925) published in *RO*, his article in *La Gaceta Literaria* of 15 March 1928, and his famous 'Poética' in Gerardo Diego's 1931 anthology. In the third of these, for example, he refers to 'esa nueva objetividad que yo persigo hace veinte años' and in the last to his advocacy of 'una lírica otra vez inmergida en *las mesmas vivas aguas de la vida*'. In the first he had redefined his ideal as 'la poesía integral totalmente humana'. As *modernismo* gave way to *creacionismo* and the poets of the Generation of 1927 began to make their appearance, Machado insisted repeatedly on two new features which seemed to him to stand in the way of progress towards that ideal. The first concerned the use of metaphor. Machado believed, like Bécquer, that poetic creation was not in the first instance a conscious activity. It emerged from what he called in *La Gaceta Literaria* 'aquella zona central de nuestra psique donde fue siempre engendrada la lírica', in the form of intuitions. Behind these intuitions lay what Machado elsewhere called the world of poets' 'valores emotivos' his 'íntimo sentir'. Hence, he asserted 'la imagen [=metaphor here] aparece por un subito incremento del caudal del sentir apasionado'.[6] The importance of feeling is in turn its universality. For, as Meneses asserts in *De un cancionero apócrifo*: 'todo sentimiento se orienta hacia valores universales o que pretenden serlo'. Of course, neither the poet's feelings nor the language in which he expresses them can ever be totally his own. 'El sentimiento no es una creación del sujeto individual, una elaboración cordial del yo con materiales del mundo externo. Hay siempre en él una colaboración del tu, es decir, de otros sujetos'.[7] We thus have three elements which, according to Machado, underlie a genuinely poetic metaphor: intuition, emotion, and a necessary relevance to shared human experience which precludes excessive subjectivity. What worried him about the sort of metaphors which came into use with the vogue of the Chilean poet Vicente Huidobro's *creacionismo* from about 1916 onwards was that they derived from concepts and not from intuitions. He regarded them in consequence as frequently gratuitous, mechanical, and merely ingenious. The reasoning behind this opinion is to be found in the severe critique of baroque poetry for basically the same reason (excessive conceptuality) which Machado made in 'El "Arte Poética" de Juan de Mairena'.

Both there and in the 'Poética' of 1931, where Machado criticized the younger poets of the day for 'el empleo de las imágenes más en función conceptual que emotiva', he also develops his argument against the second feature of their work which he thought militated against the writing of great poetry: *destemporalización*. Redefining his view of poetry in 1924, Machado wrote that it was:

> Ni mármol duro eterno
> ni música ni pintura
> sino palabra en el tiempo.
> ('De mi cartera', CLXIV)

The first two lines reject (or subordinate) two nineteenth-century views. One, which we associate chiefly with Théophile Gautier, emphasized the triumph of art alone over Time. The other, which we associate with Verlaine and the Parnassians, as well as the *modernistas* in Spanish, stressed the unity of the arts expressed by musicality and visuality in poetry. In place of these Machado stresses temporality. 'Todos los medios de que se vale el poeta: cantidad, medida, acentuación, pausas, rima, las imágenes mismas, por su enunciación en serie, son elementos temporales . . . Pero una intensa y profunda impresión del tiempo sólo nos la dan muy contados poetas'.[8] Just as he disliked mental concepts in poetry because of their conflict with emotion and intuition, so he objected to them also on this second ground. In the 1931 'Poética' he writes:

> El pensamiento lógico, que se adueña de las ideas y capta lo esencial, es una actividad destemporalizadora. Pensar lógicamente es abolir el tiempo . . . Pero al poeta no le es dado pensar fuera del tiempo, porque piensa su propia vida que no es, fuera del tiempo, absolutamente nada.

What Machado is saying is not, of course, that the poet should write about Time, i.e., that the *explicit* theme of his poetry should be man's ephemerality. The poet 'piensa su propia vida', expresses intuitions which are the fruit of his own experience, especially his own emotional experience. In his contrast between the *coplas* of Manrique and Calderón's flower-sonnet Machado emphasizes the fact that while the latter frigidly expresses abstract reflections, the former transmit the concrete remembered experience of an individual in a time-scale which is simply that of his own life.

All Machado's writings about poetry, then, can be seen to culminate in the two imperatives enunciated in his 'Poética' of 1931: 'esencialidad y temporalidad'. Essentiality in poetry for Machado involved recognition of the ultimate primacy of life over art, that is, of lived experience over the creative imagination. He insisted on poetry of 'hondos estados de conciencia' (including 'los enigmas del hombre y del mundo' [prologue to *Campos de Castilla*, 1917] and 'Inquietud, angustia, temores, resignación, esperanza, impaciencia . . . revelación del ser en la conciencia humana' ('Poética'). Essentiality also involved recognition of the primacy of emotions and intuitions over ideas and concepts, and of 'objectivity' (practical awareness in the fact that 'un poema es – como un cuadro, una estatua o una catedral – antes que nada, un objeto propuesto a la contemplación del prójimo')[9] over narcissistic subjectivity. Temporality involved the poet in the task of conveying, not the *idea* of time, but the *emotion* of time.

I. MACHADO'S EARLY VERSE

The part of *Soledades* which remained after the suppressions of 1907 represents Machado's first real achievement. In it and in the new additions we still notice, alongside some of his best-remembered verse, poems which illustrate his earliest uncertainties of direction. One is 'En el entierro de un amigo', an attempt at poetic realism with a setting quite unlike the dreamy parks, gardens, and squares of the more characteristic early poems, which appears to date from as late as 1907. Its adjectives (and pairs of adjectives), '*roja* flor', '*cielo pura azul*', '*aire fuerte y seco*' '*sueño tranquilo y verdadero*', flat and obvious when they are not jejune: '*podridos* pétalos', '*áspera fragancia*'; and its emphatic placing of harsh adverbs: *pesadamente, perfectamente, definitivamente,* are not offset by the acoustical effect of '*sonó* con recio golpe solemne' as the coffin strikes the earth. Though often mentioned in connection with the pervasive presence of death in Machado's work, it is not a successful poem. What really distinguishes it from most of the other poems in *Soledades* is the fact that it appears to describe a specific event. It is, to put it bluntly, a poem of crude 'anecdote'. This is why it stands out. One of the chief claims of *Soledades* to a place of historical importance in the evolution of modern Spanish poetry arises from Machado's own statement in 1914 that 'El libro *Soledades* fue el primer libro español del cual estaba íntegramente proscrito lo anecdótico'.[10]

In contrast, in one of the first poems we can date, number VIII, originally called 'Los cantos de los niños', written in 1898, some basic motifs of the authentic early Machado appear. One is the setting: 'la sombra de una plaza vieja'. Here for perhaps the first time Machado introduces the static, often silent, background of shady squares, labyrinthine streets, empty patios, neglected buildings, and cypress-planted parks and gardens in a dead deserted city, which he was to use in a dozen or more poems later.[11] It symbolizes, like the

tarde cenicienta y mustia,
destartalada, como el alma mía (LXXVII)

but more concretely, the poet's feelings of 'soledad de corazón sombrío' (ibid.). The poems of *SGOP* are full of a sense of lost youth and its associated love and happiness, but also underlying these a deeper loss: that of general existential confidence. Though the children in the square sing of 'tristezas de amores', and more sombrely of 'un algo que pasa/y que nunca llega', their song is neither happy nor sad, for it is innocent of insight. In a later but similar poem the 'alegría infantil' animating the 'plaza en sombra' evokes

> algo nuestro de ayer. que todavía,
> vemos vagar por estas calles viejas (III)

the spiritual serenity of childhood which Machado, like Unamuno, longed to recapture. The fountain, on the other hand, and flowing water generally, are a threatening presence. Deriving ultimately from the famous lines of Jorge Manrique which Machado glossed in the 1903 *Soledades*, the water-symbolism of his poetry is associated above all with time's ever rolling stream, with life's inexorable onward flow towards 'la mar, que es el morir', and with the bitter monotony of an existence whose values have been eroded.

> Dice la monotonía
> del agua clara al caer:
> un día es como otro día
> hoy es lo mismo que ayer. (LIV)

'Los cantos de los niños', then, is a song of innocence and experience, the voice of the fountain impassively conveying the latter.

By far the most important poem to be salvaged (with only slight changes) from the 1903 *Soledades* is the one which was there called simply 'Tarde'. Both the time and place of the setting are characteristic: the slow, sad, lifeless summer afternoon, and the silent, solitary park with its monotonous fountain. This subjective opening is already fraught with implications of time and decay, leading to the poet's exploration of the past in the centre of the poem. There we notice two essential features, the first of which is the dialogue form. One of Machado's most commonly employed poetic devices, it introduces many different interlocutors:

Me dijo *un alba* de la primavera . . .	(XXXIV)
¡ Oh, díme, *noche* amiga . . .	(XXXVII)
Me dijo *una tarde*/da la primavera . . .	(XLI)
Pregunté a *la tarde* de abril . . .	(XLIII)
Y era el *demonio de mi sueño* . . .	(LXIII)
Desde el umbral de un sueño *me llamaron*	(LXIV)
Llamó a mi corazón un claro día . . . el *viento* . . .	(CXVIII)

but its consistent function is to throw into contrast antithetical aspects of the poet's personality, chiefly his hopes and his fears. The other feature is the changed tone of the song attributed to the mountain. In the early, discarded, poems the fountain's song is happy, a 'loco borbollar riente' ('Fuente'), an 'agua clara que reía' ('Cenit'). It survives as such in 'Jardín':

> El agua
> de la fuente de piedra
> no cesa de reír sobre la concha blanca. (LI)

So, too, originally in 'Tarde' (1903 version), whose fourth line was:

> Lejana una fuente *riente* sonaba;

Line 11 referred to

> ...La fuente que *alegre* vertía

and lines 48–9 to

> tu monotonía
> *alegre* ...

In the 1907 version these adjectives were removed. Now the 'copla riente' and the 'claro cristal de alegría' of the fountain, instead of existing 'objectively', are relegated to the poet's subjectivity, and associated with his hope that the fountain retains some memory of his 'alegre leyenda olvidada'. But such hope is vain. The fountain's song is not of legend, but of harsh reality, which the poet has preferred to forget

> — Yo no sé *leyendas* de antigua alegría
> sino *historias* viejas de melancolía.

Villegas's cogent analysis of the poem falters at this point.[12] The poet struggles to organize meaningfully three fragments of the past into what he assumes will be a happy memory: the symbolic 'fruta bermeja' of a nearby tree, his *amargura* (now distant), and 'antiguos delirios de amores'. He longs, that is, to find that the bitterness of lost love has mellowed into ripe experience. But the fountain dismisses his aspiration, forcing him implacably to recognize that the passage of time, which its flow symbolizes, has brought no comfort. The tempting fruit overhanging the fountain, far from being sweet to the taste, contained only a deceitful promise of happiness, as Machado explained explicitly when he returned to the image in a later poem:

> mísero fruto podrido,
> que en el hueco acibarado
> guarda el gusano podrido. (xviii)

It was, indeed, fruit of the Tree of Knowledge. The poet's original *pena* and *sed* have undergone no change or diminution. Recalled to total consciousness of them, the poet turns bitterly away, reproaching the fountain for increasing his unhappiness by adding to it the realization that time has failed to attenuate it. Worse than pain itself is the recognition of its changelessness. It can now be seen that the poet's 'lejana amargura' refers to the moment when, deprived of love's protecting illusion, he first awoke to unhappy insight (*pena*) and to an anguished desire (*sed*) for a life-directing ideal.

In contrast XI, the famous 'Yo voy soñando caminos de la tarde' with its strong reminiscence of Rosalía Castro in the poet's *cantar*, expresses Machado's allegiance to emotion, life-enhancing even when unhappy, in preference to this bleak rational consciousness of life's enigma. The opening sentence juxtaposes three central Machadian symbols: dreaming (insight), the road (life), and the evening (disillusionment, *cansancio vital*, death). The first twelve lines present the poet advancing through life consciously towards the unknown. The gradually gathering dusk conveys both the passing of time and its hostility, since evening bears away the light, with all its associations of confidence and hope; while in the middle of the poem the poet's *cantar* implies that not even the pain of love remains to offset his awareness of life's shadows deepening around him. It is followed by an instant in which the natural setting is suddenly plunged into sombre silence, an instant of anguished vision: life drained of emotion is bereft of comfort. The sighing of the wind, nightfall, and the blotting-out of all directions confirm the poet's intuition, leaving him to lament afresh his inner emptiness. The poem's key-adjective is *dorada*. Appearing twice, symmetrically, once near the beginning and again near the end, it emphasizes cunningly the light-imagery which is the main structural feature. After the opening notation: the joyful golden light of afternoon on the hills, the colours fade through green to the grey-brown of the oaks merging with the darkening sky, its deepest hue emphasized by the contrast of *blanquea* in line 19. As all is engulfed in darkness, the opening reappears, with accumulated effect, to create a metaphoric parallel to its earlier use. The *espina*, at first mention unqualified, becomes

Aguda espina dorada

cruelly sharp, yet invested with the golden associations of the lost sunshine. In this poem perhaps more than in any other we perceive the characteristic Machadian technique of juxtaposing an external setting and an internal mood which exert a reciprocal influence, rather than the setting's merely expressing concretely the mood. The same technique is visible, e.g. in cvi, 'Un loco'.

It would be misleading, however, to class Machado as a poet of thought, in quite the same way as Unamuno was. 'El intelecto no ha cantado jamás, no es su misión', he wrote in his 'Poética' in 1931.

> Sirve no obstante, a la poesía, señalandole el imperativo de su esencialidad. Porque tampoco hay poesía sin ideas, sin visiones de lo esencial. Pero las ideas del poeta no son categorías formales, cápsulas lógicas, sino directas intuiciones del ser que deviene, de su propio existir . . .

Already it is apparent that one of Machado's central intuitions had to do with the role of Time. In 'A Narciso Alonso Cortés, poeta de Castilla' (1913) he wrote:

> Al corazón del hombre con red sutil envuelve
> el tiempo, como niebla de río una arboleda.
> ¡ No mires; todo pasa; olvida; nada vuelve!
> Y el corazón del hombre se angustia . . .¡ Nada queda! (cxlix)

Another symbol of Time's all but invincible power is that of the wind,

el soplo
que el polvo barre y la ceniza avienta. (xiv)

It reappears at the climax of one of Machado's most deeply pathetic
poems on this ancient theme of man's impermanence:

¿Y ha de morir contigo el mundo majo . . . (lxxviii)

The poem is all interrogation. Before the mystery of Time's ultimate
triumph the poet expresses not despair or rebellion, but man's
bewilderment and sense of waste. The pronounced rhythmical
alliteration of the opening line emphasizes his instinctive reluctance
to accept the annihilation of what for him is the very stuff of the soul
itself: memory. Nothing is more characteristically Machadian than
this lament for the extinction, not of the personality, but of those
surviving recollections of pure emotion (symbolized once more in a
comforting handclasp) which he held to be its true essence. Lines 9
and 10 repeat the original question:

¿Y ha de morir contigo el mundo tuyo,
la vieja vida en orden tuyo y nuevo?

We notice as in 'Recuerdo infantil' (Monotonía/de lluvia tras los
cristales . . . monotoniá de la lluvia en los cristales) Machado's tendency to introduce slight alterations in his repetitions to increase
their poignancy and impact. The alliteration of line 1 has given place
to the cunning balance of the tonic accents of line 9:

¿Y ha de morir contigo el mundo tuyo

underlined by the similar vocalic pattern of the following line:

la vieja vida en orden tuyo y nuevo?

The contrast *vieja/nuevo* is the contrast which exists between the
unique configuration of the world-vision of each individual and the
common daily experience from which it is selected. It is the unique-
ness forged and distilled by living, loving, and suffering, which Time
disintegrates, which the wind of Time blows away for ever.

Time, then, for Machado and for all the long tradition which links
him through Calderón and Quevedo to Jorge Manrique and the
classics, is inevitably death-orientated. A lapidary poem included in
the 1907 edition of the *Soledades* brings together in four lines Time,
death, and the symbol of the path or road – of life:

Al borde del sendero un día nos sentamos.
Ya nuestra vida es tiempo, y nuestra sola cuita
son las desesperantes posturas que tomamos
para aguardar . . . Mas ella no faltará a la cita.   (xxxv)

In line 4 we notice again an acoustical effect similar to that of the
last line of lxiv. The fact that eleven of the fourteen syllables
contain 'a' sounds is the prime reason why the line echoes in the

memory. While the meaning of the line is stark and threatening, its sound is soft and lulling, in tune with the curious, resigned restfulness of the image in the opening line.[14] The tension of the poem derives from the contrasting lines 2 and 3 (essentially the words *cuita* and *desesperantes*). Although there is no interlocutor here, we still feel intuitively that the poem is in a sense a dialogue between one of Machado's selves and another. In 'Hacia un ocaso radiante' (XIII) once more several elements of symbolism are present. The time is the early evening, when light struggles with growing darkness, and the inevitable triumph of the latter accords with the poet's mood of melancholy. The individual is presented as a boat on the river of life, but both are degraded by the repeated adjective (*pobre* barca, *pobre* río). To the water-symbolism is added light-symbolism. At first the river is 'agua clara'; but as it runs beneath the bridge, whose dark arches are intuitively connected by the poet to the crypts of the analytic mind, and hence to

> la vieja angustia que hace el corazón pesado

in the previous line, it becomes 'El agua en sombra' and finally 'el agua sombría', voicing its fateful warning. Mindful of it, the poet senses his insignificance and approaching annihilation. The final image recurs more explicitly in 'El poeta':

> Él sabe que un Dios más fuerte
> con la substancia inmortal está jugando a la muerte
> cual niño bárbaro. Él piensa
> que ha de caer como rama que sobre las aguas flota,
> antes de perderse, gota
> de mar, en la mar inmensa. (XVIII)

No faith in God or an afterlife upheld Machado in the face of death. To call him a believer, as Concha Espina does, is simply to ignore the evidence.[15] Critics are generally agreed that, unlike Unamuno's, Machado's religious position is plainly recognizable. His *angustia* is less strident than Unamuno's precisely because only a residue of nostalgia for faith remained. What Machado shared with Unamuno was a deep attachment to spiritual values, but in a less specifically religious context. Like Unamuno, he could not – at least until the Civil War – identify himself fully with the Left in Spanish politics because of its aggressive rejection of such values. Like him he bitterly criticized Spain as a 'país beocio y sin respeto a todo valor espiritual'.[16] Like him, in spite of his taste for using practical sounding words like 'maza' and 'yunque' in connection with the regeneration of Spain, he seems to have seen the problem basically in the usual '98 spiritual terms. But when he described himself as:

> Siempre buscando a Dios entre la niebla (LXXVII)

it would be wrong to see him engaged on the quest in Unamuno's way. He is far more explicit:

> amargura
> de querer y no poder
> creer, creer y creer. (cxxviii)

At the end of the road stretching into the dusk lies the threat of nothingness. The sea into which the stream of life bears our frail craft is a sinister sea of unknowing. Existence is overshadowed by interrogation:

> de arcano mar vinimos, a ignoto mar iremos . . .
> Y entre los dos misterios está el enigma grave. (cxxxvi)

His desire for faith burgeoned into desperate hope in the years after Leonor's death. It produced two of his most poignant poems: 'Dice la esperanza: un día/la verás' (cxx) and 'Soñé que tu me llevabas' (cxxii), both of which imply reunion after death. But this hope of a divinely ordained afterlife, which would make sense of this one, had no deep roots in Machado's nature or upbringing. It is contradicted by the other later tendency, that of the 'Cancioneros apócrifos' of Martín and Mairena. The God referred to there, so ironically and ambiguously that it is difficult to know what is to be regarded as serious, has nothing in common with orthodoxy.

Several of Machado's early poems express a lyrical vision of death as appearing like a beloved woman. Hence perhaps the use of the word *cita* and the gentle anticipatory effect of the final line in poem xxxv reproduced above. The most explicit of these poems is:

> amada, el aura dice
> tu pura veste blanca . . .
> No te verán mis ojos;
> ¡mi corazón te aguarda! (xii)

Here Machado reintroduces the mysterious female phantom who had first appeared in two discarded poems from the first *Soledades*. In them and in xlii she personifies the past with its 'cosas de ayer que sois el alma'. That is why in the latter poem she is seen partly as lovely and partly as threatening, in line with the ambivalence towards the past visible in lxxxv, originally entitled 'Nevermore'.

In other poems, notably xii, xvi, xxix, liv, and the very late 'Muerte de Abel Martín, which provides a clue to their symbolism, the phantom is identifiable with death, though not all critics are agreed on this point.[17] The synaesthesia at the opening of xii:

> el aura *dice*
> tu pura veste blanca

is reinforced in the next stanza: 'el viento me ha traído/tu nombre', The sight has become a sound, which grows from that of an echoing footstep to that of a tolling bell, and finally to those of repeated 'golpes' of hammer on coffin and spade on earth. Each sound is reiterative, implying death's unceasing activity, and as the poem progresses, the sounds become more restricted in radius until we are close enough to hear the grave being dug. Yet the poem is not one of sinister or fearful premonition, but, once more, of anticipation. This turns to supplication ('Detén el paso, belleza') in XVI, and at length in LIV almost to disappointment that the disdainful phantom has failed to choose the poet as her victim:

> —¿Eres tú? Ya te esperaba ...
> — No eras tú a quien yo buscaba.

The same disdain, the same adjectives, 'fugitiva', 'esquiva', reappear for the last time in 'Muerte de Abel Martín', included in the 1933 edition of *Poesías completas*, with the comment 'Hoy sé que no eres tu quien yo creía'. Time had by then removed all vestiges of hope and anticipation from Machado's vision, either of life or death. The question asked of death in XXIV, whether she was aspiration or fulfilment:

> —¿eres la sed o el agua en mi camino?

had lost all meaning in the presence of *El gran Cero*.

Machado's consciousness of death's ever-present companionship and occasional longing for her bitter kiss cannot be disassociated from that disenchantment with life which we have already seen he shared with others of his Generation. They are united by a common analytical insight reinforced by their scrutiny of philosophy. What this insight revealed was the same in each case so far studied: *la nada*. Sánchez Barbudo asserts that 'una viva experencia de la tuvo él en su juventud, al menos, ya que de ella brotaron sus poemas de *Soledades*'.[18] What in fact we find in the earlier poems, however, is something much less elaborate. The poet 'escucha/a orillas del gran silencio' (LX), but what he hears is the familiar message of scepticism, 'no somos nada' (XIII), and later 'Saber, nada sabemos' (CXXXVI): the same message which the eclipse conveys to Pérez de Ayala's Alberto de Guzmán (see below, p. 190). We are nothing, we know nothing (about what really matters), hence:

> todo es nada. (CXXVI)

More important and original than this sceptical pessimism which forms the common sub-stratum of much thinking about life by the Generation of 1898 is Machado's reaction away from it. Already Bécquer had associated waking dreams with poetic creativeness and Paul Valéry had linked dreaming with the real understanding of things. If the knowledge of the mind led to recognition of its own and life's nothingness, the knowledge of dreams might salvage hope.

So it is that in the above-mentioned introductory poem to 'Galerías', Machado brings together 'el laborar eterno de las doradas abejas del sueño' with what he sees in 'el profundo espejo de mis sueños' (LXI). He is referring here to the possibility, which Unamuno more emphatically insisted upon, that a non-rational or supra-rational faculty exists in man, capable of reflecting the real no less than the rational mind. What led both writers to the postulate was their ultimate hope that the reality thus reflected would be more acceptable and consoling than the one discovered by reason. The worrying aspect of the matter, in each case, is that this is just what happens.

Throughout the earlier poetry of Machado we perceive a consistent alternation between quiet despair and hope. It is tempting to see in the former a product of the poet's sense of himself as an 'oscuro rincón que piensa' (XIII) and in the latter a product of what he called the 'Colmenares de mis sueños' (LX). Nowhere, indeed, is the temptation greater than in the well-known 'Anoche cuando dormía' (LIX), whose three symbols, 'manantial de nueva vida', 'colmena', and 'ardiente sol', culminating in one of Machado's clearest expressions of his longing for religious certitude, are all deliberately associated with dream and comforting illusion. With the particular exception of 'Los sueños malos' practically every reference to dreams and dreaming in Machado's earlier poems occurs in a positive context, XLVIII, LV, and XCIII, in which the poet refers to the moment when he 'began to dream', all suggest that he did so as an instinctive reaction from *hastío* 'el estupor/del alma cuando bosteza' (LVI), which Mairena later explained was the first step on the road, 'camino de perfección', to anguish. A rapid survey shows Machado's dreams associated with an 'alba pura' (XVII), 'quimeras rosadas' (XXII), 'placidez' (XXX), 'el lindo retablo de un sueño riente' (XLII, suppressed after 1903), 'armonía (XLVI), 'abejas' (LXI), 'mágicos cristales' (LXII), 'lino' (LXXIX), 'clara luz' (LXXXIII), and 'juventud nunca vivida' (LXXXV): all more or less soothing and pleasant.

The poems most directly connected with dreaming form a special sub-group in *SGOP*, mainly because of their intimate relationship with memory. Experiences are selected by memory. In passing from perception to the mind's store of recollection (not always conscious recollection) they are, as it were, 'fixed' for ever, solid and changeless amid the flux of things. It is these enduring, comforting, and revealing memories, existing in the mind's *galerías*, that the poet's dreams can evoke. The one commonly regarded as the key-example (LXXIX):

> Y podrás conocerte, recordando
> del pasado soñar turbios lienzos . . .

has led critics to emphasize dreams in Machado's poetry as the path to self-knowledge rather than to happiness or serenity; but such emphasis poses many problems.[19] The immediately proceding poem (LXXXVIII), on the other hand, expresses in a nutshell all that unites Machado's theory of poetry with Bécquer's. Both poets aspired to see poetry as in some way tuned in, through the poet's subconscious responses, to a world of higher truth. In this way poetry comes to be thought of as fragments of truth ('Unas pocas palabras verdaderas') reported by the poet from dreams which are in some sense states of illumination.

Unlike Unamuno, who strove to convince himself of the contrary and thus clung to hope, Machado remained deeply aware that the affirmations of the non-rational mind could be no less contradictory and ultimately unenlightening as those of the conscious intellect. The 'palabras verdaderas' which the poet formulates out of his dreams may be as meaningless as the whistling of wind or the murmur of water, so that in the end 'Nada sabemos de las almas nuestras' (LXXXVII): both inner and outer reality remain bafflingly obscure. It would be natural to conclude, in defiance of those critics who persist in attributing consistently positive significance to dreams in Machado, that what they really constitute is a form of *mentira vital* which he was too self-aware to accept uncritically, but in which he was human enough to find at intervals comfort and poetic inspiration. Such a conclusion would not be incorrect; but it would be incomplete. For a poem of exceptional importance remains to be considered: XXXIV ('Me dijo un alba de la primavera'), which contains the key-line:

Sólo tienen cristal los sueños míos.

In the first two stanzas a voice from within the poet questions him concerning the 'sueño adamantino' which survives in his heart. Does any vestige of hopeful illusion, of the roses and lilies of the past, remain to perfume the brow of its fairy custodian? The poet replies with the line quoted above. Professing ignorance of his real self, as in LXXXVII, he nevertheless does not reject the possibility that death, in breaking the 'cristal cup' (a new metaphor for both life and the clear, hard dream), will find within it the roses and lilies of yesteryear. Zubiría arbitrarily associates this poem with CXXXVI, in which 'cristal' refers to a quite different metaphor, that of the mirror (cf. XLIX), though it too is one which is regularly associated with dreams (LXI, XXXVII). In this way Zubiría is able to base his interpretation on an element, 'azogue': the silvering which causes the mirror to reflect, which does not appear in the poem, and is in fact irrelevant and misleading.[20] The real clues are to be found instead in a poem of exactly the same period, XXVII, with its reference to 'la honda gruta, donde fabrica su cristal mi sueño', and above all in a poem of 1904 exhumed by Dámaso Alonso, 'Luz', which includes the lines: 'Pero, en tu alma de verdad, poeta/sean puro cristal risas y lágrimas'. Clearly Machado was elaborating here an alternative to the dream of joyful illusion and its symbol, that of the bee creating honey.

In two poems written before 1903, XLIII and LXVIII, both closely related in theme to the one now under consideration, the poet also insists that no roses, no happy memories, remain. The poet's 'corazón maduro/de sombra y ciencia' (XLVI) contains no raw materials for the bee to work on, its *galerías* are empty. Instead of secreting honey, joy, his heart now secretes 'cristal': the alternative dream of clear-eyed stoicism, 'orgullosa resignación',[21] which the poet in XLI calls his 'secret'.

II. *Campos de Castilla*

Meantime the first manifestations of a new direction had begun to appear during 1909–10 in the form of poems which were to form part of *Campos de Castilla* (1912). The contrast with Machado's earlier work can be seen in the comments in the 1917 prologue to *Poesías escogidas*. Of *Soledades* he wrote: 'pensaba que el hombre . . . puede también mirando hacia dentro, vislumbrar las ideas cordiales'; while of *Campos de Castilla* he declared: 'pensé que la misión del poeta era inventar nuevos poemas de lo eterno humano, historias animadas que, siendo suyas, viviesen, no obstante, por sí mismas'. The last three words are crucial. His poetry in *Campos de Castilla* was to be, in a sense which was absent from *SGOP*, independent of the poet's inner private reality, however much the end-product remained characteristically 'his own'. Among the main features of the new collection which directly illustrate the change are Machado's treatment of landscape and his response to the figures in it, the rural Spaniards.

The original edition of *Campos de Castilla* was, as had been the case with *Soledades*, very different from the one we now read. It contained, apart from the *romance*-sequence 'La tierra de Alvargonzález' and 'Proverbios y cantares' which at that time consisted of a prologue and 28 short poems, only 15 of the 56 poems now conventionally numbered XCVII–CLII, i.e., XCVII–C; CVII–CXIV; CXXXVI–CXXXVIII; and CLI–CLII.[22] CX ('en tren') originally figured with CXXXVII ('Parábolas', which then consisted only of IV and V). CXXXVI ('Proverbios y cantares') at that time contained as XXIII the *cantar* 'Eran ayer mis dolores' which now figures in *Soledades* as LXXXVI. The remainder, except for two (CXLVI and CXLVII) dating from 1904, were originally published for the most part in a variety of periodicals between 1912 and 1916, and were collected into *Campos de Castilla* as it is now, with slight variations, in the 1917 edition of *Poesías completas*.

When we take a critical look at the earlier poems in *Campos de Castilla*, those of the first edition, we are arrested by the contrast between two of them: cxi, 'Noche de verano', and cix, 'Amanecer de otoño'. In the former we recognize an attempt to present Soria in terms set by the pattern of Machado's older poetry, as a silent, dead town, with its high dark houses and deserted square and even with the 'evónimos' of the earliest *Soledades*. The second, on the other hand, is a straight descriptive *transposition d'art*, a pictorial composition of static elements. There is a similar pictorial quality, rendered a trifle *modernista* in tone by the very un-Machadian lines of the facial description

> y de insólita púrpura manchados
> Los labios que soñara un florentino (cvii)

in 'Fantasía iconográfica'. If we compare this poem with 'A un viejo y distinguido señor' published in *Helios* in 1904, we perceive clear signs of Machado's evolution. In the former, a vague, 'poetic' merely ornamental figure from a more elegant past appears in the artificial, literary surrounding of 'el parque ceniciento/que los poetas aman/para llorar' (lxxxi). In the latter the background seen through the window:

> Montañas de violeta
> y grisientos breñales

is real and Castilian, as befits the symbolism. We are in the presence here, not of elegance, but of 'lo castizo'. The provincial gentleman, alone, pensive, and silent in the sleepy, golden afternoon, is clearly a representative of Spain's *casta histórica*, a traditional élite whose values and role had been overtaken by newer developments, without necessarily losing their validity in the process. In dignified retirement, his hand resting on an old book (an out-of-date culture), the gentleman muses quietly in the shadowy room. Outside, the atmosphere is full of the great old national tradition, religious, literary, and (in the eagle imperial. But in the poem's climax the sun of Castile falls ironically on 'la armadura arrinconada'.

What separates Machado from Unamuno, Baroja, and Ortega, but unites him with Azorín, is the poet's sense, not of the futility and anachronism of the old tradition, but of the pathos associated with its fate. The same sense of Time which made personal memories dear in *SGOP* makes national memories noble and attractive in *Campos de Castilla*. Machado more than any other member of the Generation of 1898 was trapped between a national past, irrevocably receding, which he could not wholly renounce, and a national future he believed in – with effort – but could not yet see. Hence the three basic constituents of the poems in *Campos de Castilla* on the theme of Spain are: consciousness of the past, rejection of the present, and cautious hope for the future.

Machado's arrival in Soria in 1907 seems to have brought him immediate awareness of the past's dual impact, beauty and decay, and to have reinvigorated his patriotism. It stimulated him to write in 1908 his important though neglected article 'Nuestro patriotismo y la Marcha de Cadiz' in its local paper. There is no doubt that whatever else Machado wrote about in *Campos de Castilla* it was the national problem that he regarded as the central theme.[23]

The metre of 'A orillas del Duero', though in couplets (not quatrains) of fourteen syllables, is perhaps intended to evoke distantly the old *cuaderna vía* with all its *castizo* associations. The first 32 lines contain a vision rather than a description of the countryside around Soria in terms (escudo, arnés, ballesta, arquero, barbacana, torre) of its medieval, warlike past, so closely associated with El Cid. But, just as in 'Fantasía iconográfica' the armour was 'arrinconada', so here it is seen as 'harapos esparcidos', a mere memory of a heroic past that time has shattered, like Soria's castle, which Machado describes with a cruel and pathetic *encabalgamiento*:

> Soria . . .
> con su castillo guerrero
> arruinado . . . (xiii)

All that the flux of time has left behind are nibbling sheep, bulls kneeling in ruminative ease, and inhabitants reduced to diminutive insignificant passers-by whose movement does not even break the lonely silence of these once historic roads. The second half of the poem applies the contrast to the present, directly and even stridently, in order to emphasize the collapse of Imperial Spain into what Machado saw before him. The whole section is an amplification of the adjectives in the key-line:

> Castilla miserable ayer dominadora.

Again what we notice, in contra-distinction to Ganivet and Unamuno, is the revival in Machado of plain nostalgia for Spain's historic greatness, for 'capitanes', 'indianos', and 'soldados'. Meanwhile the peasants (according to Don Miguel the guardians of her 'intrahistoric values') are perceived, no less unrealistically perhaps, as 'humildes ganapanes', and 'atónitos palurdos sin danzas ni canciones'. The poem ends on an ambiguous note of gathering darkness and desolation combined with a certain serene pleasure in the surroundings, which consolidates the strong dualism which underlies its whole structure.

This is, then, one of the earliest of Machado's ostentatiously *noventayochista* poems. Other poems reveal that his view of the rural common people was at this time ambivalent. In 'Pascua de Resurrección', published a year earlier, they had been referred to (in lines suppressed from the 1912 version) as

> fantasmas de los fuertos días,
> nobles palurdos que pisáis la estepa. (CXII)

Earlier still, in *SGOP*, he had presented a folksy picture of

> gentes que danzan o juegan,
> cuando pueden, y laboran
> sus cuatro palmos de tierra
> ... buenas gentes que viven
> laboran, pasan y sueñan. (II)

A less hopeful reality seems to have met his eye in Soria at first. 'Desde estos yermos se ve panorámicamente la barbarie española y aterra', he wrote to Juan Ramón Jiménez.[24] The three verbs of the last-quoted poem re-echo ironically behind the three of 'Por tierras de España':

> El hombre de estos campos ...
> ... en páramos malditos trabaja, sufre y yerra. (XCIX)

In the poem, in 'Un criminal', and above all in the long narrative *romance* 'La tierra de Alvargonzález', Machado expressed his repulsion at the moral degradation, animal cruelty, and abject covetousness which are the other face of peasant life from that which Fernán Caballero, Trueba, Pereda, Gabriel y Galán, and a host of *costumbristas* had idealized. Cain and the Centaur, the old Greek symbol of savagery, are the mythical archetypes of this 'pueblo, carne de horca'. Both A. de Albornoz and Sister Katherine Elaine[25] tend to play down Machado's initially bitter vision of the 'hombre de la tierra', which was originally shared, as Laín Entralgo has demonstrated, by others of the Generation. They emphasize the coexistence in Machado's mind of the alternative vision of

> gentes del alto llano numantino
> que a Dios guardáis como cristianas viejas (CXIII)

and of

> labriegos con talante de señores (CXLIII)

which was to produce the eulogies of the people in Machado's later prose and the proud reference in one of the last sonnets, written in Valencia in 1937, to

> la estirpe redentora
> que muele el fruto de los olivares
> y ayuna y labra, siembra y canta y llora
> ('Poesías de la guerra')

its verbs triumphantly completing the pattern established in II and XCIX.

The fact is that of all the writers of the '98 only Baroja had the honesty to remain consistently true to the group's early vision of the Spanish people. Of the others, Azorín and Machado in particular were unable to resist the temptation to take refuge in idealization. They wished to believe, as Ganivet, Unamuno, and Maeztu did, in a *moral* resurgence of Spain, preceding and overshadowing any economic or social regeneration. They could not foresee that such regeneration as was to take place, was to be largely spearheaded by a new, expanding, work-orientated middle class, supported by foreign investment and technical expertise, under the dominance of a military and oligarchic leadership. Thus they were forced to look for a different source of national improvement and found it situated, in the conveniently indefinite future, with the people. The essential poem of this mystique of a people regenerating itself by spiritual effort is 'El Dios íbero', originally published in 1913 and included in *Campos de Castilla* four years later. By this time, it is clear, Machado had revised his opinion of the rural common people and transferred his opposition to the squirearchy of provincial *señoritos*. His attack on this inert, parasitic, selfishly traditionalist social group in 'Llanto por la muerte Don Guido' and 'Del pasado efímero' unites him with the Baroja of Part V, chapter 6 of *El árbol de la ciencia* ('Tipos de casino').

Machado's bitter sense of belonging to a once great nation, now degenerated into 'un pueblo de arrieros/lechuzos y tahures y logreros', profoundly influenced his vision of its physical reality. There are relatively few pure descriptive poems, in which nature appears for its own sake, in *Campos de Castilla*. The countryside of Castile and Andalusia was for Machado, as that of Castile and the Basque provinces was for Unamuno, almost always 'tierra de alma', just as the unlocalized countryside had been in 'Yo voy soñando caminos de la tarde'. Instinctively he finds in it reflections and symbols of the state of Spain. 'Visionaria y soñolienta', 'mística y guerrera', the austere grandeur of its 'llanuras bélicas y páramos de asceta' continues to concretize the old national traditions. But this unchanging reminder of the past is not allowed to obscure the present. Thus the madman of 'Un loco' (CVI) who, Herrero suggests,[26] represents 'the hero of the Generation of '98, the idealist reduced to madness by the brutality, sterility and common-sense foolishness of a cursed country', wanders through a barren, ruined countryside of 'álamos marchitos' 'sombríos estepares', and 'ruinas de viejos encinares'. These last are especially significant since they appear in 'Las encinas' (CIII) as symbols of Spanish 'humildad y fortalez'. Amid this desolate countryside stand the decrepit towns: Soria, whose pitted walls,

blackened houses, and sordid alleys are the urban equivalent of the
'tierra/estéril y raída' of 'Un loco'; Baeza, 'destartalado y sombrío'
(CXXVIII); above all Torre de Pero Gil: 'triste burgo de España'
(CXXIII). The deliberate contrast between the heroic past and the
squalid present which Machado makes in his description of this
place:

> Allá, el castillo heróico.
> En la plaza mendigos y chicuelos:
> Una orgía de harapos. . . .

repeats more pointedly the symbolism of 'El hospicio' (C):

> entre los dos torreones
> de antigua fortaleza, el sórdido edifico.

It is rammed home by the following lines, which refer to Spain's
other great tradition apart from heroism: piety, symbolized by the
convent:

> ¡ Amurallada
> piedad, erguida en ese basurero!

The repeated question ' ¿qué guarda dentro?' reiterates the Generation of 1898's collective preoccupation not so much with religious
values as such, but with the spiritual state of Spain. When Machado
in the first section of 'Los olivos' wrote 'Venga Dios a los hogares/y
a las almas de esta tierra', and when in 'En tren' (CX), this free-
thinking, anti-clerical *masón*, who penned (and later suppressed)
those lines to Azorín which told of his 'asco de las juntas apostólicas/y
las damas católicas . . . y de esa clerigalla vocinglera', painted his
delicious picture of a nun, he did not have in mind a Catholic revival. As the last stanza of 'El Dios íbero' proclaims, what Machado
longed for was a return to authentic spiritual values, without which
(even Baroja recognized) Spain could not be regarded as fully
regenerate.

It is clear that Machado's hope of national resurgence rested on
his confidence, revealed in 'El mañana efímero' and 'Desde mi
rincón', that, after 'un mañana/vacío y ¡por ventura! pasajero', a
younger generation – which he later seems to have identified with
that of the Republic – would accede to power. His own stand in
defence of the Republic reveals that he had faith in left-of-centre
government, preferably moderate and lay-orientated. For the rest,
like his companions, he is vague; and what he does imply is unrealistic, as befits a pupil of Giner's *Institución*. His references in
the poem on Giner (CXXXIX) to 'labores', 'el sol de los talleres', and
'yunques', together with his picture in 'Los olivos' of well-tilled
olive groves teaching the lesson that 'el hombre es para el suelo',
suggest an awareness of the need for practical *labores*, as well as
esperanzas, which is depressingly absent from the corporate mentality

of the Generation when it is looked at objectively. But the naïve allusions in 'España en paz' to 'avaros mercaderes' and to

el divino altar de la pobreza (CLXV)

attest the old familiar suspicion of material progress which stems from a refusal to acknowledge the real problem and its order of priorities. It follows that Blanco Aguinaga's attempt to dissociate Machado from the others of the Generation in this respect ignores some of the evidence.

Even when Machado is not exploring the countryside for symbolic or metaphorical elements, it normally remains charged with emotion. Only very rarely is it prettified or lyricized, as when the poplars by the Duero are described as

liras
del viento perfumado en primavera. (CXIII)

More commonly Machado alternates a discreetly humanized vision of the countryside with a mythicized one, constructed from a narrow range of elements and colours. Characteristic of the former is the repeated comparison of the appearance of the ground itself, and the clothing of those who till it:

Buenos aldeanos
que visten parda estameña.   (CIII)

Campo amarillento
como fosco sayal de campesina,
pradera de velludo polvoriento.   (CII)

(tierras) ... como retazos de estameñas pardas. (CXIII)

(sementeras) ... cual sayos cenicientos.   (CXVI)

pastos) ... como raído terciopelo.   (CXXXIV)

while, in turn, shepherds are described as 'de color de los caminos' (CLXIII). Emotionally charged adjectives, too, underline this closeness of man and nature, in contradistinction to 'el tedio urbano': 'noble', 'varonil', 'humilde', 'triste', 'fuerte', 'ingrata', 'esquelética', 'guerrera'. The culmination of the whole process is, of course, the presentation not just of elements in nature (the *encina* is the typical instance) as symbolic, but of all nature as possessing 'alma', and as 'dreaming'. A reassuring answer to Machado's anguished question

Castilla ... ¿Espera, duerme o sueña? (XCVIII)

is implicit in this symbiosis of countryside and inhabitant. The dream towards which the madman wanders in CVI is safe within the soul of Castile.

Where the nature-description is direct accumulation of visual elements, we perceive a deliberate repetitiveness emphasizing the harshness of the landscape. This is not the 'wide' Castile of Unamuno;

still less is it the *meseta* in springtime which invited the essayist to roll in its lush greenness. It is the 'high' Castile, of mountain, not plain, whose predominant colours: carmín y acero, cárdeno, violeta, plomizo, plateado, de ceniza, are those of rock and mountain; whose plants are 'hierbas montaraces', or at best flowering hawthorn, violets, and tiny daisies; whose birds are birds of prey. All the softer elements of highland scenery, flora and fauna, are eliminated in favour of a single quasi-mythical vision: that of warrior-like ascetic dignity, the background to the dream of 'Una España implacable y redentora' in which 'sueño' would become 'idea'.

The best-known additions to the 1912 *Campos de Castilla* are not those poems, some of which have been alluded to, that continue the pattern of preoccupation with Spain, but those which reflect the poet's anguish at the loss of his wife and his bitter nostalgia for their life together. Three months before Leonor died, he wrote 'A un olmo seco'. In a poem published nine years earlier, he had used the symbolism of the stricken tree:

> Y ese árbol roto en el camino blanco
> hace llorar de lástima.
> Dos ramas en el tronco herido, y una
> hoja marchita y negra en cada rama (LXXX)

in contrast to 'los álamos de oro, lejos', with gold as usual in its role as the colour of joyfulness or promise. Here the contrasting elements of the earlier poem are combined into one symbolic tree. Now, however, it is 'firmemente anclado en un trozo de lo real' ('Reflexiones sobre la lírica'), not in an invented landscape, but in a real one, 'la colina/que lame el Duero', enriched with the dual associations Castile and Leonor, which are both present in the ending. Terry points out that 'temporalidad' is clearly illustrated here by the way in which the tree is seen in relation to past, present, and future.[27] But this does not submerge the poem's spatial dimension. The first fourteen lines chiefly develop the opening adjective, 'viejo'. They do so partly by cumulative re-emphasis, in the words: 'hendido', 'podrido', and 'carcomido'. But mainly they do so via contrast. There is a preliminary contrast of colours: the 'musgo amarillento', 'corteza blanquecina', and 'tronco polvoriento', indicating age, heavily offset the green of the sparse new leaves. This contrast introduces the more extended and emotionally vibrant contrast between the poplars, the trees Machado most associated with love, soon to be thronged with nightingales, and the old elm inhabited only by spiders and destructive ants. This is also a temporal contrast, emphasized as ever by the verb-forms: 'será' as against 'va trepando', a future of hope set against a present of decay. Finally, delicately humanizing the description, the word 'entrañas', with its emotive connotation, is applied to the elm's rotting interior.

The apostrophe which follows is structured around the repeated temporal adverb 'antes que'. Each following phrase suggests a possible fate for the elm, arranged in descending order of meaningfulness until in line 24:

> antes que el río hasta la mar te impuje

the elm shares the fate of man and is swallowed up in the sea just as he is engulfed after death in an empty eternity. The climax establishes the link between the poet and the tree, hinted at in the previous lines. He, as always, longs to salvage something from Time's destruction and to confer on it at least the permanence granted by poetry. Here what is saved is the beauty of the elm's few green leaves. At the same time they symbolize his own hope. That hope, in May 1912, was probably for Leonor's recovery: but perhaps it cannot be wholly divorced from hope for Spain and for the human condition.

Leonor's death was described in CXXIII with typical restraint; in sixteen lines there are only six adjectives and but one point of explicit emotion: the ¡Ay! which begins the penultimate line. But this restraint is broken in the famous quatrain:

> Señor, ya me arrancaste lo que yo más quería.
> Oye otra vez, Dios mío, mi corazón clamar.
> Tu voluntad se hizo, Señor, contra la mía.
> Señor, ya estamos solos mi corazón y el mar. (CXIX)

Four starkly juxtaposed sentences are held together by the accusing vocatives: 'Señor ... Dios mío ... Señor ... Señor'. Each alexandrine has its own different rhythm, the commas marking the irregular caesuras. In the first line the accents falling on the same sound:

> Señor, ya me arrancaste lo que yo más quería

link the main emotive words. Line 2 is, as it were, encapsulated between the two related verbs 'oye' and 'clamar', one at each end, the latter being one of Machado's very rare uses of a verb of loud sound in the climatic final position. The third line develops most explicitly the Tu/yo contrast which gives the first three lines both their superb equilibrium and at the same time expresses Machado's proud disconformity. The first part of each relates to God ('arrancaste ... Oye ... Tu voluntad'), the second to the poet ('yo más quería ... mi corazón ... contra la mía'). The last line, returning to the opening formula, 'Señor, ya ...', balances the first verb, 'arrancaste', with its consequences. The line refers, not to the poet's grief alone, his heart's anguish, nor even to the solitude which accompanies his grief. It is something more profound than either, indicated by the concluding symbol: 'el mar'. The poet is left, alone and stricken, to face death.

The return of spring in April 1913, nine months after Leonor's death, produced the loveliest poem of Machado's nostalgia for their love: 'A José María Palacio' (CXXVI).[28] Like so many of his others, it illustrates his frequent avoidance of metaphor. Its 32 lines do not contain a single example of figurative language. They depend for their effect on the balance Machado achieves between elements of visual beauty ('hojas nuevas', 'Moncayo blanca y rosa ... tan bella', 'zarzas florecidas', 'blancas margaritas', 'ciruelos', 'violetas', and the climactic word 'ruiseñores') and elements of remembered reality ('chopos', 'viejos olmos', 'camino', 'estepa', 'acacias desnudas', 'grises peñas', 'cigueñas', 'trigales verdes', 'mulas pardas', 'labriegos', 'furtivos cazadores'). In this way the body of the poem comes to be an evocation of early spring in Soria which combines lyrical emotion and simple observation. Mere accumulation of elements of beauty would have produced only a prettified, nostalgic picture. As it is, the alternation of the beautiful and the real, the first expressed in questions and exclamations, the second in reflections and statements, stimulates a dual response in the reader which enhances the poem's final impact. The features of remembered observation which have no emotional significance hold the poem close to an everyday reality which Leonor's death has not changed. Alongside the nostalgia there is an additional source of pathos: spring, with its renewal of the earth, its work, and its pleasure, while poignantly affecting the bereaved poet, remains itself unaffected. There is no illusion of Nature's reflecting his grief to reduce the poem to sentimentality. It closes with the offering of spring flowers, white lilies of hope and roses of passion, to Leonor's grave.

III. LATER POETRY AND PROSE

In 'A Xavier Valcarce' (CXLI) Machado alluded directly to the drying-up of his lyrical talent and to his preoccupation with 'el enigma grave', the enigma of existence which was the real problem for the Generation of 1898. In June 1932 he referred to philosophy as 'una afición de toda mi vida'.[29] The relevance of these remarks becomes plain as we examine the last phase of his work. Early in 1924 he published *Nuevas canciones*, to which in 1928 he added a few more poems as well as the prose and verse of the 'Cancionero apócrifo', augmenting these in turn in later editions. Reading them we can see that in later life Machado often seemed to be trying consciously to write poetry which differed from the bulk of what he had written before. A sign of this is that the alexandrine – Machado's metre in some of his most obviously *noventayochista* poems – disappears. The *copla*-form becomes predominant, and sonnets (not a feature of his earlier work) appear. The quest is for even greater 'essentiality': the reduction of poems literally to 'unas pocas palabras verdaderas'. It was already recognizable in the first set of 'Proverbios y cantares' in *Campos de Castilla*. *Nuevas canciones* contains a second set, to which can be added 'De mi cartera', whose subtitle 'Apuntes de 1902' underlines how long Machado had been bending his efforts in this direction. LXXX:

> Concepto mondo y lirondo
> suele ser cáscara hueca;
> puede ser caldera al rojo

is an illustrative example. In 'Reflexiones sobre la lírica' he had written 'Las imágenes específicamente líricas son aquellas que contienen intuiciones'. In this tiny poem he reiterates the idea through the contrast of 'cáscara hueca' (image without intuition) and 'caldera al rojo' (image+intuition). Since 'Se crea por intuiciones, pero se expresa lo creado por conceptos',[30] the result is two juxtaposed concepts, but the metaphor conveys the difference. The form of the poem is designed to appeal to the memory by cunning repetition: the '*on*' sound of 'C*on*cepto m*on*do y lir*on*do; the alliteration linking 'concepto', 'cáscara', and 'caldera'; and especially the repetition of the diphthong in 's*ue*le', 'h*ue*ca', and 'p*ue*de'. While at the end of line 2 we hear the hollow sound of the empty shell, the contrast 'suele ser'/'puede ser', slight in terms of sound, great in terms of meaning, underlines the difference, at once subtle and substantial, between poetry of logic and poetry of intuition.

The often quoted 'Hoy es siempre todavía' reduces to four words Machado's vision of permanent duration: the confluence of past and future in an ever-changing continuous present. Number XCIII of the series:

> ¿Cuál es la verdad? ¿El río
> que fluye y pasa
> donde el barco y el barquero
> son también ondas del agua?
> ¿O este soñar del marino
> siempre con ribera y ancla?

similarly condenses into its three questions the essence of Machado's spiritual position: his consciousness that each human life is no more than a particle of time in an aimless onward flow, and his longing to cast anchor in some time-defying transcendence. The anchor-symbol, which had recurred at intervals since CXXV of *Campos de Castilla*, is complemented by the references to church-bells at the waking hour ('Proverbios y cantares': LXXXII; 'Consejos, coplas, apuntes': XII), perhaps a reminiscence of Darío's 'La dulzura del ángelus', and may suggest a slight recrudescence of hope in an afterlife. With these two hopeful symbols goes the desire to reject the desolate conclusions of the conscious mind:

> Confiamos
> en que no será verdad
> nada de lo que pensamos.
>
> ('Abel Martín')

The other important group of 'Proverbios y cantares' along with 'De mi cartera' refers to poetry, either repeating Machado's own views:

> Despertad, cantores:
> acaben los ecos,
> despierten las voces. (N° XXIX)

(authenticity, not imitation)

> No es el yo fundamental
> eso que busca el poeta
> sino el tu esencial. (N° XXXVI)

(communication, not subjectivity)

> Abejas, cantores
> no a la miel, sino a las flores,

(poetry is to be derived from life, not from art), or attacking the *neobarroquismo*, aristocratic poses, and experimentalism in diction of his younger contemporaries:

> ... no aséis lo que está cocido (N° XXII)
> ... no busquéis disonancias (N° XXX)
>
> Mas no te importe si rueda
> y pasa de mano en mano:
> del oro se hace moneda (N° LXXII)
>
> El tono lo da la lengua,
> ni más alto ni más bajo. (N° LXXVI)

Unfortunately not all these fragments achieve a happy combination of technical skill and epigrammatic synthesis of thought. Even if thought of as pure intuitions, they tend to lack that emotional reference which Machado himself recognized as essential to poetic communication, or what he called 'intersubjetividad'.

Related to this reflective poetry is 'Olivo del camino'. A solitary, untended olive-tree stands apart 'junto a la fuente ... al borde del camino'. These two familiar symbols, the fountain and the road, link it at once to Machado himself and his most persistent preoccupations. Its fruit is not destined for common consumption, its dark shade is not sacrificed to utility as in the harvested olive-tree. But with this lonely tree are associated wisdom ('el buho insomne de la sabia Atena') and the fertility of the earth (the reference to Demeter). Its wood contains promise of a divine fire (light, hope, enthusiasm) in the hearths and more especially in the hearts of men. In this poem, Machado is expressing the hope that his work may help to unite Spain's mental and physical energies.

A few later poems, including 'Iris de la noche', 'Parergon', 'En tren', and part of 'Los sueños dialogados', continue the themes of nostalgia for Leonor and Soria together with the search for spiritual comfort. These are the most popular and accessible part of his work at this time. But the essential love-poetry of *Nuevas canciones*: 'Glosando a Ronsard', the last two sonnets of 'Los sueños dialogados', and the two sets of 'Canciones a Guiomar' express a lucid vision of a love which is deeply corroded by that belief in the impossibility of breaking through the barriers to 'otherness' which is insistently repeated by Machado's mouthpiece, Abel Martín. 'Se canta lo que se pierde', Machado wrote to Guiomar. What he had lost by this time was not only Leonor, but also his confidence in love's power to overcome isolation. What he longed for now was to lose himself and his desolate insight completely in the 'otherness' of the beloved. While momentarily his longing seems to be fulfilled in the dream-garden of CLXXIV where lion and gazelle (he and Guiomar) slake their thirst together and seem to have found a ray of hope, the two images chosen – animals of completely different species, a tiny flash of light in the darkness – reveal Machado's sense of love's insufficiency.

Finally, a unique place in his poetry is occupied by his last major poem, 'Recuerdos de sueño, fiebre y duermivela', which is completely unlike any of his others. Dramatically developing the stream-of-consciousness manner he had used in 'Poema de un día', Machado constructs an allegorical nightmare of death on the gallows and descent into hell. No accepted interpretation of it has yet been evolved.[31] Sections I–V inclusive are linked together by the contrast *dormir/despertar*, resolved in the last line of V:

> Duerme. ¡Alegría! ¡Alegría!

Sections IX–XII contain the descent into hell. It is not difficult to perceive in the opening group of sections an allegory of death in terms of an arbitrary execution. The victim, man, is innocent; fate is the hangman; the church is in attendance, intent on its own benefit. The insistent

> Masón, masón, despierta

seems to represent the call of the poet's conscious mind to stand by his rationalistic, agnostic principles to the bitter end, rejecting comforting, eleventh-hour pseudo-clarifications of the human condition. A momentary recollection of Leonor brings no comfort either.

The central sections are the most difficult. The poet returns to the olive-tree symbol of himself used in CLIII to contrast his *canto* 'de un instante' with the eternal silent song of the universe. The hell-sequence is an allegory of life. It is a *calle larga* at the end of which death spins her thread, memory gives way to forgetfulness; love to disillusionment. Dominating all is the corpse of Leonor:

Cuajadita con el frío
se quedó en la madrugada
... Amor siempre se hiela.

The basic idea behind the presentation of life as hell is that love in all its forms is merely part of the torment. The poem ends with the poet's voices still contending. One suggests prayer, the other rational inquiry. Neither has the clue to the enigma of life: the *madeja* remains tangled.

Nor do Machado's writings on being and reality unravel the thread very much. Attributed to two invented figures, Abel Martín and Juan de Mairena, *De un cancionero apócrifo* and *Juan de Mairena* belong, like Baudelaire's intimate jottings and Leopardi's *Zibaldone*, to a type of work which offers more clues – sometimes baffling ones – to the poet's outlook than systematic explanations. The most interesting parts are those which expound Machado's poetic theory, and his poetry criticism, though most of what is said develops views expressed elsewhere in his work. Otherwise the main theme is the relationship between poetry and philosophy. Machado was intuitively convinced of the reality both of the inner and outer world which his poems deal with. 'Lo poético es ver', he insists in *Mairena* xv.[32] For him, as for Unamuno, rational analytic thought offered no certain answer to the problem of recognizing the really real. Rational thought, he believed, is 'homogeneizador', that is to say, obsessed with seeking out an all-embracing principle of unity: 'un algo que lo explique todo' (xxi, 449). In contrast, poetic thought according to Machado, is essentially 'heterogeneizador': 'el mundo visto, al fin, de derecho' (iv, 362). Poetic thought is a hook which, instead of trying to catch itself, to resolve the insoluble, catches 'pescados vivos' (ix, 380). Provided always that it is not poetry of mere intellection, it can eternalize intuitions of the really real. But if, as a poet, Machado had confidence in poetry as 'un acto vidente, de afirmación de una realidad absoluta', as a man, he felt the need for a structure of philosophical supports, and in any case believed that a poet has the duty to explain his metaphysics. The difficulty connected with his attempt to do this in the 'Abel Martín', 'La metafísica de Juan de Mairena', and the *Mairena* itself, is that what they express combines coherent rational analysis, the conclusions of which are always negative, and Machado's innermost 'poetic' convictions, which are always positive.

The main topics in these writings are: being and nothingness, individual existence and otherness, and God. Abel Martín equates being with *substancia* and hence, as in modern physics, with energy, which reveals itself universally as consciousness. His central idea is that of a constantly evolving consciousness, which cannot be thought of conceptually, but only intuited, as the really real. Everything else is mere appearance. The problems posed by this reduction of all things to a single (pantheistic) unity concern movement, physical extension, the limits of our knowledge of the real, and the relationship between our individual consciousness and universal consciousness. The paradox of the first problem, that what perpetually changes cannot be said to move, is simply enunciated. Concerning the objective existence of the physical world, Abel Martín asserts categorically that it is 'una realidad firme e indestructible', even though the individual consciousness may not possess objective knowledge of it. The contradiction here is left unresolved.

In the matter of knowledge Machado's rational position was plainly one of total scepticism. But he was saved by his confidence in 'poetic' intuition. The reality which reason disintegrates is reconstructed by poetry. But a problem of expressing this process is that concepts are too rigid to convey intuitions. Moreover, if A is never A for two minutes together, if consciousness is flux, then the static forms of language (especially in prose) cannot adequately transmit meaning. There is no 'lógica temporal'. Hence the caution with which we must treat these writings. This is especially the case when we come to Machado's description of the ultimate. His vision of it is at first sight pantheistic, as Mairena recognizes (XXXIX, 484). The really real is defined as 'el ser que todo lo es al serse a sí mismo',[33] also hinted at in the phrase 'una autoconciencia integral del universo entero'.[34] But no sooner is his view thus defined than Machado affirms the existence of certain undefined 'essences' of which being is itself composed, and which are more accessible to the emotions than to the mind.[35] The contradictory feature of them is that they are at once 'lo absoluto real que pertenece al sujeto' and that they aspire constantly to 'otherness'.

Machado is in fact trapped between his two contradictory premises: the diversity of being and the existence of a single monad. For if universal consciousness exists and if individual consciousness is no more than a reflection of it (i.e., if there is no plurality of monads), it is hard to see how there can be anything outside itself for consciousness to aspire to. Actually Machado comes down firmly in the end on the side of the diversity of being. In a late article, 'Sobre una lírica comunista que pudiera venir de Rusia',[36] he even admitted the possibility of 'una realidad espiritual, transcendente a las almas individuales, en la cual éstas pudieran comulgar' and hence of a poetry of 'comunión cordial entre los hombres' related to it. In a nutshell, while the abstract single-monad theory of being appealed to Machado intellectually, it precluded an acceptable theory of the self. This was its downfall; for Machado's thought, especially in relation to poetry, can never be divorced from the self, its feelings and intuitions. His intuition of the self is that of 'una mónada sin puertas ni ventanas' existing in irremediable isolation (*Mairena* 1, 354). Yet its fundamental feature is love, defined as 'la sed metafísica de lo esencialmente otro':[37] a desperate, but essentially vain, attempt to cross the frontier of the self 'hacia lo otro inasequible'.[38] Ultimately this 'other' is God.

Looked at like this, the essence of the self is its impossible quest for faith. From this futile but continuous struggle of the spirit ideas are born: 'Hijas del amor y en cierto modo del gran fracaso del amor'.[39] Their essential revelation is the negativity of all rational cognitive effort in regard to transcendence: 'Ni Dios está en el mundo, ni la verdad en la conciencia del hombre'.[40] But while poetry, which Abel Martín defines as 'aspiración a la conciencia integral', is also 'hija gran fracaso del amor',[41] its vision, as we know, is different from that of the intellect. Abel Martín postulates two distinct phases in the process which leads 'De lo un a lo otro' (i.e., from anguished scepticism and subjectivity to 'conciencia integral' and objectivity). The first is that of solitude and despair associated with rational ideas. The second is that of 'serse en plena y fecunda intimidad', of serene spiritual insight.[42] The latter can only be reached through the former. Hence Machado's apparently paradoxical doctrine of 'la nada' and God as its creator. Man's rational mind requires the concept of 'la nada' in order to distinguish being from it, just as white chalk needs a blackboard on which to be seen. 'La nada' is thus an emanation of being ('un milagro del ser') in order to clarify its own nature.[43] Contrariwise, 'el milagro del no ser' which Machado mentions in the poem 'Al gran Cero', refers to the poet's vision, which intuits in, or creates out of, the various 'reveses del ser', the reality of being. Thus 'Al gran Cero' is above all a poem on the theme of man's abstract reason. It calls on man to face courageously the 'huevo universal vacío' with which his mind presents him. For as the companion poem 'El gran pleno' confirms, at a subsequent stage he will be rewarded with a 'lógica divina' (of which poetry is the guardian, which will reveal all as harmony. As this point thought 'torna a ver', but now positively, and 'borra las formas del cero'.

Stripped of verbiage (especially that of certain critics), then, Machado's thought in his late prose amounts really to little more than a re-affirmation of the power of poetic intuition to overleap the gulf created by that 'escepticismo científico' which Ganivet had identified as the great characteristic of his generation.

Machado's place in the history of Spanish poetry can be established by reference both to tradition and to innovation. Serrano Poncela and Vivanco especially[44] have underlined his close links with earlier poets, but the meaning of those links was perhaps most forcibly expressed by Juan Ramón Jiménez in an untitled article in

El Sol of 24 May 1936. 'Después de Miguel de Unamuno y de Rubén Darío', is where Jiménez places him chronologically 'y antes de ningún otro, pues en él comienza, sin duda alguna y de qué modo tan sin modo, aquella fusión'. The fusion, that is to say, of existential preoccupation and artistic form, the achievement of a balance between the two, which had tended to escape Unamuno and Darío. Although a simplification, Jiménez's view is true in essence. To it must be added Machado's own recognition that he was instrumental in shaping the course of later Spanish poetry away from the nineteenth century's reliance on the unsophisticated self-identification of the reader with the content of poetry. This is of major importance, not least because, in contrast to the work of later poets who carried the process of detachment from crude 'anecdote' further, Machado's poetry happily remained 'cosa cordial'. His most important single technical contribution, as Busoño and Segre have shown, was to the renovation of symbolism. This, too, is characteristic. For in the discovery of symbols, more than in any other branch of poetic innovation, there is the possibility of fusing creative imagination and experience. The inventiveness of Machado's successors was to be in marked contrast.

Had Unamuno not turned to poetry, Machado's place as the poet of the Generation of 1898 would have been indisputable. As it is, though he wrote less poetry than Don Miguel, and less about Spain, it is his poetry in *Campos de Castilla* that is usually remembered and quoted in illustration of the Generation's outlook. His vision of the Spanish countryside complements that of Unamuno and Azorín in their essays. His rejection of 'la España de charanga y pandereta' in favour of 'la España del cincel y la maza', represented by the younger generation, most memorably synthesizes the disgust with the present and hope for the future characteristic of all the group. His disappointment with the Generation's failure in 'Una España joven' is, as we shall see in the last chapter, also typical.

But what even more than his response to the national situation makes Machado a central figure of the Generation of 1898 is his scepticism, tempered by longing for self-transcendence, his anguish (muted though it was), his deeply serious interest in philosophy, and perhaps most of all his unshakeable attachment to the ethical imperative as the last surviving existential support. These are part of the pattern we have attempted to trace in other parts of this book. The famous 'Retrato' which opens *Campos de Castilla*, with its emphasis first on the poet's moral stance:

> Soy en el buen sentido de la palabra bueno

and only thereafter on his artistic *credo* exemplifies the Generation of 1898's characteristic order of priorities: human qualities come before artistic expression. This is ultimately the case with Machado. The unchanging popularity of his poetry rests essentially on its direct human appeal.

NOTES

1. He was already a Freemason, with all that it implied in Spain at the time. A. J. McVan, *Antonio Machado* (New York, 1959), 63.
2. See, e.g., Dámaso Alonso, *Poetas españoles contemporáneos* (Madrid, 1952); J. Ángeles, 'Soledades primeras de Antonio Machado', in *Homenaje a S. H. Eoff* (Madrid, 1970); E. Carilla, 'Antonio Machado y Rubén Darío', *Cuadernos del Sur* (Bahía Blanca), IX (1971), 150–64; R. Ferreres's introduction to his edition of *Soledades* (Madrid, 1969); and especially G. Ribbans, *Niebla y soledad*.
3. Cited Ribbans, *Niebla y soledad*, 211.
4. ibid., 207, 301.
5. In *Obras*, ed. A. de Albornoz and G. de Torre (Buenos Aires, 1964), 762–4. Subsequent references are to this edition.
6. 'Notas sobre la poesía' (*Obras*, 709–10).
7. ibid. (*Obras*, 714).
8. ' "Arte poética" de Juan de Mairena' (*Obras*, 315).
9. 'Reflexiones sobre la lírica' (*Obras*, 823).
10. 'Para el estudio de la literatura española' (*Obras*, 713).
11. See in this connection the remarks of G. Caravaggi in *I paesaggi emotivi di Antonio Machado* (Bologna, 1969), 48–50 and the interesting article by J. Collantes de Terán, 'Las ciudades muertas de Antonio Machado', *Archivo Hispalense*, XLVII (1968), 1–11.
12. Juan Villegas, 'El tema del tiempo en un poema de Antonio Machado', *Hisp*, XLVIII (1965), 442–51.
13. See the remarks on this poem by F. Ayala in 'Un poema y la poesía de Antonio Machado', *La Torre* (Puerto Rico), XII (1964), nos. 45/6, 313–319.
14. One is reminded of the last part of Pascoli's famous line from 'I due fanciulli' (*Primi poemetti*): 'La morte con la sua lampada accesa'. Pascoli also uses the symbol of white linen which we find in Machado. Another example of similar acoustical effect is seen in XIII: 'pasaba el agua rizada bajo los ojos del puente'. We 'hear' the change in the colour of the water in the shift from 'a's to 'o's.
15. See the arguments of A. de Albornoz in *La presencia de Unamuno en Antonio Machado* (Madrid, 1968), Part III, ch. 1, 'El Dios de Antonio Machado', and her review there of other critics' opinions.
16. Article of 1912 in *El Porvenir Castellano*, cited Ribbans, *Niebla y soledad*, 305.
17. See J. L. Cano, *De Machado a Bousoño* (Madrid, 1955), 33–5; J. Marías, 'Antonio Machado y su interpretación de las cosas' *CHA*, 11/12 (1949), 307–21; Ribbans, *Niebla y soledad*, 155, 191; and M. Fernández Alonso, *Una visión de la muerte en la española* (Madrid, 1971), 238–73.
18. A. Sánchez Barbudo, *Los poemas de Antonio Machado* (Barcelona, 1967), 289.
19. Cf. R. Gullón, *Las secretas galerías de Antonio Machado* (Madrid, 1958), 46, 54–5, and S. Serrano Poncela, *Antonio Machado, su mundo y su obra* (Buenos Aires, 1954), 125–8.
20. R. Zubiría, *La poesía de Antonio Machado* (3rd ed., Madrid, 1966), 27–8. Concha Zardoya, *Poesía española contemporánea* (Madrid, 1961), 192–193 and A. Terry, *Campos de Castilla. A Critical Guide* (London, 1973), 80, follow Zubiría and overlook 'Luz'. See also the important article by F. Ruiz Ramón, 'En torno al sentido de "El espejo de los sueños" en la poesía de Machado', *RL*, XXII (1962), 74–83.

21. Serrano Poncela, op. cit., 101.

22. Hence Marta Rodríguez is guilty of a careless error in regarding CXIII (part viii) as reflecting Machado's memories of Leonor after her death (*El intimismo en Antonio Machado*, Madrid, 1971, 67–8).

23. Cf. his remarks in letters to Juan Ramón Jiménez in R. Gullón, *Relaciones entre Antonio Machado y Juan Ramón Jiménez* (Pisa, 1964), 46–8.

24. ibid., 48.

25. Albornoz, op. cit., 189–90, and Sister Katherine Elaine, 'Man in the Landscape of Antonio Machado' in *Spanish Thought and Letters in the Twentieth Century*, 270–86.

26. J. Herrero, 'Antonio Machado's Image of the Centaur', *BHS*, XLV (1968), 39.

27. Terry, op. cit., 54–7.

28. On which see C. Beceiro, 'El poema' "A José María Palacio" de Antonio Machado', *In*, 137 (1958), 5; 'Sobre la fecha y las circunstancias del poema "A José María Palacio"', *La Torre* (Puerto Rico), XII (1964), 387–408; and V. Gaos, 'En torno a un poema de Antonio Machado' in *Claves de literatura española*, II (Madrid, 1971), 51–80.

29. Letter to Federico de Onís, cited M. Tuñón de Lara, *Antonio Machado, poeta del pueblo* (Barcelona, 1967), 99.

30. Cited Serrano Poncela, op. cit., 66.

31. Cf. L. Rosales, 'Muerte y resurrección de Antonio Machado', *CHA*, 11/12 (1949), 435–79; R. Gullón, *Una poética para Antonio Machado* (Madrid, 1970); and R. Gutiérrez Girardot, *Poesía y prosa en Antonio Machado* (Madrid, 1969).

32. *Juan de Mairena*, section xv (*Obras*, 297). Subsequent bracketed references give the section and page number in *Obras*.

33. *De un cancionero apócrifo* (*Obras*, 306).

34. ibid. (*Obras*, 294).

35. ibid. (*Obras*, 305).

36. *Obras*, 859–61.

37. *De un cancionero apócrifo* (*Obras*, 300).

38. ibid. (*Obras*, 305).

39. ibid. (*Obras*, 305).

40. ibid. (*Obras*, 307).

41. ibid. (*Obras*, 307).

42. ibid. (*Obras*, 308).

43. ibid. (*Obras*, 311).

44. Serrano Poncela, op. cit., 67; L. F. Vivanco, *Introducción a la poesía española contemporánea* (Madrid, 1957), 18–25.

Chapter 7

AZORÍN:
THE REDISCOVERY OF A TRADITION

I. THE SENTIMENTAL ANARCHIST

José Martínez Ruiz was born in Monovar, in Alicante, on 8 June
1873. His father, the mayor of the town, was a fairly prosperous vine-
yard-owner and a law graduate who in 1881 sent his son to the board-
ing school of the religious order of the *Escolapios* in nearby Yecla
for his secondary education. In 1888 Martínez Ruiz entered the law
faculty at Valencia University, but in the end, after a decade of
desultory studies, there and elsewhere, did not take his degree. Once
freed from the restraints of home and school he had turned gradually
away from law towards literature and in the spring of 1894 under
the aggressive pseudonym of 'Ahriman' (the Persian god of destruction) made his journalistic debut as theatre critic of the newspaper *El
Mercader Valenciano*. A few articles in other local papers followed,
and in 1895–96 ten of them came out in *El Pueblo*, which belonged
to the outspoken and already influential left-wing agitator Blasco
Ibañez. The formerly retiring and lonely schoolboy was rapidly
blossoming into a rebelliously subversive young writer and critic
with the same sort of anarchist leanings that were to affect his future
friends Maeztu and Baroja.[1]

Apart from articles, Azorín's first works were a brief would-be
analytic survey of *La crítica literaria en España* and an essay on
Moratín, both published in 1893. Though creditable, they do no more
than indicate the trend of Azorín's interest towards serious literary
criticism. *Buscapiés* (1894) and *Anarquistas literarias* (1895), despite
the efforts of Blanco Aguinaga to present the latter as important,
make wearisome reading, relieved only rarely by outbursts of social
criticism. The first really revealing writings of the young Azorín are
thus his favourable review of Kropotkin's *La conquête du pain* in
late 1894[2] and the essay *Notas sociales* (1895). Here Azorín takes for
granted the inevitable, if gradual, triumph of the extreme Left.
'Indudablemente, la humanidad camina hacia el comunismo anarquista', he wrote in the review, 'pero camina con paso tardo'. Inman
Fox has amply documented Azorín's own sincere commitment,
through his writings at this time, to a concept of leftward political

evolution which, it is specifically emphasized both in the review of
Kropotkin and *Notas sociales*, does not exclude revolution. *Literatura*
(1896), the last of his Valencian *folletos*, relapses afresh into triviality.
In November 1896 Azorín arrived in Madrid and joined Baroja
and Maeztu on *El País*. He published *Charivari* (1897), a chatty
diary of the seamier side of Madrid's literary and journalistic life,
spiced with gossip and with his outspoken opinions of contemporary
writers. It was promptly suppressed by the authorities. Azorín followed it with *Bohemia* (1897) and *Soledades* (1898), two collections
of rather inconsequential miniature stories in prose or dialogue-form
and by *Pecuchet, demagogo* (1898), a laboured satire of the kind of
coarse revolutionary journalism which Azorín had come to know
well enough to detest it. What is already interesting is Azorín's
readiness to advocate inquiries into 'las causas precisas y exactas del
mal [social]' (*Obras completas* (Madrid, 1959–63, I, 283))[3] combined
with a clear disinclination to set an example of how to carry them
out. Unless, that is, we except *La sociología criminal*, a sharp attack
on traditional legal attitudes towards criminal behaviour, which
followed in 1899 *La evolución de la crítica*.

Both these works, which together mark the end of the prehistory
of Azorín's literary work, deserve attention. In the last chapter of the
latter, 'La crítica científica', Azorín discusses the theory of criticism
developed by Émile Hennequin in his book *La critique scientifique*
(1888) in contrast to that of Taine. 'Taine estudia el medio para
comprender la obra', he wrote, 'y Hennequin estudia la obra para
comprender el medio' (I, 437). We are here very close to the origin
of one of Azorín's own characteristic techniques: the attempt to
evoke the past of Spain, using as his materials works of literature and
historical documents. Once more we encounter in a new guise that
naïve assumption of historical determinism which is so prominent a
feature of thought in the Generation of 1898. The same uncritical
determinism, combined with aggressive hostility to penal legislation
on political grounds (because it treated revolutionary agitation as a
crime), characterizes *La sociología criminal*. In it Azorín not only
vehemently denied the existence of criminal responsibility, since all
actions are socially determined, but also called into question the
possibility of objectively defining crime at all. The whole work is
indeed nothing less than the application to criminology of the
anarchist dream of a humanity redeemed by absolute freedom.

With the end of the century this earliest section of Azorín's work
comes to a close. In retrospect we perceive in it a profound ambivalence. At intervals, alongside the impassioned social commitment,
the faith in man's inevitable moral progress, the revolutionary zeal,
and the admiration for disinterested intellectual effort which are the
keynotes of Azorín's first writings, appears a sense of futility and

discouragement, which, like Ganivet, he saw afflicting society as a whole.[4] 'Existe en la sociedad moderna', he wrote as early as 1894 in *Buscapiés*,

> un mal que, aunque no registrado en los más perfectos tratados de patología, hace víctimas numerosas en las filas de la juventud estudiosa. Es este el hastío temprano, que atrofiando la voluntad y aplanando el espíritu, agosta los más entusiastas ideales y derrueca los caracteres más bien templados. Es mal de nuestro siglo, así como de los pasados lo fue la credulidad cerrada, la confianza excesiva en un *ideal*, muerto para nosotros, que no creemos en nada o creemos sólo por fuera, que es peor. (I, 71)

A few pages later, in 'Impresiones literarias', the references to Buddhism in an equally important passage (I, 103) confirm the influence of Schopenhauer, which reaches its height just after the turn of the century in *Diario de un enfermo* (1901) and *La voluntad* (1902).

The first page of *Diario de un enfermo* develops the last paragraph of *La sociología criminal*. It indicates clearly that the crisis of ideals and beliefs which had been maturing in Azorín since 1894 had reached an acute stage. Its consequence, which he calls 'angustia metafísica' (I, 694), was of relatively short duration and cannot be regarded as having had the effect on Azorín's personality that similar states of mental and spiritual unrest, which were more persistent, had on those of Ganivet, Baroja, or Machado, to say nothing of the recurrent crises of Unamuno. But it marks the peak of his early intellectual evolution and links him, through *La voluntad* above all, to a central aspect of the rest of the Generation, excepting (as we have seen) Maeztu. Intellectual, corrosively self-analytic, and aboulic the diarist feels successively the attraction of 'la voluptuosa y liberadora Nada' (I, 712) and of active life lived to the utmost pitch of sensation, of philosophical inquiry and of romantic emotion, of religious serenity and 'fe en el consolador trabajo literario' (I, 718). The death of his wife, after a courtship and marriage which have symbolic overtones, leaves him, like Hurtado in Baroja's *El árbol de la ciencia*, face to face with 'la tormenta de vivir...la opaca vida, silenciosa, indiferente, muerta' (I, 732). In the first edition, he too committed suicide.

II. THE FIRST NOVEL-CYCLE

The compendium of '98 attitudes and moods exhibited by the protagonist of *Diario de un enfermo* was successfully developed a year later by Azorín in *La voluntad*, his one essential contribution to the novel of the '98. Its title and central theme are clarified by the author's reference a decade later, apropos of Baroja's *El árbol de la ciencia,* to 'el problema de la lucha entre el pensamiento y la acción: antagonismo que constituye el núcleo de la nueva novela' (I, 641). The protagonist of the novel, Antonio Azorín, from whom the author in 1904 borrowed his *nom de plume,* is presented, along with his mentor Yuste, as an intelligent and progressive-minded man, but one in whom practical considerations whether personal or collective are wholly subordinated to an invasive sense of life's futility: 'la inexorable marcha de todo nuestro ser y de las cosas que nos rodean hacia el océano misterioso de la Nada' (I, 898). This feeling of cosmic nihilism, which Azorín shared with the Generation of 1898 as a whole, he specifically identifies with that of Larra, to whose grave he, Baroja, and others made the symbolic visit described in Part II, chapter 9. This chapter, with its insistence on ideological rather than literary affinity, remains the *locus classicus* with regard to the link between the Generation of 1898 and Romanticism in Spain.

Already on his first appearance Antonio is a prey to 'mysterious speculations' and 'hondas y trascendentales cavilaciones' (I, 832). These, the author asserts, combine in 'este feroz análisis de todo', which not only in Antonio Azorín but also in an entire Spanish *fin-de-siglo* generation have produced a 'disgregación de ideales' (I, 959) and in consequence a paralysis of volition. The emphasis is placed squarely and even repetitively on the two problems to which Antonio's meditations constantly return. The first is that of finality, in a universe which, he has learned from Yuste (and Schopenhauer), 'todo: hombres y mundos! – ha de acabarse disolviéndose en la nada' (I, 835). If this is the case: '¿*Para qué?* ¿Para qué hacer nada?' (I, 974). As Baroja was to discover in the course of his earlier novels, action without purposiveness is no better than reflection without action. The second problem is that of knowledge. Again Azorín and Yuste are at one. Both are in the grip of what Pérez de Ayala was to call 'la enfermedad de lo incognoscible': the desperate need to find an answer to ultimate questions, and at the same time the obsessively conscious inability to do so. In particular the frustrated longing for a Final Cause complements the anguished longing for a transcendental aim: '¿Cuál es la causa final de la vida? No lo sabemos' (I, 975).

The only ultimate possibilities Antonio and Yuste can visualize are either an end to the whole process through the gradual loss of physical energy or a cyclic pattern of eternal repetition borrowed from Nietzsche's doctrine of eternal recurrence. The latter possibility continued to intrigue Azorín and gave rise to the famous essays 'La novia de Cervantes' in *Los Pueblos* (1905) and 'Las nubes' in *Castilla* (1912) as well as to a memorable later novel, *Doña Inés* (1925). Critics since Laín Entralgo have emphasized that Azorín introduced an important modification (in fact, a loophole) into

Nietzsche's doctrine by adding the rider that what returns cyclically is never quite the same.[5] A certain precarious purposiveness is thus salvageable. Practically, however, Antonio in the novel is reduced to two options. The first is to marry Iluminada, whose exuberantly volitive personality may thus be profitably harnessed to his own *abulia*. He marries her, but the effect is disastrous. Once again love and marriage are seen to offer no solution to the fictional hero of the '98 Generation. The second option is to retreat into total subjectivity, accepting the view obsessively repeated during his reflections that 'la imagen lo es todo', that nothing real exists outside the individual mind.

Azorín's extremism in the presentation of his fictional hero is matched by his uncompromisingly innovatory narrative technique. The famous dialogue between Antonio Azorín and Yuste in chapter 14 of *La voluntad*, in which the author explains his theory of the novel, is in essence a plea for liberation from formal structural conventions. Not, it may be noticed, for liberation from moral, sexual, or social conventions. For these Azorín, like his companions, showed in his mature work a disappointingly timid respect. What he aspired to was a fictional method in which psychological conviction was achieved not by an accumulation of observed details carefully arranged in chronological order with no gaps, but by a series of separate 'shots', each of which transmitted to the reader the exact sensation experienced by the fictional personage at a given moment. In this way what is to be conveyed is not a rational, causal account of a fictional personality, but rather a basis for intuitive understanding of it. We may notice that while Azorín asserts that 'ante todo no debe haber fábula' (i.e., plot) and advocates instead 'fragmentos, sensaciones separadas' (I, 864), he says nothing about the *arrangement* of the fragments. Thus the critical question with regard to the narrative technique of *La voluntad* is whether we can discern in it a method of composition. For his own part Azorín clearly believed that there was, insisting in 1941 that the novel was 'escrito concienzudamente' (VI, 191) and that it contained an underlying coherence (VI, 46). But it was not until the important article of Beser and the general study of Azorín's novels by Martínez Cachero in 1960 that critics began to accept this view.[6]

This is the first novel of the Generation of 1898 in which plot is really vestigial; though Azorín was to reduce its role still further in later narratives. Similarly the love-affair between Antonio and Justina, though of great importance in the former's development, is so foreshortened that the couple do not even exchange a single word in the novel. Symbolism closely connected with time and fate is prominent. Antonio's movements in the novel, like those of Sacha in Baroja's *El mundo es ansí*, are basically circular, beginning and ending in Yecla. In both cases the device suggests the futility of effort. The opening pages, minutely analysed by Amorós,[7] also present the first of several symbolic parallelisms between past and present which underline Azorín's cyclic vision of time. Another is provided by Antonio's subjection, in Part II, chapter 5, to a slight almost identical with that suffered by Yuste in Part I, chapter 5. Finally, in the descriptions of Madrid in Part II, chapter 2, and of the Rastro five chapters later, the alert reader recognizes images of life in general as an 'immensa danza de la muerte'. The presentation of the central character, Antonio, is wholly in terms of his conscious, thinking, mind. Of his emotions we know little that is reliable (the statement 'Azorín siente por Justina una pasión que podríamos llamar frenética' (I, 848) is patently untrue), and of his sub-rational personality nothing. The novel's main ideological assertions are made initially in Yuste's didactic monologues to which Antonio listens passively before his experiences and his own meditations in the rest of the work confirm them practically point by point. The text is thus almost all 'commentary' variously expressed in verbal reflections by characters, or in Antonio's internal monologues, or in passages of direct authorial statement. A final important aspect of technique is the 'open' ending in contrast to the closed, completed, structural patterns of novels written in the previous generation.

Certain criticisms of La voluntad remain. Not all the episodes and reflections are sufficiently relevant to Antonio's evolution of ideas. There is not enough divergence of outlook between Yuste and Antonio to make the two characters really independent of one another. The grouping of secondary characters around Antonio is a trifle mechanical so that their function in relation to him is always obvious. Finally the pseudo-explanatory epilogue adds complexity to the interpretation of the novel rather than, as seems to have been Azorín's intention, clarifying retrospectively the sources of Antonio's malaise. Time has shown, however, that this was a work of seminal importance in modern Spanish fiction.

The temptation to find in the rest of the trilogy, Antonio Azorín (1903) and Las confesiones de un pequeño filósofo (1904), a 'solution' to the problems enunciated by La voluntad, must be firmly resisted. The core of Antonio Azorín lies in the relationship of Antonio with two carefully selected ideological foils: Verdú and Sarrió. Verdú expresses with great pathos Azorín's regret, despite his personal scepticism, that the very real consolations afforded by traditional beliefs had been lost by all except the unthinking (I, 1071). Antonio's own longing for 'consoladoras olvidanzas' (I, 1023), the ability to set aside rational knowledge, confirms the attraction for him of Verdú's belief in the spirit's immortality.[8] Despite the sharp attack at the end of the novel on the 'catolicismo, hosco, agresivo, intolerante' (I, 1152) which Azorín, like Unamuno and Baroja, regarded as a major negative influence on the national character, it is clear that Azorín's early determined hostility to all religious belief did not survive the turn of the century. Sarrío presents a contrary option: epicurean enjoyment of life's pleasures combined with 'simplicidad de alma' (I, 1105).

It was never within Azorín's reach, and in the end his personal stance became closer to that of Verdú. Antonio, in the novel, though less nihilistic and anguished than in *La voluntad*, remains trapped within the 'terribles perpejidades de su espíritu' (I, 1106). But a certain difference of tone in this novel is marked by the reference to Antonio's 'suave congoja' (I, 1092) in contrast to his 'abrumadora augustia' in *La voluntad*, and by his recognition that there exists the possibility of cultivating a 'visión humilde de las cosas', a sense of compassionate contemplative penetration with external reality, based on the qualified realization that 'en el mundo todo es digno de estudio y de respeto' (I, 1096). Here we perceive the stimulus for his discovery of the 'primores de lo vulgar' which Ortega was to comment on so memorably.[9]

The form of *Antonio Azorín* is modelled on the same formula as *La voluntad*, but it reveals more clearly Azorín's inability to avoid the main defect associated with it. In a novel where everything is governed by the evolution of the central character, that evolution and the experiences contributing to it must remain the predominating factor of interest. In *Antonio Azorín* this is no longer sufficiently the case and the novel tends to fall apart.

Las confesiones de un pequeño filósofo (1904), which is only tenuously related to the earlier novels, is Azorín's *Recuerdos de niñez y mocedad*. Its tone is one of gentle nostalgia even when the author comes to describe the two main influences which henceforth affected his innermost being. These were the atmosphere of Yecla itself, which Azorín was to rediscover over and over again in provincial Castile, and the daily religious practices of the boarding-school. Yecla was for Azorín the archetype of the small Spanish towns in which death-orientated religious attitudes and the desolate waterless, physical surroundings had together produced an ineradicably sad, fatalistic, rutinary mentality. To this melancholy atmosphere where time seems to stand so still as to be perceptible, Azorín traced part of his own sad, Time-centred, inner vision of life. Similarly, to the daily Mass at dawn in the college chapel he traced his 'obsesión del por qué y del fin de las cosas'.

The detached tone in which these negative influences are analysed in *Las confesiones* is diametrically opposite to the furious invective which Azorín had brought to their treatment only months earlier in his articles 'La educación y el medio', 'Las confesiones de un pequeño filósofo' [!], 'La farándula'. This discrepancy between the militant socially-critical, propagandist aspect of Azorín's work and the more familiar calm, ironic fatalism which was synthesized in his two 'Cursos abreviados de pequeña filosofía' (in *Tiempos y Cosas*, 1944, but published originally in 1904) persisted plainly at least until 'Andalucía trágica' (*Los pueblos*, 1905). It reveals that the struggle between the rebellious 'Dionysian' side of his nature and the dispassionate 'Apollonian' side was certainly not resolved early, as Mrs Krause would have us believe. Whether that struggle indeed ever came to be wholly resolved remains a matter of debate affecting large areas of Azorín's subsequent work.

III. THE ESSAYIST AND CRITIC

One of the features of Azorín's earliest work is his rejection of Spain's past, both historical and cultural. In *Moratín* (chapter 1) and *La evolución de la crítica* (chapter 2) he dismissed the eighteenth century and the Golden Age in Spain respectively as periods whose reactionary intellectual atmosphere and quixotic statecraft had hurried on the nation's decadence. In *La voluntad* Part II, chapter 4, Spain's historical process after the Renaissance is interpreted in terms of the replacement of her earlier 'espíritu jovial y fuerte, placentero y fecundo' by 'la austeridad, castellana y católica', with the result that the people were turned gradually into 'esta pobre raza paralítica' (I, 930). Spanish Golden Age literature is meanwhile fiercely criticized for conforming to the rigid, uniform mentality of Counter-reformation Spain and characterized as 'insoportablemente antipática' (I, 928). As late as 1913 in his well-known essay 'La decadencia de España' in *Clásicos y modernos* Azorín was still expounding, though now with the aid of literary sources, the errors of social organization, cultural orientation, and political policy which had produced his country's decline.

Yet in 1894 he had published a snippet called 'Medalla antigua', as a puff for *Buscapiés* which was just about to be published. Valverde in his commentary on it[10] rightly emphasizes the singular way in which it portends for the first time the style and manner of the books which brought Azorín real popularity: from *El alma castellana* in 1900 to *El pasado* in 1955; half a century of evocations of a past which he had begun by rejecting! But Valverde is mistaken in regarding the article as a *near*-parody. It was clearly written in just the same spirit of literary antiquarianism as Azorín's first play, *La fuerza de amor* (1901), and is the basis for chapters 4 and 6 of *El alma castellana* itself. We cannot overlook in *La voluntad* the fact that, alongside the bitterly critical remarks apropos of the 'genio de la raza hipertrofiado por la decadencia' (I, 928), typified by Quevedo's *Buscón*, appears Yuste's unexpected regret at 'la dispersión del espíritu de aquella España' (I, 826) and Antonio's even more surprising association of 'el espíritu austero de la España clásica' with his idol, Larra!

Clearly the balance had begun to shift.[11] We perceive a further stage in its movement in the evocation of Lazarillo's *hidalgo* in *Los pueblos* (1905). In the penniless pride of this noble idler the younger Azorín could easily have seen a symbol of the Spanish past he and the Liberals spurned. But now the symbol is quite different: it is the nobleman's sword. 'Esta espada es toda España; esta espada es toda el alma de la raza; esta espada nos enseña la entereza, el valor, la dignidad, el desdén por lo pequeño, la audacia, el sufrimiento silencioso, altanero ... las raíces de la patria que ya se van secando' (II, 176, 180). The first direct confirmation of what was taking place is found in the concluding pages of *Los pueblos*: 'Confesión de un autor'. The essay begins and ends with quotations from Montaigne, whom Azorín had been reading at least since 1898[12] with absorption and dedication. Montaigne's serene mental equipoise was the ideal antidote to Azorín's youthful anguish of mind.

Azorín was now able to turn inside-out what he had called at the end of *Las confesiones* 'la percepción aguda y terrible de que "todo es uno y lo mismo"' (II, 95). The fundamental sameness of all things which had then seemed to him so dreadful now instead justified the assertion that the forces which govern human destiny can be more readily perceived in 'hechos microscópicos reveladores de la vida' than in abstract intellectual reflections. Such tiny facts, needless to say, are as available in everyday provincial and rural life as in that of the metropolis. Herein lies the justification of so much that Azorín was subsequently to write.

Los pueblos illustrates what politically biased criticism of Azorín tends to obscure: that in his mature writings he alternated among three different and in fact contradictory standpoints. These are: 'commitment', inherited from earlier left-wing enthusiasm, as in 'La Andalucía trágica', a biting attack on poverty and suffering in the south, for which he was instantly dismissed from his envied post on *El Imparcial* in 1905; the melancholy detachment of 'El pequeño filósofo que acepta resignado los designios ocultas y inexorables de las cosas' (II, 124); and nationalist affirmation in varying tones of yearning and confidence. Azorín himself confused the picture with the slogan ¡Viva la bagatela! in his two 'Cursos abreviados' abovementioned, and more especially in the prologue to *España* (1909), where he wrote: 'Si somos discretos, si la experiencia no ha pasado en balde sobre nosotros, una sola actitud mental adopteremos para el resto de nuestros días ... nos resignaremos, en suma, dulcemente, sin tensión de espíritu, sin gesto trágico, ante lo irremediable' (II, 446).

How inconsistent Azorín was with 'una sola actitud mental' of sceptical indifference – can be seen, in one respect, in his speech at Aranjuez on the occasion of the famous *homenaje* of 1913 organized by Ortega. Here his feelings are once more of 'indignación y desesperanza' before the spectacle of rural starvation, tuberculosis, and illiteracy: 'el presente trágico de España'. He returned to his earlier categoric affirmation that 'La estética no es más que una parte del gran problema social'. In the same year he was dismissed for the third time from a newspaper, this time *El Diario de La Marina* of Havana to which he had been sending regular articles, because of the aggressively critical tone in which they were written.

Before leaving *El Imparcial* Azorín had been overtaken by the tercentenary celebrations for the first edition of *Don Quixote*. His contribution was the fifteen articles that became, with another chapter, *La ruta de Don Quijote* (1905). In it he seized the opportunity to apply, more systematically than in *Los pueblos*, the notions outlined in the 'Confesión' at the end of that book. Ramsden's masterly analysis of the text[13] establishes beyond question the error of those earlier critics who have seen in *La ruta . . .* and its companion works a predominant element of straight observation of reality intended to present provincial Spain as it actually was at the time. What Azorín's mind secreted after he had achieved the indispensable 'conocimiento de las cosas concretas' was not a faithful reflection of them, but an interpretation of them, governed by subjective moods or by presuppositions. With the main presupposition we are already familiar. It is that revealing details, 'microhistoric' experiences, and sensations, can define the nation's essential spirit more clearly and reliably than 'macrohistoric' events. In turn, given Azorín's confidence in determinism, this essential spirit (*genio* or *alma de la raza*) can in some sense be explained as a product of certain 'causas y concausas'. Ramsden submits this aspect of *La ruta* to the same demolishing criticism that he had earlier applied to it in Ganivet's *Idearium español*. Azorín attempted to relate Don Quixote's personality to a certain collective mentality in Argamasilla de Alba around 1575 which was in turn due to specific physical and historic causes. However, he was obliged to doctor the evidence, changing dates and suppressing important facts. More importantly, Azorín tried to show, like Unamuno in *En torno al casticismo*, that Don Quixote (and all he symbolized in regard to Spain's national character) was the product of the flat monotonous physical environment of La Mancha where 'La fantasía se echa a volar frenética por estos llanos' (II, 315) and of the oppressive silence and inertia of village life. Here the evidence is even less convincing. Not only is

Argamasilla itself presented ambivalently, depending on Azorín's frame of mind; not only in *La ruta* ... are the same effects attributed to different physical environments; but the objection also remains that the effects themselves are apparently now no longer produced by similar causes.[14]

In chapter 15, exactly like Ganivet (cf. above, p. 28), Azorín defines the Spanish temperament in terms of 'la fantasía loca, irrazonada e impetuosa que rompe de pronto la inacción para caer otra vez estérilmente en el marasmo' (II, 317). This is the key-chapter from the point of view of the critic who is concerned to relate the book to the *Idearium* or to *El torno al casticismo*. It underlines afresh the common assumption on which the members of the Generation of 1898 founded their interpretation of the country's problem: that there existed a geographically and historically determined national character which stood in need of definition and of change. The chapter also heavily underlines the way in which Ganivet, Unamuno, and Azorín all allowed their response to the observable reality of Spain to be conditioned by their desire to justify this assumption. But otherwise chapter 15 is one of the least characteristic chapters of the book as well as the least convincing. The importance of all Azorín's writings about rural Spain, its towns, its people, its countryside, lies not in the accuracy of the descriptions, nor in the ultimately naïve attempt to interpret through them the soul of Spain. Their importance lies in their power of transmitting to the reader a vision of Spain which, even to Spaniards who knew the places described, contained elements of true discovery.

How Azorín achieved this remains a mystery, into which Marguerite Rand, in her book on Azorín as a *paisajista*,[15] hardly attempts to enter. Instead, following Laín Entralgo and the main body of those critics who avoid the trap of seeing Azorín's descriptions as realistic reportage, she relates Azorín's presentation of Castile to his ambivalent vision of the national outlook and the problem of 'regeneración'. On the other hand, we meet with a long series of descriptions of places – town or countryside – together with their atmosphere of desolation, quiet immobilism, aridity, and squalor. What they suggest to Azorín are the negative characteristics of the Spanish mentality. Their silence, he wrote in 1914 quoting Larra, is the 'silencio sepulcral de la existencia española' (III, 117). The postulate recurs of a direct causal relationship between the environment (the *paisaje físico*) and the *modo de ser* (the *paisaje moral*; III, 540). The 'Epílogo en Castilla' at the end of *Lecturas españolas* (1912) presents more than simply a telling comparison; the relationship is one of cause and effect:

El campo se extiende ante mi vista ... no se yerguen árboles en la llanura; no corren arroyos ni manan hontanares. El pueblo reposa en un profundo sueño. Ningún lugar mejor que estos parajes para meditar sobre nuestro pasado y nuestro presente . . . Reposa el cerebro español como este campo seco y este pueblo grisáceo. (II, 659–60)

On the other hand, and in contrast, Azorín just as often poeticizes his description by blending with it a nostalgic evocation of the past. In this mood the emphasis shifts radically. The product of physical determinism is not negative now, but positive: the enduring qualities of the Spanish race. Azorín's interest is now entirely centred on the element that unites his sense of the past with Unamuno's and Ganivet's: the element of continuity. The most obvious links are naturally with Spain's cultural or imperial past: a *casa solariega* suggests a conquistador or a 'capitán de Flandes'; an old inn, the wandering students of Quevedo's *Buscón*; the Escorial Palace calls to mind Spain's former 'vasto y poderoso imperio'. Conversely 'unas páginas de *La Celestina* o del *Lazarillo* nos hacen compenetrarnos hondamente, *dolorosamente*, con el paisaje' (*Un pueblecito*; III, 532). But this sort of continuity, in spite of his numerous references to it, is not what really appeals to Azorín. It is too obvious and too specific. We come closer to his genuine response in proportion as the sensation which is evoked is more 'atmospheric' and subjective, less tangible and direct. A distant *pueblo* 'que emana efluvios de historia y heroísmo' (V, 354); 'Infinitud de la llanura, que nos lleva a la infinitud del espíritu' (V, 398); these suggest, not so much a simple association with Pizarro or St Teresa, as an intuitive awareness by analogy of the spirit of conquest and mysticism. The ultimate source of this 'effluvium' of heroism and austere spirituality, and the fundamental element of continuity, is the daily life and mental configuration of the people nurtured by the soil of Spain which 'no sólo produce frutos espléndidos, sino que ha formado también un ideal finísimo'. What guarantees the survival of the soul of Spain is the unchanging *alma del pueblo*. This attempt to find a *meaning* in what is being described fails to carry conviction with the modern reader. As we tend not to believe in the 'national essence' Azorín was looking for, so we reject his deterministic appeal to geographical and historical causality which operates to produce it.

Azorín's descriptions are not, we notice, direct transcriptions; in them reality is always *remembered* reality, tinctured with *ensueño* and as a rule enveloped in an atmosphere of tranquillity, beauty, and permanence. Haunted as he was by Time's destructive effect on all that we need to feel is reliably enduring, Azorín found in nature and in *pueblo* life close to nature, a counterforce. Just as at school in Yecla the sight of fields through a window had helped him to bear loneliness and monotony, so in later life the beauty of landscape, the sounds and sights of the countryside, provided relief from the recurrent feeling of existential oppression which remained part of his personality long after the spiritual nihilism of *La voluntad* had given way to calmer thoughts. It is in *Los pueblos* rather than in *La ruta de Don Quijote* that we first see the juxtaposition, which afterwards became characteristic, of Azorín's awareness of the contingency and fragility of our lives, 'trastrocadas por el azar y por el infortunio' (II, 193), and, in contrast, of a 'concordancia secreta y poderosa de las cosas que nos rodean' (II, 237). This last, which reveals itself in moments of 'armoniosa síntesis', points to the existence of a 'fuerza misteriosa del universo' diffusing through outer reality a beauty which transcends Time and chance. The perception of such moments of synthesis is described in 'El grande hombre en el pueblo' and in 'Una criada' (*España*, 1909). The poetic appeal of Azorín's descriptions henceforth derives from the supplanting of reality by artistic re-creation in which the selection and juxtaposition of details is governed by an affective relationship between Azorín and what he chooses to describe. The stylistic devices which he employs, and which Ramsden has analysed so perceptively in regard to *La ruta de Don Quijote*, especially his adjectivization and enumerative sequences of nouns, are designed not only to create vivid visual and auditive effects. They also transmit the author's disquiet and melancholy with, at increasingly frequent intervals, his attenuating awareness of triumph over transience. Nature and natural life persist, and by persisting console. 'Lo sencillo y primario no cambia', Azorín wrote in his memoirs, 'cambia todo, y lo irreductible permanece' (VII, 388). The secret of his *paisajismo* lies in his power to communicate not just the appeal of the simple, primary reality of rural life, but also its consoling, reliable repose, its serene resistance to forces which we too experience and fear.

Between *La ruta de Don Quijote* in 1905 and *Castilla* in 1912 the bulk of Azorín's writing was political.[16] The two exceptional works in this period are *España* (1909) and Azorín's first mature work of literary criticism, *Lecturas españolas* (1912). *España* develops the formula which Azorín had gradually been evolving since *El alma castellana* nine years earlier. Now, in his middle thirties, he had perfected the type of short prose piece with which his name has since been most associated. It is an essentially hybrid form containing elements of the descriptive essay and the short story, often in a framework of poetic evocation. Azorín's technique is to select figures from the past and to bring them alive as real people in their historical context. The secret of the method is its combination of direct appeal to the reader's instinctive self-identification with the individuals described, not as distant historical names, but as everyday human types, and the vivid evocation of the setting, using authentic details deliberately borrowed from literary sources. Thus in 'Un pobre hombre' the general ambience of inquisitorial Catholicism previously described in 'La Inquisición' (*El alma castellana*) is condensed nine years later into one telling anecdote which conveys the 'feel', not the facts, of an earlier period of national life. The general pattern is still one of idealization. It is almost with surprise that we find in the last of the pen-pictures of *España* a realistic reference to 'toda la psicología humana – lucha y egoísmo' (II, 483). Where were those factors in the preceding ones? More revealing still is Azorín's description in 'Un labrantín' of peasant life and mentality in his own time. How much less convincing it is than the life described in 'La Andalucía trágica'. Only in 'Una ciudad castellana' does Azorín briefly return to the provincial Spain of Unamuno and Antonio Machado –'Esa España inferior que ora y bosteza' – the Spain of tedium, usury, and decay. Depth has been sacrificed to charm.

Not so, however, in *Castilla* which, together with *Lecturas españolas*, stands at a turning-point in Azorín's work. Without, as we have seen, entirely abandoning his denunciatory pictures of Spain's decrepitude, lack of political direction, national disorganization, and frivolity, he turned, like Unamuno, increasingly to cultural reform as the answer. He now resolutely interpreted the problem as that of Spain's ingrained lack of intellectual curiosity and consequent mental stagnation. His aim thus became, not to alter Spanish society, as he had wished to do ten years earlier, but to disseminate through his regular press-articles and books certain cultural incentives connected in his mind with regeneration, rather in the same way as Unamuno had turned to spiritual incentives. Ideally these incentives were designed to induce his readers to meditate afresh on the contrast between Spain and Europe, and on the need to adjust more readily to European modes of life and thought. Secondly, they were meant to lead the public to deepen its consciousness of Spain's own cultural tradition. Neither direction, Azorín now believed, was complete without the other. In *Un discurso de la Cierva* (1914) he quoted with full approval Baroja's 1902 article 'Vieja España, patria nueva', in which the latter had called for renovation but within the boundaries of tradition. 'Conservar es renovar', Azorín added (III, 136).

Castilla illustrates the coexistence of the two aims. It opens with four essays, the common theme of which is Spain's stubborn reluctance to accept modernizing innovations, symbolized in the railways, and her firm attachment to old habits of life, symbolized in her noisy, dirty, comfortless inns and her (to Azorín) bestial and ignoble sport of bullfighting. In three of them British engineers appear. Their refusal to watch a bullfight and the Spanish government's refusal to give them a railway contract are deftly and ironically juxtaposed. The implication is clear; but its force is diminished by the fact that Azorín is criticizing the past, not the present. The second aim is visible in the technique Azorín employed in four other chapters of

Castilla: 'Las nubes', 'Lo fatal', 'La fragancia del vaso', and 'Cerrera, cerrera', all of which are based on Spanish literary classics. Blanco Aguinaga is nowhere more partial in his criticism of Azorín than when he describes these stories as trivializing the classics with happy endings.[17] The truth is that none of the four stories in question has, objectively speaking, a happy ending, and in this precisely resides their avoidance of triviality. What distinguishes them and their kindred group in *Castilla*, 'Una flauta en la noche', 'Una lucecita roja', and 'La casa cerrada', from the mere charm of so many chapters of *España*, is the fact that in them Azorín expresses the obsessive preoccupation with Time in which critics have found the nucleus of his thought. This preoccupation is the unifying element in nine of the fourteen chapters of *Castilla*, beginning with 'Una ciudad y un balcón'. This tiny semi-allegorical piece synthesizes three major aspects of Azorín's outlook. In the opening description of the little Castilian town in the fifteenth century we recognize once more the 'delectación estética', through which, amid the silent immobility of old streets, he was able to achieve a liberating sense of eternity. In the successive descriptions of the same town in the eighteenth and twentieth centuries we perceive Azorín's 'anhelo de ver esa misma realidad transformada con arreglo a un ideal de progreso' (II, 1063). But between the two, reinforcing the former response and undermining the latter, is Azorín's *dolorido sentir*, symbolized in the changeless seated figure 'meditadora y triste'. What the latter's sad meditations concern is made clear by Calixto, who is also discovered sitting and thinking in 'Las nubes'. Calixto's realization is a dual one. Concretely he has come to understand 'cómo nuestro ser y todas las cosas corren hacia la nada' (II, 708). Abstractly he has recognized the purposelessness of the time-process itself. Barja, Clavería, Rand, and others who have studied Azorín's remarks about Time do not sufficiently emphasize that it is not ultimately the passage of Time itself carrying away our experiences and sensations, nor the mystery of Time (however frequently mentioned), nor even mere awareness of living in Time – *sentirse vivir* – which distresses him most, though each expressed an aspect of his distress. What links Azorín in this respect to other members of the Generation studied here is his haunting awareness of lack of finality: 'vivimos, nos morimos, nos angustiamos y tampoco tenemos finalidad alguna' (I, 1092). Time sacrifices all things *to no purpose*. The wealth and luxury of the *hidalgo* in 'Lo fatal' comfort him no more than golden mediocrity comforts Calixto. He too meditates sorrowfully; at the centre of his thoughts is the ' ¿Para qué . . .?' so familiar to readers of Unamuno. Time's passage, and the unappeasable nostalgia or quiet desperation to which it impassively reduces men and women, is the theme of the last chapters of *Castilla*.

The inclusion in *Castilla* of short stories alongside essays and prose-poems reminds us that Azorín was perhaps the most prolific Spanish short-story writer since Pardo Bazán. He wrote nearly four hundred of them, most of which remain uncollected. The most original group, *Blanco en azul* (1929), belongs to his so-called 'surrealist' period and is indispensable for the study of it. 'Como una estrella errante', from this collection, 'El fin del mundo' (*Cuentos*, 1956), and 'Doña María de Molina' (*Sintiendo a España*, 1942) are closely related by their common theme of Time to the stories of *Castilla* which still remain Azorín's most famous contributions to the genre.[18]

After 1911 Azorín's journalistic production underwent an almost brusque alteration. His constant use of literary texts as a source of materials for re-elaboration led him directly to literary criticism. His professed desire to reawaken in his readers a sense of their national cultural tradition pointed in the same direction. The result was a series of collections of articles more or less directly connected with literature beginning with *Lecturas españolas* and eventually reaching ten volumes by 1925. The state of criticism in Spain in 1912 was frankly deplorable. There was not even an adequate history of Spanish literature written by a Spaniard until Cejador's, which was not completed until 1922. The collection of *Clásicos castellanos* had not yet begun to be published. School and university textbooks of literature were a disgrace. It is into this too-often forgotten context that Azorín's criticism must be set.

He believed that literature must be recognized as emanating from a given racial, social, and even geographical environment. 'Todo es sincrónico y coherente en la vida española: el teatro, la mística, el paisaje' (IV, 523). Literature was to be scrutinized to seek evidence of the national spirit and the physical background as formative influences. The ideal result would be to find in literature testimony of the continuity of *alma española*. The other major (and far less suspect) aim of Azorín's literary criticism was that of bringing the classics alive by stripping away conventional critical judgements in order to underline the reflection of our present-day sensibility which true masterpieces always contain. In the dedication of *Clásicos y modernos* Azorín succinctly restated his combined aim: 'deseo de buscar nuestro espíritu a través de los clásicos que, dejande aparte enseñanzas arcaicas, deben ser revisados e interpretados bajo una luz moderna' (II, 741).

His real contribution lay in leading an attack, from the position of pre-eminence with the reading public, on conventional Spanish pedantic and moralizing criticism and very largely bringing about its fall. There is little that is systematic or genuinely analytic in his writings on literature. His target audience was in the first instance the readership of the newspaper *ABC*, not fellow specialists. Hence his aim was not to present facts or conclusions, but to stimulate curiosity and interest. This he did primarily by transmitting his own interests and enthusiasms. Chiefly these related to themes and content. In regard to form (with the exception of prose-style) Azorín has much less to say; his great concern was to get over to his readers the way in which classical authors saw and responded to life and reality around them.

His articles are not as a rule in any real sense explanatory. They make statements about works of literature, particularly about their meaning. These are supported, not by critical arguments, but by building up an image of a poem, for example, in the reader's mind, either by relating it suggestively to his own experience ('La noche serena') or by inducing him to 'imaginar, un poco fantásticamente, el momento y el lugar en que los versos se trazaron' (III, 188), as in the case of Góngora's 'Las rosas'. Elsewhere a hint or two of biography is combined with a commentary on the ideas of a work or on the impression it leaves behind. Freshness, spontaneity, imaginative sympathy, and apparent simplicity of approach, these are the qualities of Azorín's criticism. 'He ido leyendo por placer', he wrote, looking back, 'Después he resumido en unas pocas páginas mi sentir' (IV, 211). In this straightforward-seeming formula lies his secret: to transmit, briefly, his own enjoyment of literature.[19] The result was a virtual rediscovery of the classics, especially by the younger generation, comparable to the rediscovery of the Castilian landscape and *pueblos*.

How much remains of Azorín's criticism, now that this process has advanced so far, is difficult to estimate. Nowadays his approach seems impressionistic, subjective, and insufficiently technical. His pioneering re-evaluation of Berceo, Juan Ruiz, Manrique, and Santillana, his high estimate of Góngora, Saavedra Fajardo, and Fray Luis de Granada, his discovery of the pre-Romantics and of Rosalía Castro, his views on his own Generation: all these have been absorbed into modern criticism. Some of the rest has been rejected. In spite of his claim to belong to a Romantic generation (II, 784) he had no real understanding of Romanticism. His book *Rivas y Larra* contributes little to the study of the movement, His views on Clarín's *La Regenta* would be dismissed completely today. Nor can we overlook the fact that his attempt to trace backwards from 1898 critical interest in the problem of Spain led him away from the problem itself. By putting it into increasingly distant perspective he was able to avoid discussing the urgent issues of the day. But the fact remains that between 1912 and 1925 he did much to change the face of Spanish criticism of literature.

IV. DISPERSAL AND EXPERIMENTATION

Critics since Clavería have persistently emphasized the dynamic aspect of Azorín's literary personality which in middle age led him to attempt an almost total renovation of his manner, beginning with his play *Old Spain* (1926). Like Ganivet and Unamuno, Azorín cherished the hope of regenerating the Spanish theatre. Between 1925 and 1935 he published over a hundred articles analysing the state of the theatre in Spain and systematically directing attention to developments in France, Italy, and Russia, particularly in experimental and surrealistic directions. They fully bear out Inman Fox's conclusion that 'Azorín fue claramente el publicista que más abogaba por una renovación en el teatro español'.[20]

His dramatic output after his translation of Maeterlinck's *L'intruse* in 1896 and his historical play *La fuerza de amor* (1901) consists of *Old Spain* (1926), *Judit* (1926), *Brandy, mucho brandy* (1927), *Comedia del arte* (1927), *Lo invisible* (1927), *Angelita* (1930), *Cervantes, o La casa encantada* (1931), *La guerrilla* (1936), and *Ifach* (or *Farsa docente*), staged in 1942 but perhaps written as early as 1933.[21] In addition, in 1928, Azorín wrote and staged in collaboration with the comic dramatist Pedro Muñoz Seca a satirical play *El clamor* which raised a furious storm by attacking the popular press, and in the same year staged a translation of *Dr Fregoli* by the Russian *avant-garde* dramatist Nicholas Evreinoff. Though these plays have received critical attention, and in the case of *Lo invisible* and *Angelita* even praise, none of them was a genuine success. Read nowadays they produce the impression of being fantastic, but not imaginatively inventive. Azorín was trying to combine reality, fantasy, and ideas. Lorca succeeds in doing exactly this (and more, of course) in *Bodas de sangre*, for example. But he does so in a context of overriding passion, and with heavy reliance on poetic and symbolic effects. All these are missing in Azorín. Arrabal has acknowledged his debt to Azorín as a playwright and it is probable that in both his articles and plays the latter consciously indicated new paths to follow. But in the last analysis he belongs to that surprisingly wide range of important writers including Unamuno, Valle-Inclán, the Machados, Grau, Gómez de la Serna, Aub, Alberti, Salinas, Sender (and others of lesser talent such as Jardiel Poncela) who all tried unsuccessfully to establish an alternative pattern of Spanish drama to that which has predominated from Benavente and the Quinteros to the present.

Meanwhile Azorín had returned, after a gap lasting more than a decade, to prose fiction. His novels, after the first trilogy, fall clearly into three chronologically successive groups. The first, *Tomás*

Rueda (originally *El Licenciado Vidriera*; 1915), *Don Juan* (1922), and *Doña Inés* (1925), is the most significant. It was followed by *El caballero inactual* (originally *Félix Vargas*; 1928), *El Libro de Levante* (originally *Superrealismo*; 1929), and *Pueblo* (1930). The last group followed after a twelve-year interval, and comprised *El escritor* (1942), *Capricho* (1943), *El enfermo* (1943), *María Fontán* (1944), *Salvadora de Olbena* (1944), and *La isla sin aurora* (1944).

The technique of *Tomás Rueda* is basically familiar. Once more a single central character, reflecting the author's own preoccupations, dominates the novel. Once more the shape of the narrative is imposed by a process of developing insight to which everything else in the work is subordinated. The filiation of Tomás is not with Cervantes's Licenciado Vidriera, who suggested the character to Azorín, but with earlier fictional heroes of the Generation. His upbringing, his experiences, his love-affair, his interlocutors, combine to reinforce his natural meditative tendency and to concentrate his thoughts around one topic. It is that of Time's ceaseless current flowing between him and those elements in the past – sympathetic human contacts; happier, less conscious states of mind – which brought momentary release and serenity. By the end of the novel Tomás has achieved clear-eyed consciousness of life as a dolorous process in which Time snatches away all that comforts and supports the spirit. But saving him from the suicidal anguish of the sick man in *Diario de un enfermo*, of Andrés Hurtado, or of Apolodoro Carrascal, is his discovery of 'una realidad interior que le hace vivir ... [y] ... puesto que le hace vivir, es una verdad' (III, 330). The next paragraph, however, reveals that it is merely an illusion or *mentira vital*.[22]

Azorín's preoccupation with Time involves, as we have seen, the problem of finality; his theory of the novel, perceptively explored by Livingstone, involves directly the problems of truth, particularly with regard to our vision of reality. For, as he stated in *Tomás Rueda*, 'El gran misterio está insito en la realidad misma que nos circuye y que no sabemos, ni sabe, en fin de cuentas, un Kant, lo que es' (III, 280). Here, then, are two of the three underlying problems of the Generation of 1898: truth and finality. Direct involvement with the third – the ethical question, so prominent in Ganivet, Unamuno, and Baroja – is not a consistent feature of Azorín's work. In *Don Juan*, however, we find in the much-quoted epilogue, and sporadically throughout the work, an emphasis on simple goodness and compassion which is almost naïve. The novel ends on the note of separation and frustrated emotion which is a constant in Azorín's fictional work from *Diario de un enfermo* onwards, and is inseparable from his haunting awareness of Time's destructive action. But the comforting effect in Don Juan of his conscious *bondad* and almost Franciscan *piedad por todo* is not explicit. It is to be questioned whether an ethical solution is really relevant to Azorín's *dolorido sentir*.

Doña Inés, his only uncontestably important novel apart from *La voluntad*, contains the major artistic formulation of Azorín's interest in Nietzsche's idea of Eternal Return, already mentioned apropos of *La voluntad* itself and 'Las nubes'. The attraction of this idea, in the absence of religious belief, lies in its implications of continuity, in the sense which it brings of solidarity and connection with the past by the thought of one's belonging to an unchanging, infinitely repeated pattern. This pattern is expressed in *Doña Inés* by the carefully modulated parallelism which Azorín establishes between the situation and experiences of the heroine Doña Inés and her ancestor Doña Beatriz. Differences of detail prevent the parallel from becoming mechanical; but at length Inés and Beatriz are virtually identified. When their respective love-affairs give rise to scandal and come to grief, each retires into obscurity. But in Buenos Aires, where her poet-lover had spent his childhood, Doña Inés in old age discovers another child who seems destined to be his reincarnation, as he in turn had reincarnated the lover of Beatriz. Despite the fragmentation of the plot, its basic shape remains clear-cut. A secondary structural feature which adds unity to the narrative is provided by a series of contrasts: of character (Inés–Plácida; Pablo–Pompilia); of stages of historical evolution (Spain, old and static – Argentina, new and dynamic); and of abstract concepts.

These centre on Pablo, Inés's uncle. Like Calixto in 'Las nubes', he stands at the crossroads of Time. He has the power, at times, of total recall of his own past; equally, he can perceive the future consequences of each present moment. That these consequences are always unhappy must be regarded as symbolic. Azorín is not concerned with the healing, consoling aspect of Time; only with its constant erosion of the fragile basis of our serenity. What is common both to Pablo's 'visión total del tiempo' and to the idea of Eternal Return is that both have tragic implications. What is continuous in both cases is suffering. We must not overlook the fact that when Yuste in *La voluntad* speaks of *identical* repetition, he is talking of unhappiness; when Félix Vargas in chapter 39 of *El caballero inactual* appears to repudiate the idea, he is thinking of happiness. The Generation of 1898 as a whole tended to write as though the lack of a benevolent divine pattern in existence meant the triumph of a malevolent hostile fate, instead of mere blind chance, neither kind nor cruel. Correspondingly, Azorín tends to write as though the lack of a spiritually satisfying goal toward which time bears us along, meant in fact that time bears us away from all fulfilment whatsoever. This makes it difficult for the reader to share his standpoint.

It is now, as Livingstone cogently argues in one of the best books on Azorín, that the latter seeks his final solution.[23] We saw above (p. 173) how at intervals Azorín referred to magical moments of synthesis, in which the wall of mystery surrounding human existence appears to present a tiny fissure through which we perhaps faintly perceive the infinite, the enduring, the eternal. Don Juan enjoys one while watching the morning star (IV, 237). Such moments represent, not an escape from Time, but a brief escape from Time's onflowing tide. Time stands still, and is thereby somehow transcended. This is another source of Azorín's love of tiny rural towns whose timeless atmosphere is propitious for these visionary instants. Livingstone demonstrates the extent to which the later novels are dominated by the desire to fix artistically the *momento único*, to find release in cultivating a superhuman, 'divinal' perspective in which present, past, and future are fused. However, it is difficult to agree with this critic in his parallel attempt to reduce Azorín's philosophical position to a merely aesthetic one.

El caballero inactual (Félix Vargas) is generally accepted as the turning-point in Azorín's later fiction. Certainly it is the point at which it ceases to be possible to relate his novels, however distantly, to the preoccupations and prevailing method of the novel of the Generation of 1898 as a whole. From here on the doubts expressed by critics about the technique of his previous novels tend to turn into outright condemnation, while the tone adopted by his defenders becomes openly polemical. Against those critics who insist that Azorín was incapable of creating unified, coherent narratives, with rounded convincing characters whose lives involve real passion and dramatic conflict, it can be argued that these were not Azorín's aims. In the later novels themselves, where the problems of fictional writing are a recurrent theme, and also elsewhere, Azorín made it quite plain that he was consciously trying to evolve a new fictional method to which such criticism is hardly relevant. To those critics, notably Livingstone, who argue that any novel which fulfils its author's aims is *ipso facto* entitled to favour, it can be answered that other criteria do exist. Experiment and innovation in the arts, even in extreme cases, are valid for what they help to destroy: outworn conventions and methods, but they are not genuinely creative in themselves. Only when new techniques are needed to express a new sector of reality or a new vision of life or behaviour are they any more, as a rule, than gimmicks or once-only effects. The critical question with regard to Azorín's novels of 1928, 1929, and 1930 is whether their method of writing really transmits enough original insight to justify the effort required by the reader to adapt himself to it. In the main they do not. They are interesting in relation to contemporary and subsequent developments, just as are the novels of Gómez de la Serna; they rest on a firm foundation of theory; but they do not induce us to reconsider our view of reality in the way that the best experimental fiction and theatre tend to do.

El caballero inactual, El libro de levante, and *Pueblo* are the high-water mark of Azorín's ongoing attempt, begun in *Diario de un enfermo* thirty years before, to break away at one and the same time from the nineteenth-century ideals of realism and of the well-made novel. They represent the furthest extreme in this direction to be reached by any member of the Generation of 1898. Subsequently the tide begins to turn. Narrative method becomes more conventional – that of the third-person omniscient narrator reappears in *El enfermo, María Fontán,* and *La isla sin aurora.* It is modified only slightly in chapters 30 to 35 of *Salvadora de Olbena* to produce a certain impression of multiple perspective. An extension of the same technique had been used in *Capricho,* where an initial situation was explored from a dozen different angles, while in *El escritor* there is a shift from one first-person narrator to another, the novel being about the relationship of both. By fitting together references to fragments of individual texts it is possible to present Azorín's last novels as a progressive sequence moving towards an ever-more-complete synthesis of observed reality and creative imagination. But read individually they fail to carry complete conviction. Deliberate suppression of conflict, suspense, and strong human emotions together with regular use of 'open' un-climactic endings means that appreciation of Azorín's later fiction depends on the reader's readiness to share his contemplative enjoyment of a largely static reality. To increase the appeal of this reality, on which the novelist's eye lingers sensitively intent above all on 'la captación y gradación de matices' (VII, 41), its uglier and harsher aspects are deftly excised until not even the pathos of parts of *Castilla* remains. In *María Fontán* the result is triviality, which, despite the subtitle ('Novela rosa'), can hardly be intentional.

V. CONCLUSION

What survives, here and in the last phase of his work, which is dominated by Azorín's memoirs: *Valencia* (1941), *Madrid* (1941), *Paris* (1945), and *Memorias immemoriales* (1946), is Azorín's incomparable style. Looking back, as early as 1913, to the decade before he began to publish, he was able to perceive the revolution in literary expression which his own efforts and those of his comrades in the Generation of 1898 had already brought about: 'En 1885', he wrote in *Los valores literarios,* 'domina en el estilo la nota solemme, amplia, enfática, de la oratoria. Es la época en que Castelar lo llena todo ... Hoy no comprendemos ni sentimos aquella prosa' (II, 998). He himself played the leading role in that revolution. As Valverde has pointed out, his early ideological prose was far from innovatory.[24] But by the turn of the century he had begun to make that systematic use of the present tense which was to become one of his distinguishing characteristics, and to unravel the oratorical periods of Castelar's style, with their wealth of subordinate clauses, into short, deceptively simple-seeming, juxtaposed sentences. Right up to the end of his creative life, style remained a live issue for Azorín. His own main comments on it were collected by A. Cruz Rueda in *El artista y el estilo* (VIII, 609–867). His theory and practice of style have both been repeatedly analysed and illustrated by critics, perhaps most perceptively by Ramsden in his edition of *La ruta de Don Quijote* and by Livingstone in the fourth chapter of his *Tema y forma en las novelas de Azorín*, the periods and aspects dealt with by each being in a sense complementary.[25] There is no single Azorinian style, no single consistent solution to the problems of expression Azorín repeatedly explored. None of his pronouncements, especially those which advocate spontaneity and simplicity, can be accepted without modification in the light of others made elsewhere, or of his practice at different periods of his working life. It is regrettable that no satisfactory detailed study of the evolution of modern prose style in Spain has yet been published. When that gap in our knowledge is closed, there is no doubt that Azorín's contribution to the formation of a new mode of expression in the first decades of this century will be recognized as decisive.

After his return from Paris, after three years voluntary exile, in 1939 Azorín accommodated himself to the new regime in Spain. His repudiation in the preface to his *Obras completas* (Aguilar edition) of his early left-wing writings, the incorporation into the *obras* of *In hoc signo* (1948), collecting those of his writings most acceptable to orthodox Catholic readers, his acceptance successively of the Grand Cross of Isabel the Catholic, the Grand Cross of Alfonso the Wise, and of literary prizes to the tune of a million pesetas, all contrast sadly with the dignified detachment of Baroja, unforgettably described by his nephew in *Los Baroja*. Despite these honours, or perhaps because of them, for a decade or more before his death on 2 March 1967 Azorín's popularity with the public (especially the young) and to some extent his prestige as a writer, suffered a decline. It is normal for this to happen and for it to be accentuated for a time after an author's death. Of the Generation of 1898 only Unamuno and Machado escaped it completely. Baroja's prestige diminished a little in the 1960s (though less than Gullón suggests), but recovered triumphantly in the 1970s. It seems doubtful whether Azorín's work will enjoy a general revival. His first trilogy of novels and *Castilla* are established classics. His memoirs, especially *Madrid*, and his writings on the Generation of 1898 will be read by critics as long as the Generation itself is studied. *La ruta de Don Quijote* and *Una hora de España* will probably survive chiefly as school texts, though apart from *La voluntad* Azorín's work has largely disappeared from university courses. Neither his vision of Spain nor his vision of life commend themselves to the post-war generations. In retrospect, despite his enormous output and versatility, we must conclude that the creative level of all but Azorín's best work was below that of the major figures in his Generation.

NOTES

1. The major contribution to the re-valuation of the earliest work of Azorín was made in 1965–66 by E. Inman Fox. It has been supplemented by Rafael Ferreres, *Valencia en Azorín* (Valencia, 1968); Rafael Pérez de la Dehesa, 'Azorín y Pi y Margall', *RO*, 26, no. 78 (1969), 353–62; and P. Smith, 'Seven Unknown Articles by the Future Azorín', *MLN*, LXXXV (1970), 250–61. Jorge Campos, 'Hacia un conocimiento de Azorín', *CHA*, 226/7 (1968), 114–138 covers the same ground as Fox and Ferreres adding nothing new.
2. Included in the extremely useful *Artículos olvidados de José Martínez Ruiz*, ed. J. M. Valverde (Madrid, 1972), 73–6.
3. All subsequent bracketed references are to this edition.
4. Thus, after forecasting an inevitable 'revolución futura', *La sociología criminal* ends on an oddly contradictory note by stressing the utter futility of all political struggle. M. D. van Biervliet, 'José Martínez Ruiz's Obsession with Fame', *FMLS*, VIII (1972), 291–303 suggests that Azorín's frustrated ambition was a crucial factor conditioning his outlook at this time. There is plenty of evidence to support the view.
5. See Pedro Laín Entralgo, *La Generación del 98* (Madrid, 1945), 164. The first serious reference to Time in Azorín's work was made by César Barja. It was developed by Carlos Clavería in *Cinco estudios de literatura española moderna* (Madrid, 1945). Important clarifications were introduced by Ana Krause, *Azorín, the Little Philosopher* (Berkeley and Los Angeles, 1948); Gonzalo Sobejano, *Nietzsche en España* (Madrid, 1967); and José Antonio Maravall, 'Azorín, idea y sentido de la microhistoria', *CHA*, 226/7 (1968), esp. 44–8.
6. Sergio Beser, 'Notas sobre la estructura de *La voluntad*', *Boletín de la Sociedad Castellonense de Cultura*, XXXVI (1960), 169–81; José Martínez Cachero, *Las novelas de Azorín* (Madrid, 1960). Inman Fox in his excellent edition of the novel (Madrid, 1968) asserts Azorín's 'fuerte voluntad de construcción' in it, but hardly substantiates his assertion. Leon Livingstone regrettably avoids discussing *La voluntad*'s technique in his otherwise illuminating *Tema y forma en las novelas de Azorín* (Madrid, 1970).
7. Andrés Amorós, 'El prólogo de *La voluntad*', *CHA*, 226/7 (1968), 339–354.
8. For Azorín's early defence of religion as a consoling illusion, see the important article by E. Inman Fox, 'Galdós' *Electra* . . . the polemic between Azorín and Maeztu', *AG*, I (1966), 131–41.
9. José Ortega y Gasset, 'Azorín, primores de lo vulgar' in *El Espectador, Obras completas* II (Madrid, 1957), 158–92.
10. Valverde, op. cit., 277–81.
11. Indispensable for the understanding of this shift is Azorín's own essay 'Proceso psicológico' in *Palabras al viento* (1944; *OC* VII, 402–5).
12. See Blanco Aguinaga's note, correcting Inman Fox, in *Juventud del 98*, 153.
13. *La ruta de don Quijote* (ed. Herbert Ramsden, Manchester, 1956).
14. Manual Granell, *Estética de Azorín* (Madrid, 1949), 71–8 and

Marguerite Rand, *Castilla en Azorín* (Madrid, 1956), 33–4 both cast doubt on Azorín's attachment to determinism. Certainly he seemed more deterministic in proportion as he thought of collective situations, less so in proportion as he thought of individual ones. For his later attitude see his prologue to *Clásicos redivivos* (1943).

15. Rand, op. cit.
16. e.g., *La obra de un ministro* (1910); *Un discurso de la Cierva* (1914); and *Parlamentarismo español* (1916).
17. Blanco Aguinaga, *Juventud del 98*, 312.
18. See Mirella D'Ambrosio Servodidio, *Azorín escritor de cuentos* (Madrid, 1971).
19. For a note on the contradictions which Azorín's subjective approach as a literary critic led him into, see César Barja, *Libros y autores contemporáneos* (Madrid, 1935), 284–6.
20. E. Inman Fox, 'La campaña teatral de Azorín', *CHA*, 226/7 (1968), 376.
21. *Judit* was never staged or published. *Lo invisible* consists of three one-act plays: *La arañita en el espejo, El segador*, and *Dr Death, de tres a cinco*. *Cervantes* was not staged.
22. A brilliant interpretative analysis of *Tomás Rueda* is Gonzalo Sobejano's 'Azorín, el separado', *CHA*, 226/7 (1968), 239–65.
23. Leon Livingstone, *Tema y forma en las novelas de Azorín*.
24. Valverde, op. cit., 24–8, 278.
25. Other important studies of Azorín's style include Heinrich Denner, *Das Stilproblem bei Azorín* (Zurich, 1932); Mariano Baquero Goyanes, 'Elementos rítmicos en la prosa de Azorín', *Clavileño*, XV (1952), 25–32; Ángel Cruz Rueda, 'Azorín prosista', *Cuadernos de Literatura contemporánea*, 16/17 (1947), 331–68; and Robert E. Lott, *The Structure and Style of Azorín's El caballero inactual* (Athens, Georgia, 1963).

Chapter 8

NEW DIRECTIONS

By the middle of the second decade of this century the initial creative impulse of the Generation of 1898 had spent itself. Much important writing by the Generation was still to appear; the members of the Generation still dominated the literary scene throughout the 1920s and the 1930s; but, with the possible exception of Unamuno, what they published after about 1915 belongs clearly to a second stage of their work. Baroja specifically accepted that his novels could be divided into two phases separated by the beginning of the Aviraneta series (*OC* VII, 831). A clear change of emphasis can be perceived in the poetry of Machado after the additions to the first edition of *Campos de Castilla*, most of which were published between 1912 and 1916. Maeztu's war experiences created a watershed in his work, accelerating his evolution from Guild Socialism to the authoritarian theories he embraced at the end of the conflict. Azorín's *Doña Inés* (1915), while not providing quite such a dividing-line, still marks a turning-point in his production. It was about this time that Machado wrote his famous poem 'Una España joven' expressing disappointment with the Generation's achievements. The key-stanza is the fifth:

> Mas cada cual el rumbo siguió de su locura
> agilitó su brazo, acreditó su brío;
> dejó como un espejo bruñido su armadura
> y dijo: 'El hoy es malo, pero el mañana . . . es mío'.

In the poem as a whole, each member of the Generation rode off on his own hobby-horse, achieved his own reputation, and pursued his own private interests (the last word in the quotation is crucially important). The disintegration of the group was associated with the triumphant survival of all that they had initially tried to overthrow. Sadly, the problem of national regeneration was handed on unresolved to the next generation.

Already two younger writers had appeared to take up the challenge. These were Ramón Pérez de Ayala (1880–1962) and José Ortega y Gasset (1883–1955). The latter, like Ayala in the 1942 prologue to his novel *Troteras y danzaderas*, referred directly to a Spanish *crisis de conciencia* just before the turn of the century and to the emergence of the Generation of 1898 in response to it. 'Lo que había de valor nuevo en ellos', Ortega wrote grudgingly, 'era su mentalidad catastrófica. De aquí lo específico de su acción fuera negativo' (*Obras completas*, Madrid, 1946–69, IX, 494).[1] In contrast, Ayala and Ortega set out consciously to re-examine the problems which preoccupied their elders and to discover a positive, rational solution to them. Our purpose is to consider whether that re-examination produced in the end a more successful response to the Spanish crisis of conscience.

I. RAMÓN PÉREZ DE AYALA

Ayala was born in Oviedo, Asturias, on 9 August 1880.[2] From eight to fourteen he went to Jesuit schools and then, after completing his secondary education in Logroño and Oviedo, he took a degree in Law at Oviedo University in 1902. His earliest writings were in the local Republican (i.e., left-wing and anti-clerical) paper *El Porvenir de Asturias* and included translations of French Symbolist poets, which drew the attention of Benavente, Villaespesa, and Valle-Inclán. In 1902 he moved to Madrid and joined Juan Ramón Jiménez and others in founding the important literary review *Helios*. His first collection of poems, *La paz del sendero* (1903), was followed in 1916 by another, *El sendero innumerable*, and finally in 1921 by a third, *El sendero andante*. His first fictional work, 'Trece dioses', published in *El Porvenir* before he left Oviedo,[3] was followed by short stories in *Helios* and elsewhere and by his first novel, *Tinieblas en las cumbres*, finished in 1905 but not published until 1907.

In December 1907 his father's suicide and the collapse of the family business recalled him to Spain from Britain, where he had been working as correspondent of *El Imparcial* and other Madrid newspapers. Henceforth he had to make his living in earnest as a writer and journalist. His second novel, *AMDG* (1910), was followed by *La pata de la raposa* (1912) and *Troteras y danzaderas* (1913). His marriage in America to Miss Mabel Rick (1913) and the outbreak of the First World War mark the great divide in his life and work. Between 1916 and 1928 he published the remainder of his fiction and poetry, along with important collections of literary criticism and political articles.[4] In 1928 he was elected to the Royal Academy, but never took his seat. During the Republic he was Spain's ambassador to London. Thereafter he lived in exile, chiefly in Buenos Aires, until his return to Spain in 1954. Like Azorín he appears to have made his peace with the regime. In 1960 he was awarded the exceptionally substantial Juan March Prize for writing. The republication of his work, which began immediately after his death (5 August 1962), and the critical response which followed, have gone far to restore his true stature as a writer which was partly obscured by his many years of silence and exile.

Two influences which cannot be dismissed are those of his school-days and of the novelist Clarín, his Law Professor at Oviedo. Of the former he wrote to the critic Andrés González Blanco in 1906: 'Lo que no sabe Vd., y es muy importante, es que he perdido hace algún tiempo otro divino tesoro, que es la fe. Pero en cuanto le diga que estudié seis años con jesuítas (dos en Carrión de los Condes y cuatro en Gijón) se explicará Vd. fácilmente esta pérdida' (*Obras completas*, Madrid, 1963, I, xxxvii).[5] Earlier, on 11 April 1904 in *El Imparcial*, he had written of Clarín: 'La inquietud religiosa, la inquietud metafísica, sintióla él en la misma entraña, como adivinando este período espiritual por que atraviesan hoy las almas'. These two quotations reveal that Ayala, in his early twenties, was not only conscious of a spiritual disquiet in himself, but was also aware that it existed in the collectivity. From there it is but a step to his subsequent formulation, in line with that of the Generation of 1898, of the Spanish problem in terms of a crisis of confidence caused by lack of normative convictions rather than by concrete circumstances.

A final influence, overlooked hitherto, but clearly visible in his poetry, is that of the French Symbolist poets and the Latin American *modernistas* whom he avidly read and imitated. The deeply negative view of life, to which their cult of beauty was a reaction, is present in a number of Ayala's earliest poems. It remains present at least until his reminiscence in 'Canción del hombre macilento' (*El sendero innumerable*) of Darío's anguished and profoundly Schopenhauerian poem 'Lo fatal'. In general, however, the poems of *La paz del sendero* show Ayala finding relief from tension in erotic love, the contemplation of Nature, and in the exercise of his creative ability as a poet. Each of these sources of fulfilment appears as an option to Alberto de Guzmán in Ayala's first novel, *Tinieblas en las cumbres*.

Alberto is the last great fictional hero of the Generation of 1898. He takes his place alongside Pío Cid, Andrés Hurtado, Augusto Pérez, and Antonio Azorín as a typical representative of the Genera-tion's outlook. Agnes Muncy has written that Unamuno's main fictional characters are 'personajes cuya función principal es ... que a través de ellos llegue su creador a ahondar en el conocimiento de [sus propios] problemas'.[6] Ortega made an almost identical comment on Baroja's characters. It is just as relevant to those of Ganivet, Azorín (at least up to *Tomás Rueda*), and now to Ayala's, in his first novel-cycle. This use of ideologically-conceived figures, through whom the Generation explores and 'acts out' its own dilemmas, pro-jecting them on to the nation as a whole, just as Ayala was to do in 1942, is one of the unifying characteristics of its fictional technique.

Like Antonio Azorín in *La voluntad*, Alberto de Guzmán is introduced as simultaneously preoccupied with aesthetic problems and ultimate why-questions: 'traía entre ceja y ceja no se qué cosquilleos trascendentales sobre arte y hasta teología' (I, 115–16). In marked contrast, his companions on the excursion which the book describes are presented as 'individuos para quienes el mundo exterior ... no tenía vida propia ni finalidad evidente como no fuera la de subvenir a las necesidades humanas' (169). Thus once more we meet the Generation of 1898's two basic human categories: the few possessed of analytical insight, and the great mass of *ilusos*. As usual, experiences and conversational partners are employed to draw Alberto towards the moment of anguish and spiritual collapse symbolized by the eclipse of the sun which provides the climax of the story. In the 1942 prologue to *Troteras y danzaderas* (whose omission from the *Obras completas* is sadly typical of the whole collection) Ayala discussed the technical characteristics of his early novel in a way which relates them directly to what we have consistently observed heretofore, especially in Baroja. Of the role of the major secondary characters Ayala wrote: 'aquellos personajes episódicos representan (o pretenden representar) actitudes fundamentales de la conciencia individual ante la vida'. Their function in relation to the central figure is to 'provocar o estimular en el protagonista reacciones de conciencia'. Similarly the stuff of the novels themselves comes to be defined as virtually composed of states of mind.[7]

Structurally *Tinieblas en las cumbres* appears to be made up of two separate stories artificially fastened together. Rosina's story occupies more of the text than is justified by her role when Alberto's crisis occurs at the end. Equally, the events and characters of the excursion to see the eclipse do not constitute an organized pattern of experiences designed to provoke Alberto's collapse into *angustia metafísica*. His contacts with Rosina cannot be compared to those of Fernando Ossorio with Laura, with the nun, and with Adele in *Camino de perfección*, and do not merit the significance attached to them by Amorós.[8] Travesedo, though promising, fails to emerge as an adequate interlocutor for Alberto and it is not until the arrival of Warble that the narrative can adopt the familiar 'discussion-fiction' form of the '98 novel. Alberto's spiritual collapse is thus violently telescoped.

The conversation with Warble opens with a critique of the slightly pantheistic vision of Nature adumbrated in *La paz del sendero*. Ayala abandoned this youthful attitude, but without abandoning the corollary he was to add in the 1923 edition of the poems, and which is now stated here: 'el hombre es el sentido de la tierra' (191). The question now is how to use to the full the gift of conscious life, to which all the hierarchy of Nature is subordinated: '¿cómo acrecentar, intensificar y dilatar este precioso don, mezquino en las proporciones en que se nos otorga?' (192). From this point on Ayala's outlook must be seen as totally vitalistic. The problem of death is important to him only to the extent that it concentrates his thought on the life which death constantly threatens, and which, because of that threat, is rendered ever more precious. For the moment, Alberto is able to postulate the creation of beauty through Art as an adequate means of fulfilment now, and as a source of hope in future immortality. But the eclipse coincides with a sudden change in his outlook. By now the technique of the novel is densely symbolic. The tuberculosis patients who momentarily appear stand for man's pathetically cheerful unawareness of death's rapid approach. The thickening mist represents Alberto's growing 'aguda crisis espiritual',[9] which now causes him to lose sight of the solace of Art. The eclipse itself symbolizes both the eventual loss of solar energy, bringing with it the inevitable end of life on this planet, and the final collapse of Alberto's positive beliefs. Warble's light-hearted reaction provokes one of the clearest formulations of the Generation of 1898's existential pessimism we possess:

> No se ría Vd. El que no seamos nada; el que no sepamos nada; el que sospechemos que el universo es una cosa ciega, estúpida y fatal; el que pasemos por la vida como la sombra ha pasado sobre las montañas sin dejar nada detrás de sí; todo esto no es cosa de risa. (216)

The examination of Alberto's education in *AMDG* does not explain the process which set him on the road to this anguished involvement with the familiar problems of death, truth, and human destiny. The defect of the work in relation to the rest of the series is that details of Alberto's early religious crisis are swamped by the violence of Ayala's attack on the Jesuits. But its effectiveness as propaganda is attested by the fact that it is still banned in Spain.

La pata de la raposa, the most important of Ayala's early novels, opens with a reaffirmation of Alberto's spiritual desolation:

> era un mozo a quien el azacaneo de la vida había despojado, prematuramente, una por una, de todas las mentiras vitales, de todas las ilusiones normativas. (I, 246)

The pursuit of beauty is specifically rejected, after the works of Schopenhauer have been hurled out of the window.[10] Alberto's aspiration is now simply to escape from consciousness and insight. Like Ossorio in *Camino de perfección*, he sets out on what is less a journey than a pilgrimage or spiritual quest. The countryside induces a characteristically sudden poetic redefinition by Alberto of the choices before him, symbolized in a group of creatures. His dog, Sultán, stands for Christian submission to a supposed divine will, however cruelly this last may manifest itself. Alectryon, the cockerel, stands for active sensuality and self-fulfilment through power;

Calígula, the neutered cat, represents passive, selfish hedonism. Finally, the workaday ant, ignorant of abstract preoccupations, though envied, suggests no solution to the 'terrible morbo de la moderna patología espiritual; la enfermedad de lo incognoscible' (267).

Life remains for Alberto 'como una caja vacía . . . limitada de muerte por todas partes'. His question is still: ' ¿Con qué hemos de llenar la caja?' (266). After chapter 8 we perceive the beginnings of an evolution towards 'las ideas matrices y las normas morales de una vida renovada, toda serenidad y aplomo' (279). Before this acquisition of *ideas madres* is complete, however, Alberto has to pass through three stages of development. The first, and least convincingly treated, centres on his fiancée Fina. Despite the obvious attraction for Alberto of a solution via love and marriage (he returns to Fina three times in the course of the novel) it is, as in the fiction of the '98, arbitrarily rejected. A second stage of Alberto's development is sketched in chapters 15 to 19, when as a circus performer he turns his artistic ability into a source of mass entertainment. This stage, which Ayala calls *humorística*, is one of completely negative subjectivism and rejection of all 'objective' values. Antonio Azorín and Fernando Ossorio had also passed through it.[11] In it Alberto has no other resource than to 'obrar conscientemente sin finalidad' (337): to fill up the *caja* with mere activity. He is shaken out of it into the last stage of his evolution in a familiar way: by a test-situation (his brief imprisonment) and by a conversation with a specially selected interlocutor (his gaoler). Reawakened to a sense of moral responsibility by his realization of the relativity of human justice, and to a sense of urgency by the spectacle of degeneration presented by his friend Mackenzie and by the death of his childhood nurse, Alberto rapidly achieves serenity. His final position, enunciated at the end of Part II and the opening of Part III, is equidistant from total scepticism and mystical aspiration. It rests on three postulates. The first is conscious vitalism: overcoming preoccupation with death by the resolve to 'intensificar la sensación de la vida como placer supremo', or what Ayala calls less comprehensibly: 'equiparando el placer de vivir a la incertidumbre de conocer' (445). Alberto, that is, now accepts as his aim the exploration of life's mysterious potentialities, disregarding their annihilation in the end by death. The basis of his new-found confidence is the second postulate: that 'todo lo que es está bien, porque es' (I, 375): all reality is ultimately harmonious. The last postulate is that of the need for unselfish moral effort, in his case as a writer committed to the task of helping his country to overcome its crisis of national ideals.[12]

Alberto arrives at this position suddenly, almost intuitively, without convincing psychological justification. This was because Ayala was reflecting an already completed process in his own experience. As early as 1903 in an article in *Helios*, 'Letras o lanzas', he asserted that he had overcome his crisis of anguish and despair, and that he had attained a 'prudente escepticismo ecléctico' (I, 1128). The theory of universal sympathy and the idea of archetypes, which dominate Ayala's subsequent point of view, were already well developed before 1912. Two scenes from *Troteras y danzaderas* clarify Ayala's outlook further. In the first, a conversation with Tejero (Ortega y Gasset), Alberto explains the relevance of his ideas to the regeneration of Spain, asserting that literature can contribute to it by modifying the collective mentality via 'una educación estética' (I, 598). In the second, Ayala developed the central tenet of his subsequent literary philosophy: the requirement that the writer should accept a double imperative, of insight and 'la clara comprensión de todo lo creado, la justificación cordial de todo lo que existe' (576). Ayala's later work consistently expressed this ideal. The final embrace of Belarmino and Apolonio in the novel of that name (1921) symbolizes the two men's achievement of universal tolerance based on the recognition of a superior harmony. Equally in *Los trabajos de Urbino y Simona* (1923) and *El curandero de su honra* (1926) we perceive a process which leads through conflict to ultimate acceptance of a law of universal equilibrium.

The essays on Galdós in *Las máscaras* (1917) and other references in *Política y toros* (1918) develop Ayala's ideas into the affirmation that beneath the conflicts of earthly existence there operates an inner harmony in which can be perceived the manifestation of 'el sentido común cósmico' working towards 'la gran armonía universal' (III, 59). Whilst accepting 'la lucha perpetua entre . . . lo vital y lo intelectual' (III, 40), that is, the struggle between man's instinctive will to live and his corrosive analytical intelligence, Ayala refuses to agonize about it. Instead of suggesting the need for a *mentira vital* to protect us against it, he asserts the existence of an 'agente superior y armónico' capable of synthesizing the two opposing forces and producing 'la solución o equilibrio de tendencias o leyes entre sí diversas' (III, 55). This agent is universal tolerance: the 'simpatía cordial con cuanto existe' (III, 53) which Alberto finally discovered. To possess it is to possess what Ayala called 'el espíritu liberal': a quasi-mystical awareness of ultimate universal equilibrium.

The awareness rests on Ayala's belief in a pattern of universal archetypes:

El creador imprime en el tuétano o más encerrada sustancia de cada creatura un anhelo simple, un elemental, una ley o arquetipo . . . todo es bueno en cuanto obedece a su naturaleza y cumple el fin a que es destinado . . . el mal . . . aparece cuando las cosas son desencajadas de su fin propio. (III, 53, 55)

The solution to the problem of life is to be found in the discovery by the individual of his archetypal vocation, and in conscious conformity to it thereafter. Ayala's term for this is *seriedad*.[13] Alberto's discovery of his vocation as a writer, and his decision to conform to it, signal his emergence from his previously anguished state of mind. *Luz* has triumphed over *tinieblas*. Similarly Don Rodrigo in *El ombligo del mundo* (1924) exemplifies the emergence in an individual character of a hidden archetypal personality, in conforming to which he finds fulfilment and happiness. Colás in *El curandero de su honra* refers consciously to 'mi arquetipo congénito' (IV, 786).

Ayala's second manner, therefore, not only contains differences of theme and technique compared with his first series of novels, but it also illustrates a more serenely confident outlook on life.[14] Without embracing any specific creed, Ayala had found within himself what he called 'la emoción religiosa:

La emoción religiosa implica la idea siempre presente de la muerte, sí; y por esto mismo, por la perentoriedad del plazo que se nos ha asignado en el mundo, por el misterio finalista de la vida, implica deberes actuales y apremiantes. (IV, 938)

With this, one of the major problems of the Generation of 1898, that of finality, ceased to preoccupy Ayala. Life became its own finality, on condition that it was lived responsibly and usefully. In answer to the question '¿Cómo me he de salvar en la vida misma?', Ayala answers resolutely: 'Sumando los actos de mi vida pasajera a lo eterno de la vida humana' (IV, 938) and pursuing 'todo aquello que redunda y trasciende en beneficio de la especie' (IV, 789). To live fully according to this man- and life-centred ideal two further imperatives must be accepted. The character of Tigre Juan, Ayala's last great fictional creation, reaches its peak of significance when he enunciates them. The first is that of cultivating the widest possible sympathetic understanding of human behaviour, so as to achieve the maximum of tolerant insight. The second is that of deliberately refusing to convert what is only part of 'la razón de ser de la vida' (e.g., the aspiration to eternal life) into the whole of it. In these two imperatives Ayala finds the answer to another of the Generation of 1898's problems: that of duty. On the third great issue, truth, Ayala adopts a broad and comprehensive standpoint in accord with his belief in an overriding harmony in which all truths concur: 'la armonía total, donde cada cosa que es (y, cuanto es, obedece a un razón de ser) encaja sin estridencia ni coacción, espontáneamente en el conjunto' (IV, 805). The affirmation at the end of *Belarmino y Apolonio* that 'hay tantas verdades irreductibles como puntos de vista' (IV, 218) is confirmed by the equally harmonizing statement of *Divagaciones literarias*: 'A la verdad nada le puede ser ajeno, ni siquiera el error' (IV, 888). This affirmative tone contrasts markedly with the anguished interrogations of the Generation of 1898. Ayala's mature opinion that writers were nothing if not 'intérpretes, aunque falibles, de un presunto plan providente que rige los destinos mortales' (IV, 946) is diametrically opposed to the Generation's view that their role was precisely that of questioning the existence of such a pattern.

To assert the existence of a cosmic harmony unsupported by a divine presence, or to postulate a pattern of archetypes without explaining their origin, is simply to make private, oracular statements. Nevertheless, in Ayala's case they represent a sincere attempt, coinciding with the end of the first creative phase of the Generation of 1898's work, to break away from its pessimistic negativism and to reassert positive *ideas madres*, or what Ayala called 'los valores fundamentales de la vida ... las eternas verdades que exaltan el alma' (IV, 938, 949). It is tempting to suggest that they illustrate the beginning of a new movement of ideas.

II. JOSÉ ORTEGA Y GASSET

Undoubtedly the greatest contribution to restoring a positive consensus of intellectual thought in Spain was made by Ayala's friend Ortega y Gasset (9 May 1883–18 October 1955). The son of a leading newspaper editor, Ortega too studied with the Jesuits before graduating in Philosophy and Letters in Madrid in 1902. He took his doctorate with a thesis on history in 1904. In 1905, urged by Maeztu, he studied philosophy in Germany for two years, before returning to Spain to preach in articles and lectures the doctrine of *europeización*, already abandoned by Unamuno and others of the Generation of 1898. In 1910 he was appointed to the Chair of Metaphysics at the University of Madrid. During the next twenty years he carried out almost single-handed the renovation of philosophical studies in Spain as well as founding in 1923 *La Revista de Occidente*, Spain's most influential intellectual review since Perojo's *La Revista contemporánea* fifty years before. At almost the same time, with *La deshumanización del arte* (1925) he published the best-known Spanish literary manifesto of the inter-war period. Tirelessly active in public and political life, he was a founder in 1914 of the *Liga de Educación Política Española*, aimed at modernizing Spain's political outlook. His influence was significant in bringing about the fall of Maura's Conservative government in 1909 and the fall of the monarchy in 1931. In that year he, Ayala, and Marañon formed a second league of middle-class radicals, the *Agrupación al Servicio de la República*. His most famous works, *España invertebrada* (1921) and *La rebelión de las masas* (1930), were attempts to deal with the phenomenon of mass participation in political decision-making,

which he came to see as the main threat to progress in the democratic countries. His misgivings on this and other scores produced
disenchantment with the Republic. From the outbreak of the Civil
War until 1945 he shared the exile of so many Spanish intellectuals.
He spent the last decade of his life under official displeasure. Certain
sections of Catholic thought in Spain have remained bitterly hostile
to Ortega (as they were to Galdós and Unamuno), but otherwise
there is absolute unanimity as to his overwhelming influence on the
history of Spanish ideas in the first half of this century.

Beginning, like Ayala, from much the same point of departure as
the Generation of 1898, he set out to restore his readers' faith in the
capacities and destiny of Spain. At the same time he attempted to
formulate a system of ideas which would bring about a rebirth of
confidence in human reason as a source for ideal goals for existence
or, at the very least, a means of obtaining satisfaction and self-
fulfilment in the hunt for them. As late as 1937 he referred to this
hunt as 'un esfuerzo que se complace en sí mismo y no en su resultado'
(V, 439). This distinction emphasizes a duality which runs through
Ortega's thinking almost from beginning to end. Once the Nietzschean assertiveness of his earliest writing had been sloughed off,
Ortega's position (around 1906) became remarkably similar to
Unamuno's. Life is seen as pure contingency ('una casualidad', I, 54;
'Una incógnita dolorosa, opresora y obsesionante que es preciso
resolver', I, 436). Later he condensed this potentially tragic view of
the human condition into one word, a *naufragio*. Disciplined intellectual effort offers man the possibility of surviving the shipwreck
and of swimming purposefully in the sea of *circunstancia*:

> existir [es] un hallarse náufrago en algo que se llama mundo, y no se sabe lo
> que es . . . hallarse cercado, inseguro y prisionero de otra cosa misteriosa y
> heterogénea, la circunstancia, el Universo. Y para buscar en ella alguna
> seguridad, como el náufrago mueve sus brazos y nada, se ha puesta a
> pensar . . . El pensamiento . . . tiene sus raíces y su sentido en el hecho
> radical, previo y terrible de vivir. (V, 472)

The questions how do we swim? what do we swim towards? depend
for Ortega on the question what is the nature of reality? The originality of his position (which has been exaggerated) lies in the fact that
he rejected both of the traditional answers to this question. The real
for him lies not in the substantiality of things, nor in categories of the
mind, but in individual human life, defined in a special way. Life is
understood as a *situation* in which we willy-nilly find ourselves and
in which we must act if we are to go on living. 'El hombre . . . al encontrarse con que existe, al acontecerle existir, lo único que encuentra o que le acontece es no tener más remedio que hacer algo para
no dejar de existir' (VI, 32). Life is therefore a task, an inescapable
quehacer. By the same token it is the reverse of an abstraction,

since it cannot be abstracted (i.e., taken out) of its operative context. It is this last which turns it into a 'task' or 'drama'. Both words imply effort and perhaps conflict. In relation to what?

So far we have alluded to Ortega's first cardinal affirmation: that the life of each individual is his 'radical reality', not in an absolute sense, but as the reality in which *for him* everything else is rooted:

> el hecho radical, el hecho de todos los hechos – esto es, aquel dentro del cual se dan los demás como detalles e ingredientes de él – es la vida de cada cual. Toda otra realidad es una realidad secundaria. (VI, 347)

Now we come to Ortega's second affirmation: 'La vida es circunstancia' (VI, 348). All that surrounds individual human life, obstructing or facilitating it, and in the context of which the individual must act and live, is for Ortega life's 'circumstance'. Outside or separate from its circumstance, individual existence is unthinkable. Life and circumstance are indissolubly one:

> Yo soy yo y mi circunstancia. (VI, 347)

Life can only be defined and understood in relation to its circumstance; contrariwise, the reality of the objects which make up that circumstance resides for the individual solely in their 'importance' to him, that is, in their impact on his personal existence in the form of *vivencias* (by which Ortega translated the German *Erlibnis*). Neither he nor they exist absolutely.

The individual is thus subject to circumstance in the sense that he has only the limited choice of possibilities that his circumstance offers him, just as a pianist has only a finite number of keys on his keyboard to play. Within this limitation the individual is free, in the sense that he can choose at will among these possibilities. Living is deciding. For if 'la vida es quehacer', then

> lo más grave de estos quehaceres en que la vida consiste es ... que nos encontramos siempre forzados a hacer algo, pero no nos encontramos nunca estríctamente forzados a hacer algo determinado. Antes de hacer algo tiene cada hombre que decidir, por su cuenta y riesgo, lo que va a hacer. (VI, 13)

Thus each individual 'constructs' his own life (IV, 288) or 'invents' it (VI, 366) by a continuous series of decisions and actions. Ortega does not hesitate to affirm that what a man *is* consists simply in this: a potential for action which goes on being continuously realized (VI, 32; II, 80). His position here is at variance with both the spiritual or religious outlook, in which life is the manifestation of the soul's activity directed towards transcendence, and with the materialist outlook, in which life is the activity of a particularly complex organization of physical matter into which it will ultimately be reabsorbed.

Morality, for Ortega, is rooted in this need to decide or choose a particular action. The actual performance of actions he calls 'occupation'; the preceding state of mind in which decisions or choices leading to actions are made he calls 'preoccupation'. But in contrast to the anguish, 'care', or preoccupation of thinkers like Kierkegaard, Unamuno, or Heidegger, which is ultimately concerned with the implications of death, preoccupation for Ortega is solely concerned with life. The state of man, the swimmer attempting to survive his *naufragio*, is a state of insecurity. Likewise his decisions are attended by insecurity. Since his life is what his decisions and acts make it, it is not only 'inexorablemente seria' (V, 85), but also by its nature intrinsically ethical.

Ortega locates the decisive factor operating on the individual's concrete ethical performance in the very depths of his personality, far below the level of the intellect. For 'toda nuestra vida intelectual es secundaria a nuestra vida real o auténtica', the basis of which is formed by beliefs and convictions which function latently, at a lower than conscious level (VII, 61). Beneath these in turn lies a mysterious area of the personality, which Ortega never satisfactorily defined, and concerning the origin of which no coherent theory is advanced in his work. He refers to it as different times as, *inter alia*, 'una intuición o sensación primaria', a 'sentimiento radical', or a 'fondo insobornable'. This 'hontanar profundo y único' (II, 291) is both the source of man's intimate sense of anguish, solitude, and insecurity (his awareness of life as a 'problem') and at the same time the fount of an irrepressible impulse to overcome the problem, to achieve that clarity which is for Ortega a form of dominion over life and a release from disquiet. Acceptance of this 'imperativo de luz' is a metaphysical necessity since 'todo lo que el hombre hace no es sino un conato de solución del problema de la vida, y para el hombre es su vida "el centro del universo"' (I, 480). But it is also an ethical requirement: from a stratum of the psyche much deeper than that of the rational mind or the moral conscience, there emerges a demand to achieve what Ortega calls 'authenticity', 'acertar consigo mismo' (VI, 350): the fulfilment of one's own unique potential 'siempre irreductible al de los demás' (IV, 366). When this 'deseo radical' is not thwarted by the temptation to accept passively inherited patterns of belief and conduct, or patterns which are in any way whatsoever those of others, it manifests itself as what Ortega came to call 'vocation', 'project', or 'programme'. The essence of moral behaviour, for Ortega, consists in each individual's 'esfuerzo original' to execute his own inherent project (IV, 402). Not to do this is to live the inauthentic 'fictitious' life of the average man. To accept the imperative of one's own inherent vocation is, on the other hand, to achieve happy self-fulfilment. It is the condition of belonging to a select, superior minority. The distinction which Ortega went on to make, between the *mejores* and the *hombre masa*, was thus ultimately a moral distinction.

The fact that the essence of the individual's morality resides in that individual's *modo de ser*, and not in the nature of his separate acts, only means that each man's moral behaviour is intrinsically *his*: his choice of pre-existent values, dictated by his own personal *razón vital*. But the existence of objective values, independent of the individual's acceptance or rejection of them, is specifically accepted by Ortega in his *Introducción a la estimativa* (1923) and in '¿Qué son los valores?'

Ortega's ethics were, from the point of view of his relationship with the Generation of 1898, a most important area of his thought, since all the Generation tended to see philosophy as a source of practical existential orientations and not as abstract speculation. But they were inseparable from his metaphysics:

> Nuestra vida se nos presenta constituída por dos dimensiones, inseparables la una de la otra y que quiero dejar destacadas con toda claridad. En su dimensión primaria vivir es estar yo, el yo de cada cual, en la circunstancia, y no tener más remedio que habérselas con ella. Pero esto impone a la vida una segunda dimensión consistente en que no tiene más remedio que averiguar lo que la circunstancia es. (V, 24)

We must now therefore glance at Ortega's conceptions of truth and knowledge. The essence of his doctrine here is contained in the idea of perspectivism, which appeared in his earliest writings and evolved continuously, enriching and complicating its meaning, to the very end of his work.[15] Perspectivism is the logical corollary of what we have seen already: that while Ortega does not question the existence of a reality outside the mind of the individual (II, 338) since this is implicit in the notion of 'circumstance', he held that knowledge of it is rooted, like everything else, in the 'realidad radical' of the individual's unique and concrete existence. It follows that we can only perceive reality, or attain any sort of knowledge of it, from the viewpoint or perspective of our own individual lives. All knowledge is thus 'perspectivistic' in its very essence:

> Cada vida es un punto de vista sobre el universo . . . la realidad, como un paisaje, tiene infinitas perspectivas, todas ellas igualmente verídicas y auténticas. La sola perspectiva falsa es esa que pretende ser la única . . . la utopia, la verdad no localizada, vista desde lugar ninguno. (III, 200)
> La verdad integral solo se obtiene articulando lo que el prójimo ve con lo que yo veo y así sucesivamente. Cada individuo es un punto de vista esencial. (III, 202)

Ortega rejected the view that this was a form of philosophical idealism, arguing that the viewpoint of the individual did not create its object; the object existed independently of the individual who looked at it. The criticism that his theory was basically subjectivistic he answered by admitting that the individual *punto de vista* contained an objective element, since it was always a point of view about something outside, a part of 'circumstance'. The most dangerous accusation, that his doctrine was a form of philosophical relativism, he tried to counter chiefly by arguing that the absolute was a fallacious concept of old-style rationalism outmoded by his *racio-vitalismo*, and secondly that every pseudo-absolute belonged to a time and place, so that in the end, inevitably 'el puro o absoluto pensamiento se convierte en un pensamiento histórico' (VI, 183).

Truth, then, for Ortega, was in the first place the truth which I personally need in my own time and place in order to 'saber a que atenerme', the product, in other words, of a *razón vital* which is 'sólo una forma y función de la vida' (III, 178). I need this truth ultimately in order to understand my circumstance well enough to be able to recognize my 'project', to justify it to myself and others, which is the ethical aspect of truth-seeking, and finally to carry it out. Truth is my purposive, functional (and selective) interpretation of a 'mundo común y objetivo', the reality of which the consensus of others sufficiently guarantees. The test of whether truth was 'vital' or not lay for Ortega in its power to stimulate enthusiasm, sincerity, and delight. A culture pattern, individual or collective, which rested on passively accepted truths which no longer stimulated such responses, had outlived itself.

Truth is not static. Change is not an accident of the individual's life but the very substance of it (VI, 35). Movement in time changes man's point of view on life just as physical movement from one place to another changes his point of view on what he sees before him. Thus man has no definite time-defying nature. Being is historical. As each man creates his life and personality in a continuous flow of decisions and actions, so mankind creates its history. It is only through history that man 'perceives mankind'. The radical reality of man, whether we see him individually or collectively, is different from epoch to epoch (II, 517), but at the same time continuous. In Ortega's work therefore, after *Las Atlántidas* (1924), *razón vital* is progressively complemented by *razón histórica*, the latter being in fact a dimension of the former: 'acontece que la razón misma, la auténtica [i.e., razón vital] es histórica'.[16] History, that is, constitutes that aspect of man's circumstance which contains his previous collective *proyectos de vida*, each of which has been found insufficient and outgrown. These survive as positions to which he cannot return, and thus in a sense force him to discover others in an endless series (V, 238). History is a chain of human experiences: man's being in the past. Ortega regarded it as intelligible and progressive when viewed from the angle of what he called 'la dialéctica de la razón viviente' (V, 135) in contrast to Hegel's purely rationalistic interpretation of historical development.[17] In so far as human life forms part of an infinite transcendence, that transcendence *is* history (IV, 521). Regrettably Ortega did not live to write his projected book *Aurora de la razón histórica*, which would have filled out the affirmations of *Historia como sistema* (1941).

It follows that the task of the historian, for Ortega, was to escape from the 'fetichism of facts' and attempt to define the 'drama vital' of men and peoples in history – their struggle to fulfil their various *proyectos*. His own writings on the problem of Spain (especially *España invertebrada*, 1921) and by extension that of Europe and the West in general (*La rebelión de las masas*, 1930) develop this approach in what seemed for a time a most persuasive way. However, they are now something of an embarrassment to his apologists and are no longer taken very seriously. But their relevance to the ideas of the Generation of 1898 is considerable. In Ortega the naïve historicism which we have criticized in Ganivet, Unamuno, Maeztu, and Azorín reaches a climax of intellectual abstraction. In broad outline Ortega's stance is familiar. The individual is conditioned by his racial origin. 'Esto soy yo', he wrote in 1917, in his essay on Azorín, 'un hasta hendiendo el viento que fue lanzada por el brazo secular de mi raza' (II, 188). Unlike Azorín, however, and more especially unlike Unamuno, Ortega did not see race in terms of enduring 'intrahistoric' characteristics, but in terms of a historical succession of racial goals and achievements. Three years before he had defined race as 'un estilo de vida', and in 1915 as 'una manera de pensar' (I, 414). Hence, once again, change was part of its essence. In *El tema de nuestra tiempo* (1923) he defined race afresh as 'un repertorio de tendencias vitales' (III, 154) evolving coherently, each new racial 'project' growing organically out of the last. The dynamics of change are mysterious, but their operation can be observed by regarding each historical moment as embodying the perspective of a particular generation.[18] The generation forms the nexus between the individual and the race. The individual enters the historical process with a general racial heritage together with a specific generational imperative to bring nearer to fruition an existing racial (or national, for the distinction is not always clear) 'project'. The individual project is thus ideally a component of a generational project which is in turn a component of a racial or national project.

Within the bosom of each generation coexist those whose vital pulse beats strongly, and who respond positively, clear-sightedly, to the personal, generational, and racial/national imperative, as well as those whose response varies from passive, uncritical acceptance of the inherited pattern of norms and ideals, to negative indifference to them or actual betrayal of them. The former Ortega does not scruple to call 'los mejores'; the latter are accused of *plebeyez*, and ultimately form the *masas* on whom Ortega blamed the plight of

Western civilization. Not surprisingly Ortega attributed the unhappy state of Spain in the 1920s to a chronic lack of *mejores*, capable of formulating a new national project to replace the old Catholic and imperialist one which had collapsed at the end of the sixteenth century. He believed that the 'European idea' (now after half a century painfully taking concrete shape) could supply the purposive collective ideal Spain needed.[19]

It is clear, then, that Ortega took as his starting-point the same crisis of ideas and beliefs which the Generation of 1898 had recognized and projected on to the nation. But in *raciovitalismo* he believed that he had found, for our time at least, an answer to the 'desazón radical ante la existencia' (II, 163) with which he and the '98 writers were primarily concerned. To test the validity of this belief a thoroughgoing review of Ortega's system of thought would be necessary. All that can be undertaken here is the briefest survey of his central affirmations in relation to the Generation of 1898's collective aspiration to rediscover a satisfying pattern of *ideas madres*.

We must begin from Ortega's position with regard to any possible transcendental finality, since it is loss of faith in this which more than anything else is behind Ganivet's *escepticismo científico*, the *agonismo* and *congoja* of Unamuno, the *angustia metafísica* of Azorín in 1901, the instinctive shift of Maeztu's thought from economics to philosophy and theology, and Baroja's unconcealed longing for a *mentira vital*. Ortega maintained a prudent reticence about his religious position. That he was not only fiercely anti-clerical but also fiercely anti-Catholic is beyond all question. 'Yo, señores', he declared in 1931, 'no soy católico, y desde mi mocedad he procurado que hasta los humildes detalles de mi vida privada queden formalizados acatólicamente'.[20] But references to God and to an afterlife are frequent throughout his work and create an ambiguous impression. In *Renan* (1909) he seemed to define God as immanent and identify Him with cultural ideas in general. In *Meditaciones del Quijote* (1914) he was able to assert that 'Dios es la perspectiva'. In *Adán en el Paraíso* he had declared: 'Dios, con efecto, no es sino el nombre que damos a la capacidad de hacerse cargo de las cosas'. In *El tema de nuestro tiempo* God becomes 'también un punto de vista' and 'símbolo del torrente vital'. Alongside these affirmations are those in which Ortega insists on history as 'la realidad trascendente' (VI, 49) beyond which there is no ulterior transcendence, and those in which he asserts that thought can never attain its final goal: security. Nor, as we have noted, is there any discussion of the origin of the life from which 'la razón vital' springs. It is hard to avoid the conclusion that Ortega's thought does not meet the demand for the kind of finality which the Generation of 1898 so desperately sought.[21]

On the issue of man's ability to perceive truth rationally Ortega's position was much stronger. His whole system constituted a determined attempt to assert a third position between the two horns of Unamuno's dilemma: 'todo lo vital es anti-racional . . . y todo lo racional anti-vital' (*OC* IV, 488). Nothing is more opposed to the '98 view than Ortega's confident belief in the intelligibility of life as an ascending creative process. By insisting, in an almost pragmatistic way, on truth not as an abstraction, but as 'una forma y función de la vida' (III, 178), Ortega attempted to detach the search for it from the pursuit of 'eternal' universally valid and unchanging norms, a pursuit which he regarded as sterile, and to attach it to the here and now. The truth of each epoch was that epoch's selection from a general repertory of values; not an arbitrary choice, but one which grows organically out of the previous selection and prefigures the next one, in an ongoing series (V, 533). This is undoubtedly the part of Ortega's thought which is most related to the main problem faced by the Generation of 1898: the need to rediscover an intelligible explanation of life and a source of practical values. Ortega's ideas promised an answer here in the very terms of the question, a means to 'convertir en punto de apoyo aquello mismo que engendró la impresión de abismo' (VI, 23). Within its limits Ortega's system offered a real alternative to metaphysical despair. But these limits were, for the '98, too narrow. For to accept them was to accept the loss of the absolute. For Ortega all values, all truths, all interpretations of human destiny, were condemned to pass away in the end and give rise to others. This serene acceptance of 'el flujo histórico de lo corruptible' (VI, 417) ran utterly counter to the outlook of the Generation of 1898. Indeed, it is arguable that it ran counter to Ortega's own acceptance of man's need for 'security'. Truth as 'functional', 'instrumental', contingent, and in perpetual metamorphosis, was not truth as the Generation (trapped as it was in what Ortega regarded as the old-fashioned world of 'Kantian pure reason') wanted it to be.

In the field of ethics Ortega's thoughts were more clearly formulated than those of his immediate predecessors. For the Generation an austere conception of ethical behaviour offered a refuge from uncertainty about other aspects of existence and the possibility of nobly defying the injustice of man's ultimate annihilation by death. It was, as Aranguren writes, 'una ética existencial, ética del hombre menesteroso, indigente, cuando no angustiado o desesperado . . . una ética de crisis'.[22] Ortega's ethic of 'magnanimity', with its emphasis on the creative task of each individual and its call for enthusiasm and impetuosity, is, like the rest of his thought, more positive and appealing. But it is open to serious objections. Morality, for Ortega, consists in fidelity to one's authentic self, expressed as a mission or 'proyecto vital'. But it is not clear why all authentic *proyectos* are *ipso facto* moral by standards of morality other than Ortega's own. Again, since Ortega wrote little systematically about ethics, no exploration of the moral individual's concrete relationship with his circumstance is undertaken. Ortega's ethics lack content and precept. Finally, despite all attempts to explain it away, there subsists the fundamental duality of all Ortega's writings:[23] the vital imperative as a *necessary* response to a tragic reality into which man is born, and the vital imperative (seen here in its ethical dimension) as essentially superfluous, sportive, delighting in its own activity irrespective of aim or goal. Of all the '98 only Baroja momentarily adopted this sportive view of life, behaviour, and ethics (see Hasting's speech quoted above, pp. 102–3); only, in Hasting's own character, to emphasize its inconsistency.

Finally, with regard to the problem of Spain, Ortega appears to prolong the '98 approach rather than to offer an alternative. Like the *noventayochistas* he views it as a philosophical thinker and theorist of historical processes, rather than as an economist or social scientist. Hence when he comes to discuss the issue of the individual's relationship with the collectivity he falls into the same double error of postulating a false antithesis between the individual and society and asserting a false relationship between the individual and his race or racial tradition. Ortega's definition of society as 'una masa organizada, estructurada, por una minoría de individuos selectos' (III, 93) ignores fundamental questions of class and social function. It not only completely misinterprets the composition of any society's ruling élite, but also grossly simplifies and overestimates its role. At the same time Ortega's version of the familiar idea of the 'social myth', now seen as a 'national project' with strong overtones of racial tradition, into which the individual project fits, is plainly naïve. It assumes a primacy of abstract, almost spiritual goals over concrete collective aspirations to (for example) material wellbeing, which is in defiance of historical experience. At best it applies only briefly to moments of national crisis. However, Ortega's vision of a nationally unifying Spanish project, linking her racial heritage fruitfully to a European future, was one which all the Generation to some degree shared.

What can we conclude? Ortega's central intuition: that reason is a function of man's existential situation, without minimizing the anguish and insecurity which he in common with the Generation of 1898 felt in the presence of life's enigma, did offer the possibility of interpreting the human condition positively and hopefully. In 1901 the manifesto of Baroja, Azorín, and Maeztu had emphasized, in terms only slightly different from those employed by Unamuno and Ganivet, that the crisis of Spain was a crisis of ideals at both the individual and national level. Increasingly as the impact of the Cuban disaster faded, the Generation of 1898 perceived that this 'Spanish crisis of conscience' was part of a general Western crisis of beliefs and values. Like *krausismo* half a century earlier *raciovitalismo* seemed for a time to restore an affirmative consensus among the younger cultured minority. Providing what seemed to be renewed metaphysical certitude and persuasive ethical imperatives, it stood out as an alternative both to the scepticism of the '98 and to the dogmatism of the church. In retrospect we can see that it did not entirely fulfil the aspiration of its creator to formulate an all-embracing answer to the anguishing questions of our time. Despite its internal coherence and its considerable originality, Ortega's system of thought is vulnerable at the very point which to the Generation of 1898 was crucial: that is, as 'un sistema de convicciones *últimas* sobre la vida' (VI, 114; my italics). We may perhaps see in the satire of Ortega contained in Luis Martín Santos's *Tiempo de silencio*, a major novel of the late 1960s in Spain, and in the obvious relationship of its hero, Pedro, to the fictional hero of the Generation of 1898, symbols of the survival of the Generation's *Weltanschauung*.

NOTES

1. All subsequent bracketed references to Ortega's work are to this collection.

2. No satisfactory biography of Ayala exists. M. Pérez Ferrero's *Ramón Pérez de Ayala* (Madrid, 1973) ends at the year 1908 and consists chiefly of gossip. Its treatment of facts is vague and many of these remain conjectural. Agustín, Rand, and others all provide fragmentary information.

3. Pérez Ferrero, op. cit., 72. The piece seems to be uncollected.

4. i.e., *Tres novelas poemáticas de la vida española: Prometeo, Luz de Domingo*, and *La caída de los Limones* (1916); *Hermán encadenado* (war correspondence; 1917); *Las máscaras* (literary criticism), 2 vols. (1917 and 1919); *Política y toros* (Political and social articles: 1918); *Belarmino y Apolonio* (1921); *Luna de miel, luna de hiel* and its sequel *Los trabajos de Urbano y Simona* (1923); *El ombligo del mundo* (short stories; 1924); *Bajo el signo de Artemisa* (short stories; 1924); *Tigre Juan* and its sequel *El curandero de su honra* (1926); and *Justicia* (1928).

5. All subsequent bracketed references are to this edition.

6. Agnes Muncy, *La creación del personaje en las novelas de Unamuno* (Santander, 1963), 14.

7. Ayala's shorthand term for this was 'Biometría espiritual' (cf. the note added in 1930 to the title of *La pata de la raposa*, OC I, 238). He defined *biometría* in *Amistades y recuerdos* (Barcelona, 1961), ('El senso galdosiano') as 'de una parte descripción atenta de unas cuantas vidas . . . y por otra parte, comprobación de su textura e intensidad respectivas, mediante el juego recíproco de acciones y reacciones al choque, roce o contacto de las unas con las otras' (p. 47).

8. In his edition of *Tinieblas en las cumbres* (Madrid, 1971), 198, note 270.

9. On the persistence of the mist-symbol in Ayala's subsequent work see M. Fernández Avelló, *Pérez de Ayala y la niebla* (Oviedo, 1970). Unfortunately the author limits himself to a descriptive survey, accumulating references rather than advancing any convincing explanation of the symbolism.

10. In a later essay, 'El arte del estilo', part v (IV, 1067–70), Ayala ex-

plains Schopenhauer's theory of the aesthetic act as the only valid source of ultimate knowledge. This theory Alberto now abandons.

11. Compare with Ayala's remark apropos of Alberto at this point, 'Las cosas no tenían otro sentido o trascendencia que los que él, humorísticamente, quisiera otorgarles', with Antonio Azorín's reflection in *La voluntad*: 'La sensación crea la conciencia. La conciencia crea el mundo. No hay más realidad que la imagen' (Azorín, *OC* I, 816), and especially with Fernando Ossorio's 'El mundo de afuera no existe, tiene la realidad que yo le quiero dar' (Baroja, *OC* VI, 58).

12. K. W. Reinink, *Algunos aspectos literarios y lingüísticos de la obra de Ramón Pérez de Ayala* (The Hague, 1959) appears confused about this point. On p. 35 he appears ready to concede Alberto's emergence from 'crisis espiritual', but on p. 76 seems to regard it as illusory. H. S. Tracy, 'Nota sobre *La pata de la raposa*', *NRFH*, XI (1957), 198–200, fails sadly to see the process of emergence from anguish at all. The views of both critics suffer from inattention to the positive outlook formulated especially in *Las máscaras* and developed subsequently.

13. The idea is clearly very similar to Ortega's idea of authenticity as stemming from fidelity to a 'programme' or 'proyecto vital'. The whole question of the effect of Ortega's ideas on the work of Ayala remains unexplored. It is clear that a similarity exists between Ayala's theory of vocation, his postulate of archetypes, his advocacy of universal tolerance and comprehension, and his later literary theories on the one hand, and well-known views of Ortega on the other.

14. M. Azaña in his review of *Belarmino and Apolonio* in *La Pluma*, II, no. 8 (1921), 54–8 was perhaps the first critic to stress Ayala's new-found *armonismo*. I agree with Leon Livingstone, 'Interior Duplication and the Problem of Form in the Modern Spanish Novel', *PMLA*, LXXIII (1958), 393–406 as against C. H. Leighton, 'The Structure of *Belarmino y Apolonio*', *BHS*, XXXVII (1960), 241 in believing that this *armonismo*, the technical result of which is Ayala's perspectivism, does not imply any return to absolute criteria of belief.

15. See Antonio Rodríguez Huéscar, *Perspectiva y verdad* (Madrid, 1966), esp. 257–415, 'Trayectoria y problemática de la idea de perspectiva en los textos de Ortega'.

16. Cited ibid., 182 from the uncollected 'Orígen y epílogo de la filosofía', 36.

17. See Ortega's unfinished prologue to Hegel's *Philosophy of History* (1928).

18. For accounts of the generational theory see Yves Renouard, 'La théorie des générations de José Ortega y Gasset', *BH*, IV (1951), 413–21; and P. Garagorri, *Introducción a Ortega* (Madrid, 1970), 147–63. A more elaborate treatment is J. Marías, *El método histórico de las generaciones* (Madrid, 1949).

19. Ortega's literary theories need not be discussed here. Although their most famous formulation, *La deshumanización del arte e ideas sobre la novela* (1925), grew out of a debate with Baroja, they had no serious influence on the work of the Generation of 1898.

20. 'Rectificación de la República', a speech made on 6 December 1931. For the Catholic reaction to Ortega see, *inter alia*, P. Santiago Ramírez, *¿Un orteguismo católico?*' (Madrid, 1958) and J. L. Aranguren's reply in *La ética de Ortega* (3rd ed., Madrid, 1966); also J. Marías's defence of Ortega against Iriarte, Sánchez Villaseñor, and Gironella in *Ortega y tres antípodas* (Buenos Aires, 1950).

21. But see *per contra* Aranguren, op. cit., ch. 1 and H. Larraín Acuña, *La génesis del pensamiento de Ortega* (Buenos Aires, 1962), esp. 154–6.

22. Aranguren, op. cit., 43.

23. See in this connection N. R. Orringer's articles 'Ortega y Gasset's Sportive Theories of Communication', *MLN*, LXXXV (1970), 209–13 and 'Ortega y Gasset's Sportive Vision of Plato', *MLN*, LXXXVIII (1973), 264–280. Morón Arroyo, Ferrater Mora, and Aranguren tend to deny that the duality exists.

Chapter 9

CONCLUSION

I. THE UNITY OF THE GENERATION

Despite the disclaimers of some of its members and the dissent expressed by Federico de Onís, Juan Ramón Jiménez, and a few of their followers, Azorín's postulate of the existence of a Generation of 1898 in Spanish literature has been generally accepted at least since the publication of Pedro Laín Entralgo's fundamental book in 1945. Azorín's views about who belonged to the Generation and his approach to it in terms of 'crítica social y política' have had to be modified, but the central assertion of his 1913 articles is no longer in doubt. Nor can the unity of the Generation of 1898 be seriously questioned. It rests, not on similar dates of birth, allegiance to a common leader, or other adventitious factors, but on a comparable attitude to a common set of problems. In the preceding chapters we have seen repeatedly that the major effort of the group was directed at exploring the position of the individual in a world bereft of absolutes. Their hope of social amelioration in general, and of the regeneration of Spain in particular, was conditioned by their determination to see progress primarily in terms of a recovery of values. Hence their aim became that of discovering collective national values rather than advocating a programme of reforms designed to bring about greater social justice or material prosperity. The direction taken by their creative work was in turn governed by this quest for normative ideas and new vital orientations. It follows that their literary output should be judged first and foremost in relation to its ideological content, to which innovations of form and expression were in practice subordinated.

II. THE FAILURE OF AN IDEAL

In attempting to assess the Generation of 1898's achievements, we must examine its aims separately, beginning with an evaluation of its response to the problem of Spain. Laín Entralgo in chapter 5 of his book, 'Amor amargo: El amor a España', has amply documented the deep involvement of each of the *noventayochistas* with the state, and the fate, of Spain. All angrily rejected the Spain of the

206

Restoration. For a brief period at the start of their careers many of the group used the more extreme section of the left-wing press to advocate radical social and economic changes, and attempted, without concrete results, to intervene practically in public life. The key-documents for this early phase are Maeztu's *Hacia otra España*, the 1901 manifesto of 'Los tres', and the parable contained in chapter 6 of Azorín's *La voluntad* which explains the latter's discouragement at the lack of public response. Alongside these we may mention afresh Unamuno's refusal to join 'Los tres' in advocating practical economic reforms and Baroja's despairingly negative review of *Hacia otra España* (*OC* VIII, 861–2), in which he affirms the impossibility of bringing 'another Spain' into being. Azorín's 'La Andalucía trágica' (1905) was the last significant manifestation of this aspect of the Generation's work. Thereafter, despite Unamuno's political activities and Baroja's attempt to enter political life in 1909, the initiative passed to Ortega and his *Liga de Educación Política Española* whose programme, expounded in Ortega's 'Vieja y nueva política' (1914), reads pathetically like that of 'Los tres' a decade earlier and was destined for equally ignominious defeat.

The Generation of 1898's failure to stick to its early ideology has drawn criticism, especially from the Left, taking its cue from Maeztu's original question in 1913: why did the group's rebellious indignation produce no call for revolutionary action? This current of criticism survives powerfully in Luis Cernuda's attack on the Generation in 1964 as 'traidores y apóstatas'[1] and Blanco Aguinaga's *Juventud del 98* (1970). The straight answer to it is that the objective conditions for effective action simply did not exist. Azorín in *Pueblo* (1930) summed up the position once and for all with uncharacteristically brutal realism. 'Aprendí', he wrote, 'que cuando no se tienen medios para hacer la revolución, todo lo que se haga es como orinarse en las paredes de la Banca de España' (*OC* V, 582). We have also repeatedly stressed lack of specialized intellectual training which might have enabled the members of the Generation of 1898 to define adequately and confront realistically the problems of their country in the first third of this century. All that they could do was to maintain a generally critical, opposing stance to the Spain of their time, and through their writings to keep 'the problem of Spain' alive in the public consciousness. To the extent that they inoculated successive generations of Spaniards with their own *dolor de España* they performed a continuously positive function.

Had this been all, we might have left the matter there; but it was not. We have seen how, one after another (with the exception of Baroja), the members of the Generation of 1898 reinterpreted the problem of Spain as a crisis of individual and national ideas and beliefs, and how all of them bent their energies towards rediscovering *ideas madres*. It must be categorically stated that this reinterpretation was decidedly reactionary. It diverted attention from concrete national needs. Secondly, it led, through a scrutiny of the nation's supposed cultural tradition, to theories of racial and historical determinism founded on myths and emotionally charged assumptions. Such theories, we now recognize, are not only intellectually unsound, but also in their very nature anti-progressive. Fascinating as the whole series of works from *En torno al casticismo* and *Idearium español* to *Defensa de la Hispanidad* appears, we must recognize these books for what they are: speculations about unverifiable postulates which only obscure the issue. That these postulates appealed to José Antonio Primo de Rivera and other right-wing Spanish intellectuals was natural; that they survive in a sense in Américo Castro's approach to Spanish history is regrettable; that they were allowed to confuse the thinking of a subsequent generation of Latin American writers is perhaps the most depressing part of the Generation of 1898's intellectual legacy. Finally, the interpretation of Spain's problems in 'spiritual' terms was intrinsically harmful because it led to a confusion between the collective need for a better society and the need of many individuals for a recovery of belief in transcendence. To try to convert a whole nation to a new outlook, albeit within an allegedly continuous tradition, is a task utterly different in kind and magnitude from that of modifying social abuses. Pérez de Ayala in his essay on the '98 in *Política y toros* put the matter succinctly and realistically: 'tratar de sustituir un pueblo por otro pueblo que no sea el mismo, sin poder dejar de ser el mismo, tiene toda la traza de un problema sin solución imaginable' (*OC* III, 1018). The basic assumption of the Generation of 1898 in regard to *regeneración* came to be that changing people must take precedence over changing the economic and social environment. The modern tendency is to think in precisely the opposite terms.

III. THE LITERARY ACHIEVEMENT

Parallel with the *noventayochistas*' rebellion against the Spain of their youth was their rebellion against her literary establishment with the possible exception of Galdós. 'La insurrección contra el orden literario establecido', Azorín asserted, 'era la nota distintiva de ese grupo' (*OC* II, 782). Their efforts to renew poetic diction and prose style were made simultaneously with those of the *modernistas*. But whereas the *modernistas*' interest in formal innovations was essentially aesthetic in character and stemmed from their conception of the artist primarily as a creator of beauty, the *noventayochistas* were concerned to explore new ways of writing above all to express more effectively what they wanted to say. When Unamuno wrote in 1899: 'Tengamos, primero, que decir algo jugoso, fuerte, hondo y universalmente humano, y luego, del fondo, brotará la forma',[2] he spoke for the entire '98 group. This resolute subordination of conscious form to significant content is what distinguishes *noventayochistas* from *modernistas* as writers.

It led them inevitably to the essay, which in their hands became for a time the dominant literary genre. Nothing in the work of the '98 group so far outshines the achievement of the previous generation as does their contribution to this branch of writing. Practitioners of the stature of Valera and Pardo Bazán, whose reputation seemed assured, were suddenly eclipsed and have never since recovered their former prestige. The range of the essay was vastly extended; its traditionally impersonal mode of expression was replaced by a wide variety of tones ranging from the violently denunciatory to the quasi-lyrical. All the members of the Generation of 1898, including even Machado, were memorable essayists. Collectively they transformed the genre and made it the main instrument for the dissemination of their ideology. But if for the most part their essays were dominated by ideas, there was one area in which feelings came close to the surface. One of the most positive by-products of the Generation of 1898's deep involvement with Spain itself was its members' acquisition of a new vision of the Spanish countryside. Whether we see this simply as a natural offshoot of their love for their homeland or as a means of taking refuge from the issues which that love raised, the fact remains that the '98 group colonized a whole new area of literary creation in Spanish. If we compare their *paisajismo* with, for example, that of Pereda in his highland novels or with that of Alarcón in *La Alpujarra* (1873) or *Viajes por España* (1883), we perceive a difference not only in the quality of the writing itself and in the selection of significant details, but also and above all in the subtle inter-relationship between the writer and the countryside or township contemplated. Pereda and Alarcón merely *describe* the scene; the writers of the '98 *meditate upon* it. For the former what matters is the merely picturesque; for the latter it is the symbolic, the evocative, the *état d'âme*.

In the novel the work of the Generation of 1898 produced a series of radical modifications in fictional technique. Elaborate plots, with carefully organized chains of incidents working up to dramatic and emotional climaxes, balance of forces in play, suspense, highly developed love-interest, lengthy descriptions of social conditions, local colour, in fact most of the trappings of the well-made realist novel tended to go by the board. In their place came novels structured around a single dominant character in which the unifying element is a completed process of change in his outlook. The formal pattern of the narrative is thus dictated in the first instance by the protagonist's evolution of insight. A major feature is the replacement of incidents by dialogues, so that the novel progresses not from happening to happening, but from conversation to conversation, each marking a stage of mental development. Ganivet pioneered the new pattern; Baroja established it by sheer repetition of the formula; Unamuno produced an interesting variation of it in the *nivolas*; Azorín and Pérez de Ayala, having used it initially, strive to break away from it in the second phase of their work.

Nothing more clearly underlines the unity of the Generation of 1898 than the family likeness revealed by its best-known fictional heroes and heroines. Beginning with Ganivet's Pío Cid, they include Antonio Azorín of Azorín's first trilogy, Baroja's Fernando Ossorio, Andrés Hurtado, Sacha Savarof, José Larrañaga, and others we have referred to earlier. Unamuno's Apolodoro Carrascal, Augusto Pérez, and Don Manuel, to name again only the most obvious, and finally Ayala's Alberto de Guzmán. All of them are near-tragic heroes in a context which is not so much tragic as hopeless. Deeply self-aware and analytic, they evolve towards a spiritual boundary-situation in which only the ethical ideal survives to sustain them. Together they express the Generation's view of the modern predicament in a Spanish context. The novels in which they appear mark one of the highest peaks of achievement in the history of Spanish fiction.

In contrast to the *modernista* ideal of creating beautiful patterns of words and images, the poetry of Unamuno and Antonio Machado remained rooted in the same human predicament. While they were at one with the *modernistas* in their rejection of the bombast, the banality, the conventional values, and above all the poverty of creative achievement we associate with the poets of the Restoration period in Spain, neither Unamuno nor Machado found an alternative in conscious artistry for its own sake. Poetry existed for them not only to produce aesthetic pleasure, but also and most of all to stir the spirit. However much they participated, alongside the *modernistas*, in the general renovation of Spanish poetry which the beginning of this century saw set on foot, their work expresses a different and more profound vision of human reality. The triumph of the Generation of 1927 left Unamuno and Machado somewhat isolated. But this was only temporary. The publication of Unamuno's *Cancionero* in 1953 finally made possible a comprehensive evaluation of his poetry. It is now impossible to deny him the status of a major poet. Machado's position as a classic is undisputed; he is indeed the one figure of the Generation of 1898 who seems to be almost totally exempted from hostile criticism. Thus, of the three incontestably important poets in Spain in the first decade of the twentieth century (the other being Juan Ramón Jiménez), two belonged to the '98.

The achievement of the writers of the Generation of 1898 was not without its limitations. As dramatists they failed consistently. No attempt to include Benavente in the group can disguise the fact, nor can all the blame be placed on theatre audiences. This is the major area in which the work of the Generation of 1898 was incomplete. But it is not the only one. The group's criticism of many aspects of Spanish life and behaviour did not extend to the asphyxiating moral and sexual tabus of the period. Just as they produced no consistent apostle of social justice, so they produced no advocate of sexual freedom along the lines we think of in connection with Gide or Lawrence. More importantly, perhaps, for some readers, the work of the Generation as a whole lacks both humour and ironic detachment. Its members' whole outlook was founded on the belief that the possession of insight, however anguishing, is intrinsically superior to the enjoyment of happiness based on illusion. Yuste's remarks in Azorín's *La voluntad*: 'El dolor es bello: él da al hombre el más intenso estado de conciencia; él hace meditar; él nos saca de la perdurable frivolidad humana' (*OC* I, 890) synthesizes the attitude of the entire group. Hence their humour is seldom spontaneous. When it is not bitingly satirical, as in Ganivet's description of politics in Maya, or Baroja's presentation of Castro Duro, it is apt to contain a certain *frisson métaphysique* which turns it into what Unamuno called 'lo bufo-trágico', the only real conception of humour which the Generation possessed. This is another distinction which can be drawn between Pérez de Ayala and his seniors. Once he had discovered his solution, at a comparatively early stage of his thought, his humour evolved away from theirs towards greater spontaneity and genuinely funny situations. Similarly, no seeker after absolutes can be a true ironist. For irony accepts a basic contradiction, an irremediable irrationality in the nature of things. None of the Generation of 1898 shared the ability of Borges, for example, to contemplate existence from this viewpoint, defeating both hope and despair. They were too seriously involved with the search for 'solutions' to be able to confront life's absurdity with a smile.

IV. THE UNIVERSALITY OF THE GENERATION

What left-wing critics of the Generation of 1898 tend to overlook is that if the approach of the group to the problem of Spain was, as we have argued, an error, it was a wonderfully creative error. For it brought them into direct contact with the contemporary human situation. Their lasting importance lies in the fact that they were the first unified group in modern Western literature to explore systematically the collapse of belief and existential confidence which has been a major theme for writers and thinkers ever since. Nowhere else in Europe or the Americas in the early twentieth century can we find a similarly compact body of writers whose work illustrates so consistently the critical moment of transition from the relative stability and optimism, already hollow as it was, of the preceding period, to the philosophical and spiritual impasse in which the main part of our culture finds itself today. In the writers of the Generation of 1898 we can trace with exceptional clarity the operation of many intellectual forces which have gone into the shaping of our present worldview. Not surprisingly the Generation has been seen as portending Existentialism. This is accurate, at least in the sense that the group enunciated the general view of the human condition to which Existentialist thought attempted to formulate a positive response. They were not the only writers to do so; but what is sometimes called the 'dislocation of sensibility' in the rest of modern European literature is generally regarded as dating from the First World War. Its shattering effect repeated on a wider scale the isolated impact made by the defeat of 1898 on Spain.

While it was this defeat which triggered off the Generation of 1898's obsession with the national problem, at a deeper level it accentuated and crystallized a pre-existing sense of existential disorientation. This had been fed, as was suggested in chapter 1, by influences which had been gathering strength in Spain since the period of Romanticism.[3] What Allison Peers in his history of Spanish Romanticism mistook for 'eclecticism' dominating the post-Romantic period was not in fact, as he represents it, an attempt to strike a balance between neo-classic and Romantic literary ideas. Such a balance was impossible. The literary innovations of the mid-century, such as the *balada*, the *alta comedia*, and the *cuadro de costumbres*, all somewhat hybrid, were merely attempts, for the most part sterile, to give formal expression to the harmony-ideal of the period based on what Valera in 1860 called 'un consorcio fecundo de la razón y la fe'. The Revolution of 1868 swept away any basis for 'armonismo' and optimistic complacency. It ushered in a period of renewed awareness of what Sanz del Río had recognized as 'el vacío que todos sentimos hoy dentro y fuera de nosotros'. This sense of spiritual and ideological emptiness the Romantics had been the first modern literary group to discover in themselves and express. It was their major legacy to the Generation of 1898. The Generation found itself caught up in an effort to come to terms with a current of thought stemming from Romanticism which suggested that the ideological foundations on which life had been traditionally thought to rest had collapsed. The group's work is alternately dominated by acceptance of incertitude and the attempt to conquer it. In the end, as everywhere else in contemporary European writing, except for neo-Catholic works and those of

Socialist Realism, the quest for new absolutes failed or ended only in private solutions. But the allegiance of the men of the Generation of 1898 to the ethical imperative, while at the same time they were carrying out their searching and scrupulous critique of life, reveals that the defeat was not total. This is the positive message of the Generation [that man's integrity is not compromised by the collapse of traditional values and certainties. So long as he retains the courage to contemplate his condition honestly, finding pride in achieving the fullest consciousness of it without giving way to demoralization, his dignity is enhanced.]

In the final analysis the test of the importance of any literary group is the ability of its members to reach beyond the circumstances of their own time and place, and to express a vision of reality which men elsewhere and in other periods can find comprehensible and relevant. By moving away from the problem of Spain to the problem of modern man's alienation from existential security, the Generation of 1898 moved from the national to the universal plane. It is on this plane that its work acquires permanent validity and in this context it must in the end be judged. Writers like those of the '98, Pérez de Ayala wrote, 'son a la manera de gigantescos condensadores de ideas y prejuicios, sentimientos y pensamientos, de una gran colectividad en un momento crítico de su existencia'.[4] That the collectivity in this case was Spain has meant that the Generation of 1898 has been unjustifiably neglected by critics and historians of European literature as a whole. But the appearance of these writers as a united group when elsewhere only isolated figures were beginning to formulate a view of the human condition similar to theirs, underlines emphatically that, however underdeveloped Spain was in other ways at the turn of the century, she was in the forefront of modern cultural development.

NOTES

1. Luis Cernuda, *Poesia y literatura*, II (Barcelona, 1964), 241.

2. Miguel de Unamuno, 'Los cerebrales', *La Ilustración Española y Americana* (Madrid), 22 October 1899.

3. See above, p. 13, note 6. R. A. Cardwell's 'The Persistence of Romantic Thought in Spain', *MLR*, LXV (1970), 803–12 carries the argument a stage further.

4. Ramón Pérez de Ayala, *Amistades y recuerdos*, 300.

BIBLIOGRAPHY

The bibliography which follows is selective, with a preference for recent works and works in English. Excellent sources of additional material are *The Year's Work in Modern Language Studies* (the Modern Humanities Research Association) and *The Modern Language Association of America, International Bibliography*. Both are annual. Articles in Memorial Numbers and Collections devoted to one author are not included individually.

General Works on the Generation of 1898 and related topics

Abellán, J. L., *Sociología del 98* (Madrid, 1973)
Barja, C., *Libros y autores contemporáneos* (Madrid, 1935)
Baroja, R., *Gente de la Generación del 98* (Barcelona, 1952)
Bell, A. G. F., *Contemporary Spanish Literature* (London, 1926)
Blanco Aguinaga, C., *Juventud del 98* (Madrid, 1970)
Buffum, M. E., 'Literary Criticism in the Essay of the Generation of 1898', *Hisp*, XVIII (1935), 277-92
Cansinos Assens, R., *La nueva literatura* (Madrid, 1925)
Caponigri, A. R., *Contemporary Spanish Philosophy* (Notre Dame and London, 1967)
Caudet Roca, F., *Vida y obra de J. M. Salaverría* (Madrid, 1972)
Cernuda, L., *Estudios sobre poesía española contemporánea* (Madrid, 1957)
Díaz-Plaja, G., *Modernismo frente a 98* (2nd ed., Madrid, 1966)
Domingo, J., *La novela española del siglo XX* (Barcelona, 1973)
Durán, M., 'La técnica de la novela y el 98', *RHM*, XXXIII (1957), 14-27
Eoff, S. H., *The Modern Spanish Novel* (New York, 1961)
Fernández Almagro, M., *En torno al 98* (Madrid, 1948)
Franco, Dolores, *España como preocupación* (Madrid, 1960)
García de Castro, R. G., *Los intelectuales y la iglesia* (Madrid, 1934)
Gómez de Baquero, E., *Novelas y novelistas* (Madrid, 1918)
——, *El renacimiento de la novela* (Madrid, 1924)
Gómez Molleda, M. D., *Los reformadores de la España contemporánea* (Madrid, 1966)
Granjel, L. S., *Biografía de Revista Nueva, 1899* (Salamanca, 1962)
——, *Panorama de la Generación del 98* (Madrid, 1959)
Gullón, R., *La invención del 98 y otros ensayos* (Madrid, 1969)

Ilie, P., 'Nietzsche in Spain in 1890–1910', *PMLA*, LXXIX (1964), 80–96

Jeschke, H., *La Generación del 98 en España* (Madrid, 1954)

King Arjona, D., '*La voluntad* and *abulia* in Contemporary Spanish Ideology', *RHi*, LXXIV (1928), 573–672

Laín Entralgo, P. *La Generación del 98* (Madrid, 1945)

——, *España como problema* (Madrid, 1962)

Lida, C. E., 'Literatura anarquista y anarquismo literario', *NRFH*, XIX (1970), 360–81

Livingstone, L., 'Interior duplication and the problem of form in the Modern Spanish Novel', *PMLA*, LXXIII (1958), 393–406

López-Morillas, J., *El krausismo español* (Mexico, 1956)

——, *Intelectuales y espirituales* (Madrid, 1961)

——, *Hacia el 98* (Barcelona, 1972)

Marquina, R., 'El bautista de la 98', *La Gaceta Literaria*, 15 November 1931

Molina, A., *La Generación del 98* (Barcelona, 1968)

Nora, E. de., *La novela española contemporánea 1898–1960* (Madrid, 1968)

Paniagua, D., *Revistas culturales contemporáneas*, I (Madrid, 1964)

Pastor, J. F., 'La Generación del 98: su concepto del estilo', *Die Neuren Sprachen*, XXXVIII (1930), 410–15

Pérez de la Dehesa, R., *El pensamiento de Costa y su influencia en el 98* (Madrid, 1966)

——, 'Editoriales e ingresos literarios a principios de siglo', *RO*, 24, no. 71 (1969), 217–28

——, *El grupo 'Germinal': una clave del 98* (Madrid, 1970)

Ramsden, H., *The Spanish Generation of 1898* (Manchester, 1974)

Reding, K. P., 'The Generation of 1898 in Spain as seen through its fictional hero', *Smith Coll. Studies in Mod. Lang.*, III/IV (1935–1936), VII, 121

Río, E. del, *La idea de Dios en la Generación del 98* (Madrid, 1973)

Salinas, P., *Literatura española siglo XX* (Mexico, 1949)

Sanjuan, P., *El ensayo hispánico* (Madrid, 1954)

Sastre, J. L., *El magisterio español. Un siglo de periodismo (1867–1967)* (Madrid, 1967)

Seeleman, R., 'The Treatment of Landscape in the Novelists of the Generation of 1898', *HR*, IV (1936), 226–38

Sender, R., *Los noventayochos* (New York, 1961)

Sequeros, A., *Determinantes históricos del 98* (Alicante, 1953)

——, *Con el 98 y su proyección literaria* (Alicante, 1972)

Serrano Poncela, S., *El secreto de Melibea y otros ensayos* (Madrid, 1959)

Sobejano, G., *Nietzsche en España* (Madrid, 1967)

Tierno Galván, E., *Costa y el regeneracionismo* (Barcelona, 1961)

Torre, G. de, *Del 98 al barroco* (Madrid, 1969)
Torrente Ballester, G., *Panorama de la literatura española contemporánea* (Madrid, 1956)
Trend, J. B., *A Picture of Modern Spain* (London, 1921)
Tzitsikas, H., *El pensamiento español 1898–99* (Mexico, 1967)
Valbuena Prat, A., *La poesía española contemporánea* (Madrid, 1930)
Vásquez Bigi, A. M., *El pensamiento filosófico europeo y la Generación del 98*, *RO*, 28, no. 113/14 (1972), 171–90
Zardoya, Concha, *Poesía del 98 y del 27* (Madrid, 1968)
Zulueta, E. de, *Historia de la crítica española contemporánea* (Madrid, 1966)

Collections of articles on, or mainly on, the Generation of 1898

Arbor (Madrid) XI, no. 36 (1948)
Spanish Thought and Letters in the Twentieth Century, ed. G. Bleiberg and E. Inman Fox (Nashville, 1966)

Works on more than one member of the Generation of 1898

Albornoz, A. de, *La presencia de Unamuno en Antonio Machado* (Madrid, 1968)
Ayllón, C., 'Experiments in the theatre of Unamuno, Valle-Inclán and Azorín', *Hisp*, XLVI (1962), 49–56
Balseiro, J. A., *Blasco Ibañez, Unamuno, Valle-Inclán, Baroja, Cuatro individualistas de España* (Chapel Hill, 1949)
Baquero Goyanes, M., 'La novela como tragicomedia', *In*, 110 (1955), 1.
Basabe Fernández, A., *Miguel de Unamuno y José Ortega y Gasset* (Mexico, 1950)
Campbell, B., 'Free Will and Determinism in the Theory of Tragedy: Pérez de Ayala and Ortega', *HR*, XXXVII (1969), 375–82
Clavería, C., *Cinco estudios de literatura española moderna* (Madrid, 1945)
Fox, E. Inman, 'The Polemic between Martínez Ruiz and Maeztu', *AG*, I (1966), 131–41
Garagorri, P., *Unamuno, Ortega, Zubiri en la filosofía española* (Madrid, 1968)
——, *Unamuno y Ortega* (Madrid, 1972)
Gómez de Baquero, E., *De Gallardo a Unamuno* (Madrid, 1926)
Gómez de la Serna, R., *Retratos contemporáneos* (Buenos Aires, 1944)
——, *Nuevos retratos* (Madrid, 1945)
Mateu Llopis, F., *Baroja y Azorín* (Barcelona, 1945)

Navascués, L. J., *De Unamuno a Ortega y Gasset* (Toronto, 1951)
Quintana, J., *España entre Unamuno y Maeztu* (Bilbao, 1968)
Ribbans, G., *Niebla y soledad* (Madrid, 1971) [Unamuno and Machado]
Rodríguez Alcalá, H., 'Ortega, Baroja, Unamuno y la sinceridad', *RHM*, XV (1949), 107–14
Rovetta, C., *De Unamuno a Ortega y Gasset* (Buenos Aires, 1968)
Salaverría, J. M., *Retratos* (Madrid, 1926)
——, *Nuevos retratos* (Madrid, 1930)
Sánchez Barbudo, A., *Estudios sobre Unamuno y Machado* (Madrid, 1959)

Ganivet

(For an almost complete bibliography on Ganivet up to 1965 see Herrero, *Ángel Ganivet, un iluminado*.)

Abad, C. M., 'Ángel Ganivet', *RyF*, LXXII (1925), 18–30, 190–207
Agudiez, J., 'Ganivet en las huellas de Galdós y Alarcón', *NRFH*, XVI (1962), 89–95
——, *Las novelas de Ángel Ganivet* (New York, 1972)
Aguirre Prado, L., *Ganivet* (Madrid, 1965)
Arbó, S. J., 'La lección de Pío Cid', *Ateneo*, XXXV (1953), 12–13
Azorín, Unamuno, et al., *Ángel Ganivet* (Valencia, 1905)
Carrasco Arauz, N., *Ángel Ganivet* (Madrid, 1971)
Casalduero, J., 'Descripción del problema de la muerte en Ángel Ganivet', *BH*, XXXIII (1931), 214–46
——, 'Ganivet en el camino', *BH*, XXXVI (1934), 488–99
Castra Villacañas, D., 'Ángel Ganivet, su contradicción', *Clavileño*, XXV (1954), 49–54
Conradi, G., 'El ideal de la indiferencia creadora en Ángel Ganivet', *Arbor*, XXXII (1955), 1–20
Domínguez Rodiño, E., 'En los umbrales de Rusia', *El Imparcial*, 9 December 1920; 14, 21, 23 January 1921
Durán, M., 'Ganivet y el senequismo hispánico', *In*, 228/9 (1965), 3, 19
Espina, A., *Ganivet. El hombre y la obra* (Buenos Aires, 1942)
Fernández Almagro, M., *Vida y obra de Ángel Ganivet* (2nd ed., Madrid, 1952)
Franco, J., 'Ganivet and the Technique of Satire in *La Conquista del reino de Maya*', *BHS*, XLII (1965), 34–44
Fuentes, V., 'Creación y estética en Ganivet', *RHM*, XXXI (1965), 133–41
Gallego y Burín, A., *Ganivet* (Granada, 1921)
Gallego Morell, A., *Ángel Ganivet, el excéntrico del 98* (Granada, 1965)

——, *Estudios y textos ganivetianos* (Madrid, 1971)

García Lorca, F., *Ángel Ganivet, su idea del hombre* (Buenos Aires, 1952)

Herrero, J., 'Ganivet y su canciller en Amberes', *RHM*, XXX (1964), 271–8

——, 'El elemento biográfico en *Los trabajos de Pío Cid*', *HR*, XXXIV (1966), 95–116

——, *Ángel Ganivet, un iluminado* (Madrid, 1966)

—— (ed.), *Correspondencia familar de Ángel Ganivet, 1888–1897* (Granada, 1967)

Hutman, N. J., '*El escultor de su alma*', *PSA*, CXX (1966), 265–84

Jeschke, H., 'Ángel Ganivet. Seine Persönlichkeit und Hauptwerke', *RHi*, LXXII (1928), 102–246

Laffranque, M., 'Ángel Ganivet et le christianisme contemporaine', *BH*, LXIX (1967), 56–84

Laín Entralgo, P., 'Visión y revisión del *Idearium español*' in *Ensayos y estudios*, II (Berlin, 1940), 67–93

Lascaris Conmeno, C., 'Las ideas estéticas de Ángel Ganivet', *Rev. de Ideas Estéticas*, IX (1951), 59–73

——, 'El pensamiento filosófico de Ángel Ganivet', *Rev. de la Universidad de Buenos Aires*, XXI/XXII (1952), 452–533

López, N. M., *La cofradía del Avellano* (Granada, 1936)

Montalto Cessi, D., 'Política e storia in Ángel Ganivet' in *Tre studi sulla cultura spagnola* (Milano-Varese, 1967), 141–98

Olmedo Moreno, M., *El Pensamiento de Ganivet* (Madrid, 1965)

Osborne, R. E., 'Ángel Ganivet and Henry Stanley', *HR*, XXIII (1955), 28–32

Peers, E. A., 'Ángel Ganivet', *BSS*, XXI (1944), 199–208

Pérez, M., *Ángel Ganivet, poeta y periodista* (Madrid, 1918)

——, *Ángel Ganivet, universitario y cónsul* (Madrid, 1920)

Ramsden, H., *Angel Ganivet's Idearium español: a Critical Study* (Manchester, 1967)

Revista de Occidente, III, no. 33 (1965). Memorial Number

Saldaña, Q., *Ángel Ganivet* (Madrid, 1930)

Seco de Lucerna, F., Prologue to *El escultor de su alma* (Granada, 1904)

Seco de Lucerna Paredes, L., *Juicio de Ángel Ganivet sobre su obra literaria* (Granada, 1962)

Serrano Poncela, S., 'Ganivet en sus cartas', *RHM*, XXIV (1958), 301–11

Shaw, D. L., 'Ganivet's *España filosófica contemporánea* and the Interpretation of the Generation of 1898', *HR*, XXVIII (1960), 220–32

——, 'Ganivet's *El escultor de su alma*: an Interpretation', *Orbis litterarum*, XX (1965), 297–306

Shaw, K. E., 'Ángel Ganivet: a Sociological Interpretation', *REH*, II (1968), 1–17

Tejada y Spínola, F. E. de, *Ideas políticas de Ángel Ganivet* (Madrid, 1939)

Unamuno

Bibliography on Unamuno is immense. For the bulk of it up to the early 1960s see his *Obras completas* (Madrid, 1958–64); F. de Onís, 'Bibliografía de M. de Unamuno', *La Torre*, XXXV/XXXVI (1961), 601–36; and D. W. Foster, 'Adiciones y suplemento a la bibliografía de Unamuno', *La Torre*, XLVIII (1964), 165–72. Batchelor, *Unamuno Novelist* selects newer material and gives details of contents of Memorial Numbers and *CCMU* up to and including XIX/XX (1970). *CCMU* itself carries a progressive bibliography.

Abellán, J. L., *Unamuno a la luz de la psicología* (Madrid, 1964)

Alberes, R. M., *Miguel de Unamuno* (Paris, 1957)

Alberich, J. L., 'Unamuno y la duda sincera', *RL*, XVI (1958), 210–225

Alvar, M., 'Sobre Unamuno' in *Estudios y ensayos de literatura contemporánea* (Madrid, 1971), 111–19

Aristides, J., *Unamuno, dialéctica de la tragedia existencial* (Rosario, 1972)

Azar, I., 'La estructura novelesca de *Cómo se hace una novela*', *MLN*, LXXXV (1970), 184–206

Barcia, J. R., and Zeitlin, M. A., *Unamuno Creator and Creation* (Berkeley and Los Angeles, 1967)

Barea, A., *Unamuno* (New Haven, 1952)

Baskedis, D., *Unamuno and Spanish Literature* (Berkeley and Los Angeles, 1967)

Batchelor, R. E., *Unamuno Novelist* (Oxford, 1972)

Benítez, H., *El drama religioso de Unamuno* (Buenos Aires, 1949)

Blanco Aguinaga, C., *Unamuno teórico del lenguaje* (Mexico, 1954)

——, *El Unamuno contemplativo* (Mexico, 1959)

——, 'Sobre la complejidad de *San Manuel Bueno, martir*', *NRFH*, XV (1961), 569–88

——, 'Unamuno's *Niebla*. Existence and the Game of Fiction', *MLN*, LXXIX (1964), 188–205

Butt, J. W., 'Determinism and the Inadequacy of Unamuno's Radicalism', *BHS*, XLVI (1969), 226–40

——, 'Unamuno's Idea of *Intrahistoria*' in *Studies Presented to Helen F. Grant* (London, 1972), 13–24

Cancela, G., *El sentimiento religioso de Unamuno* (New York, 1972)

Cannon, C., 'The Miltonic Rhythms of Unamuno's *El Cristo de Velázquez*', *Hisp*, XLIV (1961), 95–8

——, 'The Mythic Cosmology of Unamuno's *El Cristo de Velázquez*', *HR*, XXVIII (1960), 28–39

Clavería, C., *Temas de Unamuno* (2nd ed., Madrid, 1970)

Collado, J. A., *Kierkegaard y Unamuno* (Madrid, 1962)

Cornín Colomer, E., *Unamuno libelista. Sus campañas contra Alfonso XIII y la dictadura* (Madrid, 1968)

Cuadernos de la Catedra de Miguel de Unamuno (Salamanca, 1948–). An important review wholly on Unamuno

Díaz, E., *Revisión de Unamuno* (Madrid, 1968)

Durand, F., 'Search for Reality in *Nada menos que todo un hombre*', *MLN*, LXXXIV (1969), 239–47

Earle, P. G., *Unamuno and English Literature* (New York, 1960)

Esclasans, E., *Miguel de Unamuno* (Buenos Aires, 1947)

La Estafeta Literaria, 300/301 (1964). Memorial Number

Falconiere, J. V., 'The Sources of Unamuno's *San Manuel Bueno, mártir*', *RoN*, V (1963), 18–22

Farre, L., *Unamuno, William James y Kierkegaard* (Buenos Aires, 1967)

Fernández, P. H., *Miguel de Unamuno y William James* (Salamanca, 1961)

——, *El problema de la personalidad en Unamuno y en San Manuel Bueno* (Madrid, 1966)

Fernández Turrienzo, F., *Unamuno, ansia de Dios y creación literaria* (Madrid, 1966)

Ferrater Mora, J., *Unamuno, bosque de una filosofía*, (Buenos Aires, 1957); trans.: *Unamuno: a Philosophy of Tragedy* (Berkeley and Los Angeles, 1962)

Franco, A., *El teatro de Unamuno* (Madrid, 1972)

García Blanco, M., *Don Miguel de Unamuno y sus poesías* (Salamanca, 1964)

——, *América y Unamuno* (Madrid, 1964)

——, *En torno a Unamuno* (Madrid, 1965)

García Morejón, J., *Unamuno y el cancionero* (São Paulo, 1966)

González Caminero, N., *Unamuno* (Comillas, Santander, 1949)

Granjel, L. S., *Retrato de Unamuno* (Madrid, 1957)

Gullón, R., *Autobiografías de Unamuno* (Madrid, 1964)

Guy, A., *Unamuno* (Paris, 1964)

Hannan, D. G., '*La tía Tula* como expresión novelesca del ensayo "Sobre la soberbia"', *RoN*, XII (1971), 296–301

Hoyos Ruiz, A. de, *Unamuno escritor* (Murcia, 1959)

Huertas Jordá, J., *The Existentialism of Miguel de Unamuno* (Gainesville, 1963)

Ilie, P., *Unamuno. An Existentialist View of Self and Society* (Madison, 1967)

——, 'Unamuno, Gorki and the Cain Myth', *HR*, XXIX (1961), 310–23

Ínsula 216/17 (1964). Memorial Number.

Kock, J. D., *Introducción al cancionero de Miguel de Unamuno* (Madrid, 1968)

Lacy, A., *Miguel de Unamuno: the Rhetoric of Existence* (The Hague and Paris, 1967)

Letras Hispánicas (São Paulo), IV (1965). Memorial Number

Lijerón Alberti, H., *Unamuno y la novela existencialista* (La Paz, 1970)

Livingstone, L., 'Unamuno and the Aesthetic of the Novel', *Hisp*, XXIV (1941), 442–50

López-Morillas, J., 'Unamuno and Pascal: Notes on the Concept of Agony', *PMLA*, LXV (1950), 998–1010

——, 'Unamuno y sus criaturas: Antolín S. Paparrigopulos', *CA*, 8, no. 4 (1948), 234–49

Luby, *Unamuno a la luz del empirismo lógico contemporáneo* (New York, 1969)

Manyá, J., *La teología de Unamuno* (Barcelona, 1960)

Marías, J., *Miguel de Unamuno* (Madrid, 1943)

Marrero, V., *El Cristo de Unamuno* (Madrid, 1960)

Meyer, F., *L'ontologie de Miguel de Unamuno* (Paris, 1955)

——, 'Kierkegaard et Unamuno', *RLC*, XXIX (1955), 478–92

Muncy, A., *La creación del personaje en las novelas de Unamuno* (Santander, 1963)

Nozick, M., *Miguel de Unamuno* (New York, 1971)

Olsen, P. R., 'The Novelistic logos in Unamuno's *Amor y Pedagogía*', *MLN*, LXXXIV (1969), 248–68

Oromí, M., *El pensamiento filosófico de Unamuno* (Madrid, 1943)

Padín, J., 'El concepto de lo real en las últimas novelas de Unamuno', *Hisp*, XI (1928), 418–23

Paris, C., 'El pensamiento de Unamuno y la ciencia positivista', *Arbor*, XXII (1952), 11–23

——, *Unamuno, estructura de su mundo intelectual* (Barcelona, 1968)

Pauker, E. K., *Los cuentos de Unamuno* (Madrid, 1965)

Pérez de la Dehesa, R., *Política y sociedad en el primer Unamuno 1894–1904* (Madrid, 1966)

Pizán, M., *El joven Unamuno (influencia hegeliana y marxista)* (Madrid, 1970)

Predmore, R. L., 'Flesh and Spirit in the Works of Unamuno', *PMLA*, LXX (1955), 587–605

Regalado García, A., *El siervo y el señor* (Madrid, 1968)

222 THE GENERATION OF 1898 IN SPAIN

Revista de Occidente, VII, no. 19 (1964). Memorial Number

Round, N. G., *Abel Sánchez. A Critical Guide* (London, 1974)

Rudd, M., *The Lone Heretic* (Austin, 1963)

Salcedo, E., *Vida de Don Miguel* (Madrid, 1964)

Sedwick, F., 'Unamuno, the third self and *lucha*', *SP*, LIV (1957), 464–79

Serrano Poncela, S., *El pensamiento de Unamuno* (2nd ed., Mexico, 1964)

Sevilla Benito, F., 'La idea de Dios en don Miguel de Unamuno', *Rev. de Filosofía*, XI (1952), 473–95

Shergold, N. D., 'Unamuno's novelistic technique in *San Manuel Bueno, mártir*', in *Studies Presented to Helen F. Grant* (London, 1972), 163–80

La Torre (Puerto Rico), IX (1961). Memorial Number

Turiel, P., *Unamuno, el pensador, el creyente, el hombre* (Madrid, 1970)

Turin, Y., *Miguel de Unamuno universitaire* (Paris, 1962)

Unamuno (Departamento de Extensión Universitaria, Universidad de Chile, Santiago, 1964)

Unamuno Centenial Studies, ed. R. Martínez López (Austin, 1966)

Valdés, M. J., *Death in the Literature of Unamuno* (Urbana, 1966)

Villamar, M., *Unamuno, su vida y su obra* (Madrid, 1970)

Villarrazo, B., *Miguel de Unamuno* (Barcelona, 1959)

Webber, R. H., 'Kierkegaard and the elaboration of Unamuno's *Niebla*', *HR*, XXXII (1964), 118–34

Weber, F. M., 'Unamuno's *Niebla*: from novel to dream', *PMLA*, LXXXVIII (1973), 209–18

Yndurain, F., 'Unamuno en su poética y como poeta' in *Clásicos modernos* (Madrid, 1969)

Zavala, I. M., *Unamuno y su teatro de conciencia* (Salamanca, 1963)

Zubizarreta, A., *Tras las huellas de Unamuno* (Madrid, 1960)

——, *Unamuno en su nivola* (Madrid, 1960)

Maeztu

The bulk of Maeztu's journalistic work remains uncollected. A series of *Obras de Ramiro de Maeztu*, intended to run into about 30 volumes, ceased to be published after ten of them had appeared under various titles between 1957 and 1967. Fortunately they include *Hacia otra España* and a fair cross-section of Maeztu's later work.

ABC, 2 November 1952. Memorial Number

Bancroft, R., 'América en la obra de Maeztu', *RHM*, XIII (1947), 236–48

Cuadernos Hispanoamericanos, 33/34 (1952). Memorial Number

D'Ors, E., 'Homenaje a Maeztu' in *Nuevo glosario* (Madrid, 1921)
Fernández Barros, E., 'Pérez Galdós y Menández Pelayo en el pensamiento de Maeztu', *Ábside* (Mexico), XXXVI (1972), no. 3
Maeztu, María de, Introductions to Maeztu's *Ensayos* (Buenos Aires, 1948) and *Antología: Siglo XX. Prosistas españoles* (Buenos Aires, 1943)
Mariategui, J. C., *El alma matinal* (Lima, 1964)
Marrero, V., *Maeztu* (Madrid, 1955)
Nozick, M., 'An Examination of Ramiro de Maeztu', *PMLA*, LXIX (1954), 719-40
Plá Cárceles, J., 'La "Kantina" de Londres', *ABC*, 3 July 1952

Baroja

Alarcos Llorach, E., *Anatomía de La lucha por la vida.* (Oviedo, 1973)
Alberich, J., *Los ingleses y otros temas de Pío Baroja* (Madrid, 1966)
Aldaola, A. de, *En torno a don Pío Baroja* (San Sebastián, 1972)
Alfaro, M., 'Pío Baroja: el pasado, la raza', *CA*, 16 (1957), 240-9
Amalel Yatko, C., *Pío Baroja y el país vasco* (Madrid, 1973)
Andrés, A. A., 'Baroja ante los alemanes y Alemania', *Iberoromania* (Munich), II (1970), 169-96
Andujar, M., et al., *Encuentros con don Pío Baroja* (Madrid, 1972)
Arbó, S. J., *Pío Baroja y su tiempo* (Barcelona, 1963)
Azorín, *Ante Baroja* (Zaragoza, 1946) and in *OC* VIII (Madrid, 1948)
Baeza, F., *Baroja y su mundo* (Madrid, 1962)
Barrow, L. L., *Negation in Baroja* (Tucson, 1972)
Bartrés, R., *La nodriza de la Generación del 98* (Barcelona, 1972)
Benet Goitia, J., et al., *Barojiana* (Madrid, 1972)
Bergaza, F., *Baroja, las mujeres y el sexo* (Madrid, 1973)
Boletín de la Real Academia Española, LII (1972) contained a memorial section on Baroja (four essays)
Bollinger, D. W., 'Heroes and Hamlets: the Protagonists of Baroja's Novels', *Hisp*, XXIV (1941), 91-4
Cangiotti, G., *Pío Baroja osservatore del costume italiano* (Urbino, 1969)
Caro Baroja, J., *Los Baroja* (Madrid, 1972)
Cela, C. J., *Don Pío Baroja* (Mexico, 1958)
Ciplijauskaite, B., *Baroja, un estilo* (Madrid, 1972)
Corrales Egea, J., *Baroja y Francia* (Madrid, 1969)
Cuadernos Hispanoamericanos, 265/7 (1972). Memorial Number
Díaz de León, M., 'Dos ensayos sobre Pío Baroja', *CA*, 16 (1957), no. 1, 71-106

Embieta, M., 'Aurora roja: una interpretación', Hispanófila, XVI (1972), 51–8

Flores Arroyuelo, F., Las primeras novelas de Pío Baroja (Murcia, 1967)

——, Pío Baroja (Madrid, 1973)

——, Pío Baroja y la historia (2nd ed., Madrid, 1973)

Fox, E. Inman, 'El árbol de la ciencia: Baroja y Schopenhauer', RLC, XXXVII (1963), 350–9

García Mercadal, J., Antología crítica: Baroja en el banquillo, 2 vols (Zaragoza, 1947)

García Sarriá, F., 'Estructura y motivos de Camino de perfección', Romanische Forschungen, LXXXIII (1971), 246–66

Gómez Santos, M., Pensando en Baroja (Madrid, 1972). Private edition

González López, E., El arte narrativo de Pío Baroja en las trilogías (New York, 1971)

Granjel, L. S., Retrato de Pío Baroja (Barcelona, 1954)

Iglesias, C., El pensamiento de Pío Baroja (Mexico, 1963)

Índice de Artes y Letras, 70/71 (Madrid, 1954). Memorial Number

Insula, 308/9 (1972). Memorial Number

Knox, R. B., 'The Structure of El Mayorazgo de Labraz', Hisp, XXXVIII (1955), 285–90

Letras de Deusto, II (1972). Memorial Number

Longhurst, C. A., Las novelas históricas de Pío Baroja (Madrid, 1974)

López Estrada, F., Perspectiva sobre Pío Baroja (Seville, 1972)

Martínez Palacio, J., 'Las mujeres de La lucha por la vida', El Urogallo, XV (1972), 106–10

—— (ed.), Baroja (Madrid, 1974)

Matus, E., La técnica novelesca de Pío Baroja (Havana, 1961)

Nallim, C. O., El problema de la novela en Pío Baroja (Mexico, 1964)

Ortega y Gasset, J., 'Ideas sobre Pío Baroja' and 'Una primera vista sobre Baroja' in OC II (Madrid, 1946)

Ortiz Armengol, P., Aviraneta y diez más (Madrid, 1970)

Owen, A. L., 'Concerning the Ideology of Pío Baroja', Hisp, XV (1932), 15–24

Patt, B., Pío Baroja (New York, 1971)

Placer, E. L., Lo vasco en Pío Baroja (Buenos Aires, 1968)

Puértolas Villanueva, S., El Madrid de La lucha por la vida, (Madrid, 1971)

Quiñonero, J. P., Una lectura de Baroja (Madrid, 1972)

Revista de Letras (Puerto Rico), XV (1972). Memorial Number

Revista de Occidente, 21, no. 62 (1968). Memorial Number

Rivera, H., Pío Baroja y las novelas del mar (Salamanca, 1972)

Santander, C., 'Camino de perfección de Pío Baroja, Aproximación psicoanalítica', *Estudios Filológicos* (Valdivia, Chile, 1964), 197–217

Shaw, D. L., 'A Reply to *deshumanización*: Baroja on the Art of the Novel', *HR*, XXV (1957), 105–11

——, 'Two Novels of Baroja. An Illustration of his Technique', *BHS*, XL (1963), 151–9

Sin Nombre (Puerto Rico), II (1971–72), no. 4. Memorial Number

Solotorevsky, M., 'Notas para un estudio comparativo de *Camino de perfección* y *La voluntad*', *Boletín de Filología* (Santiago, Chile), XV (1963), 3–64

Templin, E. H., 'Pío Baroja. Three Pivotal Concepts', *HR*, XII (1944), 306–29

——, 'Pío Baroja and Science', *HR*, XV (1947), 165–92

Tijeras, E., *Pío Baroja* (Madrid, 1972)

Ugalde, L. M., 'El supuesto antihistoricismo de Pío Baroja', *Hispanófila*, XXXVI (1967), 11–20

La Vanguardia, 28 December 1972 contained a Memorial Supplement

Villegas, J., *La estructura mítica del heroe* (Barcelona, 1973)

Yndurain, D., 'Teoría de la novela en Baroja', *CHA*, 233 (1969), 355–88

Zunzunegui, J. A., *En torno a don Pío Baroja y su obra* (Bilbao, 1960)

Machado

Editions of Machado's work are notoriously incomplete. The best is *Obras:poesía y prosa*, edited by Aurora de Albornoz and Guillermo de Torre (Buenos Aires, 1964). But see also *Antonio Machado, Antología de su prosa*, edited by Albornoz in 4 vols. (Madrid, 1970–1972); *Antonio Machado. Prosas y poesías olvidados*, edited by R. Marrast and R. Martínez López (Paris, 1964); and *Los complementarios*, edited by D. Yndurain (Madrid, 1971) for additional material. The best critical edition of the poems is *Poesie di Antonio Machado*, edited by O. Macrí (3rd ed., Milan, 1969).

Aguirre, J. M., *Antonio Machado, poeta simbolista* (Madrid, 1973)

Albornoz, A. de, *La prehistoria de Antonio Machado* (Río Piedras, Puerto Rico, 1961)

Alonso, D., *Poetas españoles contemporáneos* (Madrid, 1952)

——, *Cuatro poetas españoles* (Madrid, 1962)

Álvarez Molina, R., *Variaciones sobre Antonio Machado* (Madrid, 1972)

Ángeles, J., 'El mar en la poesía de Antonio Machado', *HR*, XXXIV (1966), 27–48

——, 'Soledades primeras de Antonio Machado' in *Homenaje a, S.H. Eoff* (Madrid, 1970)

Ávila, P. L., *Algunas variantes en la poesía de Machado* (Turin, 1968)

Beceiro, C., 'El poema "A José María Palacio" de Antonio Machado', *In*, 137 (1958), 5

Busoño, C., *Teoría de la expresión poética* (2nd ed., Madrid, 1962)

Cano, J. L., 'La espina arrancada', *Clavileño*, XXIX (1954), 49–50

——, *De Machado a Bousoño* (Madrid, 1955)

——, *Poesía española del siglo XX* (Madrid, 1960)

Caravaggi, G., *I paesaggi emotivi di Antonio Machado* (Bologna, 1969)

Carbonell, R., *Espíritu de llama* (Pittsburgh, 1962)

Carilla, E., 'La poesía de Antonio Machado', *RHM*, XXX (1964), 246–56

——, 'Antonio Machado y Rubén Darío', *Cuadernos del Sur* (Bahía Blanca), IX (1971), 150–64

Casalduero, J., *Estudios de literatura española* (Madrid, 1967)

Ciplijauskaite, B., *El poeta y la soledad* (Madrid, 1966)

Chavez, J. C., *Itinerario de don Antonio Machado* (Madrid, 1968)

Cobb, C. W., *Antonio Machado* (New York, 1971)

Cobos, P. de A., *Humor y pensamiento de Antonio Machado en la metafísica poética* (Madrid, 1964)

——, *Humorismo de Antonio Machado en sus apócrifos* (2nd ed., Madrid, 1972)

——, *El pensamiento de Antonio Machado en Juan de Mairena* (Madrid, 1971)

——, *Antonio Machado en Segovia* (Madrid, 1973)

Collantes de Terán, J., 'Las ciudades muertas de Antonio Machado', *Archivo Hispalense*, XLVII (1968), 1–11

Cowes, H., 'El motivo de la fuente en la poesía de Antonio Machado', *Sur*, 234 (1955), 52–76

'El hombre viator en la poesía de Antonio Machado', *Sur*, 245 (1957), 58–74

Cuadernos Hispanoamericanos, 11/12 (1949). Memorial Number

Darmengeat, P., 'A propos de "La tierra de Alvargonzález"', *Bull. des Langues Neo-latines*, CXXXIII (1955), 1–19

——, *L'homme et le réel dans Antonio Machado* (Paris, 1956); trans. in *Tres poetas españoles* (Madrid, 1969)

Espina, C., *De Antonio Machado a su grande y secreto amor* (Madrid, 1950)

Fernández Alonso, M., *Una visión de la muerte en la lírica española* (Madrid, 1971), 238–73

Ferreres, R., *Los límites del modernismo* (Madrid, 1964)

——, Introductions to his editions of *Soledades* (Madrid, 1969) and *Campos de Castilla* (Madrid, 1970)

Foster, D. W., 'Una contribución machadiana al romance español', *Rev. Nacional de Cultura* (Caracas), CLXVI (1964), 98–110

Frutos, E., 'El primer Bergson en Antonio Machado', *Rev. de Filosofía*, XIX (1960), 117–68

——, 'La esencial heterogeneidad del ser en Antonio Machado', *Rev. de Filosofía*, XVIII (1959), 271–92

Gaos, V., 'En torno a un poema de Antonio Machado' in *Claves de literatura española*, II (Madrid, 1971), 57–80

Gener Cuadro, E., *El mar en la poesía de Antonio Machado* (Madrid, 1966)

Gicovate, B., 'Reflexiones en torno a "La tierra de Alvargonzáles" ', *Hispanófila*, IV (1961), 47–53

——, *Ensayos sobre poesía hispánica* (Mexico, 1967)

Gil Novales, A., *Antonio Machado* (Barcelona, 1966)

Glendinning, N., 'The Philosophy of Henri Bergson in the Poetry of Antonio Machado', *RLC*, XXXVI (1962), 50–70

Guerra, N. H., *El teatro de Manuel y Antonio Machado* (Madrid, 1966)

Gullón, R., *Las secretas galerías de Antonio Machado* (Madrid, 1958)

——, *Direcciones del modernismo* (Madrid, 1963)

—— (ed.), *Cartas de Antonio Machado a Juan Ramón Jiménez* (Río Piedras, Puerto Rico, 1959)

——, *Una poética para Antonio Machado* (Madrid, 1970)

Gutiérrez Girardot, R., *Poesía y prosa en Antonio Machado* (Madrid, 1969)

Herrero, J., 'Antonio Machado's Image of the Centaur', *BHS*, XLV (1968), 38–41

Hutman, N. E., *Machado, a Dialogue with Time* (Albuquerque, 1969)

Ilie, P., 'Antonio Machado and the Grotesque', *Journal of Aesthetics and Art Criticism*, XXII (1963), 209–16

——, 'Verlaine and Machado: the Aesthetic Role of Time', *Comparative Literature*, XIV (1963), 261–5

Ínsula, 158 (1960). Memorial Number

Lascaris Conmeno, C., 'El despertar de la conciencia moral en "La tierra de Alvargonzález" ', *CHA*, 128/9 (1960), 236–47

López Landeira, R., 'A un olmo seco', *RoN*, LXXXVI (1972), 280–284

Machado, J., *Últimas soledades del poeta Antonio Machado* (Santiago de Chile, 1958)

McVan, A., *Antonio Machado* (New York, 1959)

Marías, J., 'Machado y Heidegger', *In*, 94 (1953), 1

Monserrat, S., *Antonio Machado, poeta y filósofo* (Buenos Aires, 1943)

Monte, A. del, *La sera nello specchio* (Milan-Varese, 1971)

Morrow, C., 'An Analysis of "Poema de un día"', *RoN*, II (1959), 149-53

Navas Ruiz, R., 'Guiomar y el proceso creador en Machado', *RL*, XXXV (1969), 69-70

Orozco Díaz, E., *Antonio Machado en el camino* (Granada, 1962)

Peers, E. A., *Antonio Machado* (Oxford, 1940)

Pérez Ferrero, M., *Vida de Antonio Machado y Manuel* (Madrid, 1947)

Phillips, M. W., 'La tierra de Alvargonzález', *NRFH*, IX (1955), 129-48

Pradal-Rodríguez, G., *Antonio Machado* (New York, 1951)

Predmore, R., 'La visión de Castilla en la obra de Antonio Machado', *Hisp*, XXIX (1946), 500-6

——, 'El tiempo en la poesía de Antonio Machado', *PMLA*, LXIII (1948), 696-701

Quintanilla, M., 'El pensamiento de Antonio Machado', *Estudios Segovianos*, XI (1952), 369-82

Rodríguez, Marta, *El intimismo en Antonio Machado* (Madrid, 1971)

Rodríguez Forteza, A., *La naturaleza y Antonio Machado* (Madrid, 1965)

Rosselli, F., *Contributo a una tematica generale della poesia di Antonio Machado* (Pisa, 1970)

Ruiz de Conde, J., *Antonio Machado y Guiomar* (Madrid, 1964)

Ruiz Ramón, F., 'En torno al sentido de "El espejo de los sueños" en la poesía de Antonio Machado', *RL*, XXII (1962), 74-83

——, 'El tema del camino en Antonio Machado', *CHA*, 151 (1962), 52-76

Sánchez Barbudo, A., *Los poemas de Antonio Machado* (Barcelona, 1967)

Schwartz, K., 'The Sea and Antonio Machado', *Hisp*, XLVIII (1965), 247-54

Segre, C., 'Due appunti su Antonio Machado' in *Studi di lingua e letteratura spagnola* (Turin, 1965)

——, 'Sistema e struttura nelle "Soledades" di Antonio Machado', *Strumenti Critici* (Turin), VII (1968), 269-303

Serrano Poncela, S., *Antonio Machado, su mundo y su obra* (Buenos Aires, 1954)

Socrate, M., *Il linguaggio filosofico della poesia di Machado* (Padua, 1972)

Terry, A., *Campos de Castilla. A Critical Guide* (London, 1973)

Tilliette, X., 'Antonio Machado, poète philosophe', *RLC*, I (1962), 32–49

La Torre (Puerto Rico), XII, nos. 45/6 (1964). Memorial Number

Trend, J. B., *Antonio Machado* (Oxford, 1953)

Tuñón de Lara, M., *Antonio Machado* (Paris, 1960)

——, *Antonio Machado, poeta del pueblo* (Barcelona, 1967)

Valle, R. H., *Antonio Machado, 1895–1939* (New York, 1939)

Valverde, J. M., *Estudios sobre la palabra poética* (Madrid, 1952)

——, Prologues to his editions of *Nuevas canciones y De un cancionero apócrifo* and *Juan de Mairena* (Madrid, 1970)

Villegas, J., 'El tema del tiempo en un poema de Antonio Machado', *Hisp*, XLVIII (1965), 442–51

Yndurain, D., 'Tres símbolos en la poesía de Antonio Machado', *CHA*, 223 (1968), 117–49

Zubiría, R., *La poesía de Antonio Machado* (3rd ed., Madrid, 1966)

Azorín

Abbott, J. H., 'Azorín and Taine's Determinism', *Hisp*, XLVI (1963), 476–9

Alfonso, J., *Azorín íntimo* (Madrid, 1950)

——, *Azorín. En torno a su vida y su obra* (Barcelona, 1958)

Aznar, B., *Personalidad biológica de Azorín* (Salamanca, 1973)

Azorín 1873–1947. Homenaje de la Hemeroteca Municipal de Madrid (Madrid, 1947)

Baquero Goyanes, M., 'Elementos rítmicos en la prosa de Azorín', *Clavileño*, XV (1952), 25–32

Bastianelli, E. B., *La Francia en Azorín* (Florence, 1970)

Beser, S., 'Notas sobre la estructura de *La voluntad*', *Bol. de la Sociedad Castellonense de Cultura*, XXXVI (1960), 169–81

Biervliet, M. D. van, 'José Martínez Ruiz's Obsession with Fame', *FMLS*, VIII (1972), 291–303

Campos, J., *Conversaciones con Azorín* (Madrid, 1964)

Caro Baroja, J., 'Azorín', *RO*, 20, no. 59 (1968), 138–53

Carpintero, H., *et al.*, *Azorín* (Madrid, 1964)

Catsorio, J. A., *Azorín and the Eighteenth Century* (Madrid, 1971)

Cruz Rueda, Á., '*Semblanza de Azorín*' in *Azorín: Obras selectas* (Madrid, 1943)

——, 'Nuevo retrato de Azorín', in *Azorín. Obras completas*, I (Madrid, 1947)

——, *Mujeres de Azorín* (Madrid, 1953)

Cuadernos de Literatura Contemporánea, 16/17 (Madrid, 1947). Memorial Number

Cuadernos Hispanoamericanos, 226/7 (1968). Memorial Number

D'Ambrosio Servodidio, M., 'Azorín and the Modern Short Story', *RR*, LIX (1969), 88–92

——, *Azorín escritor de cuentos* (Madrid, 1971)

Denner, H., *Das Stilproblem bei Azorín* (Zurich, 1932)

Enguídanos, M., 'Azorín en busca del tiempo divinal', *PSA*, XIV (1959), 13–32

Fernández Pombo, A., *Maestro Azorín* (Madrid, 1973)

Ferreres, R., *Valencia en Azorín* (Valencia, 1968)

Fiesta en Aranjuez en honor de Azorín (Madrid, 1915)

Fox, E. Inman, *Azorín as a Literary Critic* (New York, 1962)

——, 'Two Anarchist Newspapers of 1898', *BHS*, XLI (1964), 160–8

——, 'Una bibliografía anotada del periodismo de José Martínez Ruiz', *RL*, LV/LVI (1965), 231–44

——, 'José Martínez Ruiz. Sobre el anarquismo del futuro Azorín', *RO*, 12, no. 35 (1966), 157–74

——, 'Lectura y literatura', *CHA*, 205 (1967), 1–22

——, Introductions to his editions of *La voluntad* (Madrid, 1968) and *Antonio Azorín* (Barcelona, 1970)

García Mercadal, J., *Azorín* (Barcelona, 1967)

——, 'El carácter de Azorín', *In*, 246 (1967), 6

Gil San Juan, P., *et al.*, *Cinco ensayos sobre Azorín* (Granada, 1955)

Glenn, K. M., *The Novelistic Technique of Azorín* (Madrid, 1973)

Gómez de la Serna, R., *Azorín* (3rd ed., Buenos Aires, 1957)

Granell, M., *Estética de Azorín* (Madrid, 1949)

Granjel, L. S., *Retrato de Azorín* (Madrid, 1958)

Hommage à Azorín. Bulletin de l'Institut Français en Espagne, LXX (1953)

Hoyos, A. de, *Yecla de Azorín* (Murcia, 1954)

Joiner, L. D., 'Proust and Azorín', *RoN*, XIII (1971–72), 468–73

Krause, A., *Azorín, the Little Philosopher* (Berkeley and Los Angeles, 1948); Spanish trans.: *Azorín, el pequeño filósofo* (Madrid, 1956)

Lajohn, L. A., *Azorín and the Spanish Stage* (New York, 1961)

——, 'Surrealism in Azorín's Theatre', *KFLQ*, X (1963), 20–5

Lamiquiz, V., *Ciudad de Azorín* (Seville, 1973)

El Libro Español, X, no. 112 (1967). Memorial Number

Livingstone, L., 'The Pursuit of Form in the Novels of Azorín', *PMLA*, LXXVII (1962), 116–33

——, 'The Aesthetic of Repose in Azorín's *Diario de un enfermo*', *Symposium*, XX (1966), 241–53

——, 'Tiempo contra historia en las novelas de José Martínez Ruiz', in *Homenaje a Rodríguez Moñino*, I (Madrid, 1966), 325–38

——, 'The Theme of Intelligence and the Will in the Novels of Azorín', *RR*, LVIII (1967), 83–94

——, *Tema y forma en las novelas de Azorín* (Madrid, 1970)

Lott, R. E., *The Structure and Style of Azorín's El caballero inactual* (Athens, Georgia, 1963)

——, 'Azorín's Experimental Period and Surrealism', *PMLA*, LXXIX (1964), 305–20

——, 'Considerations on Azorín's Literary Technique and the Other Arts', *KFLQ*, XVIII (1970), 423–34

Mainer, J. C., 'Para un análisis formal de *Capricho* y *La isla sin aurora*', *In*, 246 (1967), 5, 11

Martínez Cachero, J. M., 'Clarín y Azorín', *Archivium*, III (1953), 159–76

——, 'Vísperas de Azorín. *Diario de un enfermo*', *PSA*, XXIX (1958), 121–34

——, *Las novelas de Azorín* (Madrid, 1960)

Merenciano, F. M., *Fronteras de la locura: tres personajes de Azorín vistos por un psiquiatra* (Valencia, 1947)

Montoro, A., *¿Cómo es Azorín?* (Madrid, 1953)

Ortega y Gasset, J., 'Azorín, primores de lo vulgar' in *Obras completas* II (Madrid, 1957), 158–92

Pageux, D., 'La confrontation du passé et de l'actuel chez Azorín', *MLN*, LXXVII (1968), 210–21

Palley, J., 'Images of Time in *Doña Inés*', *Hisp*, LIV (1971), 250–5

Panero, M., *En torno a la vida y la obra de Azorín* (Santiago de Chile, 1967)

Pérez de la Dehesa, R., 'Un desconocido libro de Azorín: *Pasión*', *RHM*, XXXIII (1967), 280–4

——, 'Azorín y Pi y Margall', *RO*, 26, no. 78 (1969), 353–62

——, 'Azorín en la prensa anarquista de fin de siglo', *CA*, 173 (1970), 111–18

Ramsden, H. (ed.), *La ruta de Don Quijote* (Manchester, 1956)

Rand, M., *Castilla en Azorín* (Madrid, 1956)

——, '*El Licenciado Vidriera* recreated by Azorín', *Hisp*, XXXVII (1954), 141–51

——, 'Azorín in 1960 and after', *Hisp*, XLV (1962), 32–9

——, 'Más notas sobre Azorín y el tiempo', *Hisp*, XLIX (1966), 23–9

Revista (Barcelona) V, no. 8 (1953). Memorial Number

Riopérez y Milá, S., 'El problema de la muerte en la obra de Azorín', *CHA*, 113 (1959), 126–34

Rozas, J. M., Introduction to his edition of *Castilla* (Barcelona, 1973)

Sabater, G., *Azorín o la plasticidad* (Barcelona, 1944)

Smith, P., 'Seven Unknown Articles by the Future Azorín', *MLN*, LXXXV (1970), 250–61

Stimson, F. S., '*Lo invisible*: Azorín's Debt to Maeterlinck', *HR*, XXVI (1958), 64–70

Tudela, M., *Azorín* (Madrid, 1969)

Valverde, J. M., *Azorín* (Barcelona, 1971)

―― (ed.), *Artículos olvidados de José Martínez Ruiz* (Madrid, 1972)

Vilanova, M., *La conformidad con el destino en Azorín* (Barcelona, 1971)

Villegas, J., *Azorín, autor teatral* (Santiago de Chile, 1967)

Zamora Vincente, A., 'Una novela de 1902', *Sur*, 226 (1954), 67–78

Pérez de Ayala

Agustín, F., *Ramón Pérez de Ayala, su vida y sus obras* (Madrid, 1927)

Amorós, A., Prologues to his editions of *La pata de la raposa* (Barcelona, 1970) and *Tinieblas en las cumbres* (Madrid, 1971)

――, *La novela intelectual de Ramón Pérez de Ayala* (Madrid, 1972)

Balsiero, J. A., 'Ramón Pérez de Ayala novelista' in *El Vigía*, II (Madrid, 1928), 123–269

Baquero Goyanes, M., *Perspectivismo y contraste (de Cadalso a Pérez de Ayala)* (Madrid, 1963)

Beck, M. A., 'La realidad artística en las tragedias grotescas de Ramón Pérez de Ayala', *Hisp*, XLVI (1963), 480–9

Clavería, C., 'Apostillas adicionales a *Belarmino y Apolonio*', *HR*, XVI (1948), 97–119

Concha, V. G. de la, 'Los senderos poéticos de Ramón Pérez de Ayala', *Archivium* (1970). Entire Number

Curtius, E. A., *Ensayos críticos acerca de la literatura europea*, II (Barcelona, 1959), 109–21

Derndarsky, D., *Ramón Pérez de Ayala* (Frankfurt, 1970)

Fabian, D. L., 'Action and Idea in *Amor y pedagogía* and *Prometeo*', *Hisp*, XLI (1958), 30–4

――, 'The Progress of the Artist: a Major Theme in the Early Novels of Pérez de Ayala', *HR*, XXVI (1958), 108–16

Fernández, P. H., 'Animalización y cosificación en la primera novela de Pérez de Ayala', *Bol. del Instituto de Estudios Asturianos*, XXVI (1972), 371–80

Fernández Avelló, M., 'Ramón Pérez de Ayala y el periodismo' *Gaceta de la Prensa Española*, 132 (1961), 3–13

――, 'Pérez de Ayala en su rincón', *Bol. del Instituto de Estudios Asturianos*, XXII (1968), 423–6

――, *Pérez de Ayala y la niebla* (Oviedo, 1970)

García Mercadal, J., Prologues to *Obras completas de Ayala* (Madrid, 1964) and to Ayala's *Ante Azorín* (Madrid, 1964)

Gillespie, R. C., 'Ramón Pérez de Ayala, precursor literario de la revolución', *Hisp*, XV (1932), 215–22

González Ruiz, N., 'La obra literaria de Ramón Pérez de Ayala',
BSS, IX (1932), 24–31

Hartsook, J. H., 'Literary Tradition as Form in Pérez de Ayala',
RoN, VI (1964), 21–5

Johnson, E. A., 'Sobre *Prometeo* de Pérez de Ayala', *In*, 100/101
(1954), I

——, 'The humanities and *Prometeo* of Pérez de Ayala', *Hisp*,
XXXVIII (1955), 276–81

Livingstone, L., 'The Theme of the *Paradoxe sur le Comédien* in
the Novels of Pérez de Ayala', *HR*, XXII (1954), 208–23

Lozano Alonso, M. B., 'El tiempo en *Belarmino y Apolonio* de
Ramón Pérez de Ayala', *Bol. de la Real Academia*, LXI (1971),
no. 194, 413–58

Luján, N., Prologue to *Obras selectas* of Ayala (Barcelona, 1957)

Noble, B., 'The Descriptive Genius of Pérez de Ayala in *La caída de
los Limones*', *Hisp*, XL (1957), 171–5

Rand, M. C., *Ramón Pérez de Ayala* (New York, 1971)

Reinink, K. N., *Algunos aspectos literarios y lingüísticos de la obra
de Ramón Pérez de Ayala* (The Hague, 1959)

Salgués de Cargill, M., *Los mitos clásicos y modernos en la novela
de Pérez de Ayala* (Jaen, 1971)

Sallenave, P., 'La estética y el esencial ensayismo de Ramón Pérez
de Ayala', *CHA*, 234 (1969), 601–15; 244 (1970), 178–90

Shaw, D. L., 'Concerning the Ideology of Pérez de Ayala', *MLQ*,
XXII (1961), 158–66

Sturken, H. T., 'Nota sobre *La pata de la raposa*', *NRFH*, IX
(1957), 198–200

Sullivan, C. A., 'La modificación del protagonista en *La pata de la
raposa*', *Hispanófila*, XLV (1972), 73–81

Urrutia, N., *De Troteras a Tigre Juan* (Madrid, 1960)

Weber, F. W., *The Literary Perspectivism of Ramón Pérez de Ayala*
(Chapel Hill, 1966)

Zamora, C., 'La concepción trágica de la vida en la obra novelesca
de Pérez de Ayala', *Hispanófila*, XLII (1971), 21–34

——, 'Homo impotens and the vanity of human striving: two
related themes in the novels of Pérez de Ayala', *REH*, V (1971),
no. 3

Ortega y Gasset

A useful guide to bibliography up to 1970 is U. Ruker, *Bibliografía
de Ortega* (Madrid, 1971)

Abellán, J. L., *Ortega y Gasset en la filosofía española* (Madrid,
1966)

Aguado, E., *Ortega y Gasset* (Madrid, 1971)

Aranguren, J. L., *La ética, de Ortega* (3rd ed., Madrid, 1966)

Araya, G., *Claves filológicas para la comprensión de Ortega* (Madrid, 1971)

Armstrong, A., 'The Philosophy of Ortega y Gasset', *PhQ*, III (1952), 124–39

Asomante (Puerto Rico), XX (1956). Memorial Number

Bayón, J., *Razón vital y dialéctica, en Ortega* (Madrid, 1972)

Borel, J. P., *Introducción a Ortega y Gasset* (Madrid, 1969)

Casanova Sánchez, U., *Ortega, dos filosofías* (Madrid, 1960)

Cascalès, C., *L'humanisme d'Ortega y Gasset* (Paris, 1957)

Clavileño, XXIV (1953). Memorial Number

Clemente, J. E., *Ortega, estética de la razón vital* (Buenos Aires, 1956)

Cobian y Machiavello, A., *La ontología de Ortega y Gasset* (Lima, 1960)

Conard, P., 'Ortega y Gasset, écrits politiques 1910–1913' in *Mélanges de la Casa de Velázquez*, II (Madrid, 1967)

Conway, 'Ortega y Gasset's vital reason', *Thought*, XXXII (1957), 594–602

Cuadernos Americanos, 15, no. 1 (1956). Memorial Number

Díaz Casanueva, H., *Das Bild vom Menschen bei Ortega y Gasset* (Leipzig, 1938)

Díaz de Cerio, F., *J. Ortega y Gasset y la conquista de la conciencia histórica* (Barcelona, 1961)

Fernández de la Mora, G., *Ortega, y el 98* (Madrid, 1961)

Ferrater Mora, J., *Ortega, y Gasset* (New Haven, 1957); Spanish trans.: *Ortega y Gasset, etapas de una filosofía* (Barcelona, 1958)

Gaete, A., *El sistema maduro de Ortega* (Buenos Aires, 1962)

Gaos, J., *Sobre Ortega y Gasset y otros trabajos* (Mexico, 1957)

Garagorri, P., *Ortega, una reforma de la filosofía* (Madrid, 1958)

——, *Introducción a Ortega* (Madrid, 1970)

García Bacca, J. D., *Nueve grandes filósofos y sus temas* (Caracas, 1947)

Gironella, J. R., *Lo que no se dice* (Barcelona, 1953)

Gómez Galán, A., 'El estilo de Ortega', *Arbor*, XXXIII (1956), 38–47

González Caminero, N., 'El Ortega póstumo', *Annali* (Naples), V, no. 1 (1963), 127–72

Goyenechea, F., *Lo individual y lo social en la filosofía de Ortega y Gasset* (Zurich, 1964)

Granell Muñiz, M., *Ortega y su filosofía* (Madrid, 1960)

Guy, A., *Ortega y Gasset, critique d'Aristote* (Paris, 1963)

——, *Ortega y Gasset ou la raison vitale et historique* (Paris, 1969)

Hampton, W., 'La crítica literaria de Ortega y Gasset según criterios contemporáneos', *Language Quarterly* (Florida), X (1971), 23–6

Hernández Rubio, J. M., *Sociología y política en Ortega y Gasset* (Barcelona, 1956)

Hierro S. Pescador, J., *El derecho en Ortega* (Madrid, 1965)

Livingstone, L., 'Ortega y Gasset's Philosophy of Art', *PMLA*, LXVII (1952), 609–54

Índice (Madrid), October 1956. Memorial Number

Iriarte, J., *Ortega y Gasset, su persona y su doctrina* (Madrid, 1942)

——, *La ruta mental de Ortega. Crítica de su filosofía* (Madrid, 1949)

Kourim, Z., 'Une vision marxista de Ortega', *RO*, 29, no. 86 (1970), 176–204

Laín Entralgo, P., 'Los católicos y Ortega', *CHA*, 101 (1958), 283–296

Larraín Acuña, H., *La génesis del pensamiento de Ortega* (Buenos Aires, 1962)

López Quintás, A., *El pensamiento filosófico de Ortega y D'Ors* (Madrid, 1972)

McClintock, R., *Man and his Circumstances. Ortega as Educator* (New York, 1972)

Mañach, J., *Imagen de Ortega y Gasset* (Havana, 1956)

Maravall, J. A., *Ortega en nuestra situación* (Madrid, 1972)

Marías, J., *Introducción a la filosofía* (Madrid, 1947); English trans.: *Reason and Life* (London, 1956)

——, *Ortega y la idea de la razón* (Madrid, 1948)

——, *Ortega y tres antípodas* (Buenos Aires, 1950)

——, *Meditaciones del Quijote, Comentario* (Madrid, 1957)

——, *El lugar del peligro* (Madrid, 1958)

——, *Ortega I. Circunstancias y vocación* (Madrid, 1960)

——, *Ortega ante Goethe* (Madrid, 1961)

——, *Acerca de Ortega* (Madrid, 1971)

Marrero, D., *El centauro: Persona y pensamiento de Ortega y Gasset* (San Juan, Puerto Rico, 1951)

Marrero, V., *Ortega, filósofo 'mondain'* (Madrid, 1961)

Martínez Curto, M. C., *Por el sendero a la meta* (Madrid, 1960)

Mermall, T., 'En torno a *Ideas y creencias*', *Hispanófila*, XLIII (1971), 31–43

Montoro, A., *José Ortega y Gasset* (Madrid, 1957)

Morón, G., *Historia política de Ortega y Gasset* (Caracas, 1960)

Morón Arroyo, C., *El sistema de Ortega y Gasset* (Madrid, 1968)

Oromí, M., *Ortega y la filosofía* (Madrid, 1953)

Orringer, N. R., 'Ortega y Gasset's Sportive Theories of Communication', *MLN*, LXXXV (1970), 209–13

——, 'Ortega y Gasset's Sportive Vision of Plato', *MLN*, LXXXVIII (1973), 264–80

Paris, C., 'Meditación sobre la filosofía de Ortega', *Arbor*, XXXIII (1956), 329–52

Pina Prata, X., *Dialéctica da razão vital* (Lisbon, 1962)

Raley, H. C., *Ortega y Gasset. The Philosopher of European Unity* (Alabama, 1971)

Ramírez, S., *La filosofía de Ortega y Gasset* (Barcelona, 1958)

——, *¿Un orteguismo católico?* (Salamanca-Madrid, 1958)

——, *Ortega y el núcleo de su filosofía* (Madrid, 1959)

Ramis Alonso, M., *En torno al pensamiento de José Ortega y Gasset* (Madrid, 1948)

Reid, K. S., 'Two Periods in the Philosophic Development of Ortega' in *Essays Presented to C. M. Girdlestone* (Newcastle, 1960), 263–275

Renouard, Y., 'La théorie des générations de José Ortega y Gasset', *BH*, LIII (1951), 413–21

Revista de Filosofía XVI, 60/61 (1957). Memorial Number

Rodríguez Huéscar, A., *Con Ortega y otros escritos* (Madrid, 1964)

——, *Perspectiva y verdad* (Madrid, 1966)

Romero, F., *Ortega y Gasset y el problema de la jefatura espiritual* (Buenos Aires, 1960)

Rosales, L., 'La libertad y el proyecto vital en Ortega y Gasset', *CHA*, 32 (1957), 159–74

Salmerón Roiz, F., *Las mocedades de Ortega* (2nd ed., Madrid, 1971)

Sánchez Villaseñor, J., *Ortega y Gasset* (Chicago, 1949)

Senabre Sempere, R., *Lengua y estilo de Ortega y Gasset* (Salamanca, 1964)

Soler Grima, F., *Hacia Ortega* (Santiago de Chile, 1965)

Sur, 241 (1956). Memorial Number

La Torre (Puerto Rico) IV, nos 15/16 (1956). Memorial Number

Vela, F., *Ortega y los existencialismos* (Madrid, 1961)

Walgrave, J. H., *La filosofía de Ortega y Gasset* (Madrid, 1965)

INDEX

Printed in Great Britain
by Western Printing Services Limited
Bristol